# Migrations and Belongings
## 1870–1945

Dirk Hoerder

*The Belknap Press of Harvard University Press*

CAMBRIDGE, MASSACHUSETTS
LONDON, ENGLAND

Originally published as Chapter 3 of *A World Connecting: 1870–1945*, ed. Emily S. Rosenberg (Cambridge, MA: Belknap Press of Harvard University Press, 2012), a joint publication of Harvard University Press and C. H. Beck Verlag. German language edition © 2012 by C. H. Beck Verlag.

Maps by Isabelle Lewis
Book design by Dean Bornstein

*Library of Congress Cataloging-in-Publication Data*

Hoerder, Dirk.
    Migrations and belongings: 1870–1945 / Dirk Hoerder.
        pages   cm
    Includes bibliographical references and index.
    ISBN 978-0-674-28131-8 (alk. paper)
    1. Emigration and immigration—History—19th century. 2. Emigration and immigration—History—20th century. 3. Transportation—History—19th century. 4. Transportation—History—20th century. I. Title.
    JV6029.H64   2014
    304.809'041—dc23        2013031955

# Contents

*~ Migrations and Belongings*

# Introduction

To take a worldwide perspective on migrations and belongings, we must raise a question of definition: How are migration systems and macroregions defined? We must also ask a question of periodization: How do long-lasting migration systems fit into the time frame of industrialization, transformation, and crisis from the 1870s to the end of the Second World War?[1]

Critiquing the traditional Atlantocentric perspective common in "the West," Adam McKeown has argued that three large-scale long-distance migrations in the century from the 1840s to 1940 need to be addressed and compared:

- 55–58 million to the Americas, mainly from Europe (the Atlantic migration system) and in smaller numbers (2.5 million of the total) also from Africa as well as China, India, and Japan;
- 48–52 million to Southeast Asia, the Indian Ocean Rims, and the South Pacific, mainly from India and southern China (the China Seas–Indian Ocean–Plantation Belt migration system) and in smaller numbers (4 million of the total) from Africa, Europe, northeastern Asia, and West Asia or the Middle East;
- 46–51 million to Manchuria, Siberia, Central Asia, and Japan, mainly
  1. from northeastern China (the north China-to-Manchuria migration system) and
  2. in the Russo-Siberian migration system from Russia.[2]

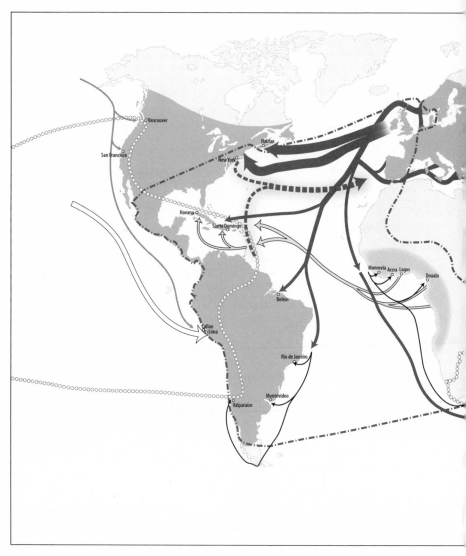

Global systems of migration, 1840–1940.

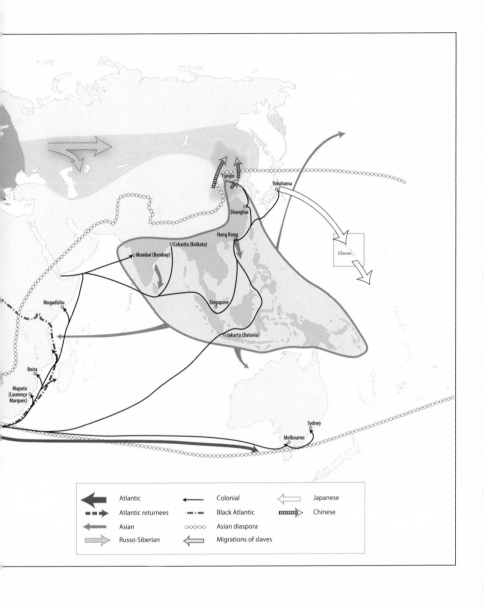

| | | | | |
|---|---|---|---|---|
| Atlantic | | Colonial | | Japanese |
| Atlantic returnees | | Black Atlantic | | Chinese |
| Asian | | Asian diaspora | | |
| Russo-Siberian | | Migrations of slaves | | |

Tianjin
Yokohama
Shanghai
Hong Kong
Calcutta (Kolkata)
Mumbai (Bombay)
Singapore
Jakarta (Batavia)
Hawaii
Mogadishu
Beira
Maputo (Lourenço Marques)
Sydney
Melbourne

In addition,

- from 1807 to the 1870s, another 2 million Africans were force-migrated to the Americas (from a total of 12.4 million shipped and, after the deaths of the Middle Passage, over 9 million arriving in the early sixteenth century to the 1870s); and
- about 1 million colonizer migrants (administrators, soldiers, merchants and personnel) from Europe to the acquired territories.[3]

The figures are still being debated, because they compare transoceanic movements and northern Asia's land-based migrations. If intracontinental land-based migrations in Europe and the Americas are included, numbers for these macroregions are far higher. But inclusion of regional and interregional migrations within the whole of the Qing Empire or any other macroregions also massively increases numbers. Each and every individual migrant also left behind his or her family—on all of whom the departure impacted. Large-scale migrations were a global phenomenon connecting societies and states that were in the process of defining themselves as nations with deeply engrained national identities—imagined and constructed ones, in fact.[4]

Transglobal migratory movements emerged over century-long periods or in the first half of the nineteenth century. These continuities will be outlined to examine the developments in the several distinct macroregions of the globe. To begin a discussion of *global* migrations and regional identities from the North Atlantic and Mediterranean worlds reflects both an adherence to the traditional perspective centered on Europe and North America, as well as these states' worldwide imperialism by armed force, economic penetration, and an ideology of the superiority of white people—or, in terms of the times, white men. Since the early sixteenth century, colonization and imperial rule involved migrations of white administrators, soldiers, and investors or their personnel. The black Atlantic's forced migrations, which did come to an end in the 1870s, had depleted sub-Saharan Africa of about

12.4 million men, women, and children before 1810, and the descendants of survivors continued to shape the economies and societies of the Americas.[5] In the world of the Indian Ocean, the migrations of free men and women and, from the 1830s, of indentured servants— never more than 10 percent of the total South Asian migration, though white racializing views labeled all of these migrants "coolies"— established a macroregion of trade and cultural exchange. The indentured and free men and women sustained production in Plantation Belts imposed by European investors.[6] In the Far East—or from a North American transpacific perspective, in the west—nineteenth-century imperial China was weakening both internally and externally. Its many regions were the arenas of expanding populations, many millions of which migrated to fertile lands and growing cities.[7] In the North Atlantic world the period 1870 to 1945 encompasses the apogee of both intracontinental and transatlantic migrations, beginning in the early decades of the nineteenth century, at the height of industrialization. It also comprises the self-paralysis of Europe during two world wars that were in many respects European wars, whose aftermaths changed the massive labor migrations that had begun before 1914 into massive refugee migrations, from 1914 to the late 1940s.[8]

Each perspective or positioning implies a point of view, particular or partisan, and marginalizes others of the many viewpoints available. Challenging a Euro- and US-centric perspective, we can discern five major migration systems across the globe in the nineteenth century, with some beginning centuries earlier:

- the dual North and South "white" Atlantic system connecting Europe and the Americas, as well as Europe with its colonies, beginning in the early fifteenth century, reaching its apogee from the 1880s to 1914, and ending in the mid-1950s;
- the African slave, or black Atlantic, migration system, beginning in the 1440s, reaching its apogee in the eighteenth and nineteenth centuries, and ending in the 1870s;

- the system of migration of Asian men and women, both free and under indenture—often within the framework of power relations mposed by the British or other European empires and US capital investments on colonies—as well as its transpacific extensions to the Americas;
- the Russo-Siberian system composed of both high-volume, often ircular, rural-to-urban migrations within European Russia and settlement of trans-Caspian and southern Siberian regions, as well as some emigration to North America and in-migration from Western Europe;
- a fifth system, the North China-to-Manchuria system, commencing in the late nineteenth century and assuming large proportions in the 1920s and 1930s.[9]

A migration system, on the level of empirical observation and geographical space, is a cluster of moves between a region of origin and a receiving region that continues over a long period of time. It is distinct from nonclustered multidirectional migrations. Gross and net quantity of migration flows, continuity over time, and ratio per thousand population may be studied on this level. Across macroregions (and similarly across meso- and microregions), migration systems connect distinct societies with a labor surplus to others with a demand for additional laborers or, from the view of the migrating men and women, more options. (The connection may also involve densely settled agricultural regions of out-migration with regions less densely settled but never empty.) The regions of origin and of destination are each characterized by the ratio of rural to urban populations, by degree of industrialization and urbanization, by political structures and current policies, by social hierarchies and the impermeability of dividing lines between classes or status groups, by specific educational, value, and belief systems, by ethnic composition and demographic factors (infant mortality, marriage patterns, dependency ratio, age structure), by gendered and intergenerational role ascriptions, and by traditions of internal, medium-distance, and long-distance migrations. These complex structures and processes are often simplified into general push-and-pull-factors. Because economic sectors and regions transcend state borders, and because migrants in pursuit of their life-course decisions often cross political borders, states are not a useful unit of analysis for the nineteenth century and earlier. However, with the invention of passports in the late nineteenth century and mainly in the first two decades of the twentieth century, as well as with exclusionary policies based on racial ascriptions, states increased their role in establishing a framework, or migration regimes, for migrants' departure or entry.[10]

Macroregions are empirically determined, interconnected, and re-lated spaces. They provide a human-agency-based spatial frame of analysis that cannot be achieved by using fixed units of physical geog-raphy, like continents, or the fixed borders of polities. Europe's regions—Iberian, then Mediterranean, Atlantic littoral, northern, west central, and east central—became one migration space in the nine-teenth century both internally and as regards out-migration. Eastern tsarist Europe remained a separate region connected to southern Si-beria by eastward out-migration. The divide between the Atlantic and the Russo-Siberian system along the Dnepr River was crossed eastward or westward by comparatively small numbers. Asia's four macroregions—South Asia, Southeast Asia, China with North Asia, and the Japanese islands—remained distinct spaces but were con-nected through sea-lanes. From Southeast Asia, migrations extended to the Pacific islands, including the islands of Australia and New Zea-land. A further region, the cultures of the Eastern Mediterranean and the Persian Gulf or West Asia, is best discussed as a hinge region con-necting Mediterranean Europe, the Russian and Ottoman Black Sea littorals, and North Africa with the Indian Ocean's littoral societies and their products. Africa's spaces include the distinct Arab and Kabyl Mediterranean North, the littoral societies of the Indian and the At-lantic Ocean and a central landlocked region. The Americas, Anglo North and Latin South, contain a French-language region in the St. Lawrence Valley, the culturally interactive Caribbean, and the Greater

US Southwest and Mexican Northwest in which Spanish and English mingle.

Periodization, as is obvious in this synthesis, varies between the macroregions; and the 1870s, in most regional migration systems, reflect continuities rather than breaking points. In the 1870s, about six decades after European governments decided to end the slave trade, slave merchants did indeed cease to buy and sell human beings. They did so more for economic reasons than for any respect of law. In the white Atlantic, the age of revolution, counterrevolution, and Napoleonic imperial warfare—extending from the 1760s in some of the British North American colonies to the reestablishment of a reactionary dynastic order in Europe at the 1815 Congress of Vienna—slowed transatlantic mobility. Migrations resumed in 1816–1817, partly induced by a particularly harsh winter, and grew steadily in conjunction with economic growth or slowed during periods of recession and the American Civil War, 1861–1865. From the 1870s and 1880s, the "proletarian mass migration" reached new heights. This Atlantic migration system came to a sudden halt in 1914 and reemerged for a decade each after 1918 and 1945. In South Asia and in the southern provinces of the Qing Empire, indentured servitude was introduced or assumed larger proportions in the 1830s. Almost a century later, India's nationalist leaders used the weakening of imperial Britain in 1914–1918 to negotiate an end to British rule, which was achieved de facto by the 1930s. Migrations in most of China, influenced by the British Opium Wars, after around 1840, which massively increased opium sales and indebtedness, show no particular caesura in the 1870s. However, in the north, the Shandong-to-Manchuria migrations began. In contrast to the continuities characterizing the 1870s, the end of the Second World War changed the parameters of (refugee) migrations almost everywhere in the world, and the decade after 1945 is characterized by resettlement of refugees and displaced persons (DPs)—people who had been moved to forced labor, internment camps, or other confinement by the warring Axis powers, Japan included. At armistice, they found themselves wherever they had been deposited, with limited means to return home.

This discussion focuses on the developments from the 1870s. Chapter 1 discusses preceding migration and migration-related developments across the globe and establishes patterns and processes specific to regions and societies. Chapter 2 turns to contemporary concepts of belonging and identities and to theorizations and interpretations of migrations. Chapter 3 describes and analyzes migrations in the Atlantic economies, in the world's Plantation Belt and mining nodes, and in all other macroregions from the 1870s to the 1910s or, depending on the region, the 1930s. Chapter 4 turns to twentieth-century (refugee) migrations induced by 1910s warfare and related to the 1930s Great Depression and includes intellectual migrations that contributed to a global critique of colonialism and racism. Finally, Chapter 5 discusses the consequences of the displacements and migrations of the Second World War for the subsequent decade.

Languages imply connotations, and scholars are socialized into them in childhood. Hidden viewpoints of languages, mother tongues spoken in fatherlands, also need to be brought into the open for critical assessment. Common usage has it that "wars break out"—they are declared, sometimes prepared. Governments are involved, and refugee migrants are aware of this. Historians need terminologies that do not imply interpretations. Migration history has been written in an emigration/immigration dichotomy. Both terms imply unidirectional permanent moves. In a further ideologization, nationalist historians often assumed that emigrants were a loss to the nation or even committed treason to a constructed national identity. Immigrants have been viewed as uncultured and uprooted, in need of immersion into a melting pot to become new and better human beings. In contrast, the term *migration* is open as to direction, number of moves, return, and variants of acculturation processes. Migration experiences and choices, it still needs to be emphasized, were gendered. In specific periods, varying by region, more women than men moved. Another problem occurs when terms with different connotations are used for similar phenomena or when one term is used for distinct phenomena. Forced African migrations have been subsumed under the catch-all label *slavery,* but they encompassed (1) forced migrations that, in the Americas and the Plantation Belt, led to a status as "chattel"—labor forces commodified as property without personality; (2) traditional rights-in-persons dependency relationships within Africa; and (3) service bondage in Asia in households, as soldiers, or as highly educated business or court administrators. *Bondage,* the generic term, and associated mobilities involve serfdom in Europe, forced labor in 1930s Fascist Germany and the Stalinist Soviet Union, and subsequently in apartheid South Africa, or bound status in Chinese societies. The binary juxtaposition of free and unfree migrations hides a continuum from voluntary to involuntary. The problematic connotations of bounded categories like "free," "coolie," or "slave" skew analyses. Most "free" migrants—from Europe to the Americas, for example—were forced to leave by severe economic constraints. They departed from known impossibilities to perceived options, but never to "unlimited opportunities." Bound migrants, whether slaves or coolies, are often assumed to have been passive (or to have been deprived of the possibility to act on their own). But all bound and constrained migrants (except for young children) came fully socialized and have created cultures. Migrants come with developed personalities even if they must adjust under extreme constraints.[11]

CHAPTER ONE

# A *Longue-Durée* Perspective

Scholars have often given priority to white migrants who moved west-ward across the Atlantic, based on the assumption that they migrated in singular quantity, an assumption that is not born out by the data. In fact, the numerically small migrations from Western Europe and, later, from the United States into the colonized regions of the world were of far larger global economic and mobilizing impact. The Euro-peans' economic activities and aggressiveness, or simply their imposi-tion of rule, set in motion local, regional, or even empire-wide migra-tions. None of the colonizer powers did ever imagine a reversal of migratory directions, a future of decolonization that would result in mass movements—for example, of Indonesians to the Netherlands, of West Africans to France, of Jamaicans to Britain, or of Puerto Ricans the United States. In conjunction with other factors the long-term ef-fects of the colonizer migrations still determine many patterns of pres-ent postcolonial migrations.

When humanist and Enlightenment thinkers in Europe began to connect the issues of inalienable human rights to human bondage, whether in regimes of serfdom or of slavery, economic transformations were beginning to change the character of work and some employers started to discuss the advantages of permanently bound versus flexibly hired labor forces. At the same time, bound human beings, who had never accepted any legitimacy of enslavement as chattel, had estab-lished subcultures under bondage that gave them collective strength, and they were aware that withdrawal and resistance would undercut the plantation regime's productivity.[1] In Europe, serfdom, which was intended to immobilize large segments of the regionally diverse peasant populations, was also more complex and involved mobility: When nobles favored hunting over husbandry, fewer serfs were needed; when they intensified agriculture, bound peasant families had to be attracted; when neighboring cities offered escape from *corvée* labor, serfs fled.[2] In Spanish America, slavery involved the forced mobilization of segments of the many West, Central, and East African peoples, as well as of many of the Native American peoples, and their immobilization at the destination.[3]

The resistance of bound men and women, the Enlightenment debates over human rights, and the discussions about perceived benefits of free or bound labor impacted deeply on human mobility in the frame of power relations. Europe's sedentary *latifundia* lords and their migrating cousins, the plantation owners in the colonized world (later augmented by those of US origin), demanded a supply of workers as cheap and as tractable as possible. If Africans could no longer be enslaved, could Europe's underclasses be induced to migrate to subtropical or tropical climates? Could laborers from colonized Asian societies be recruited, under pressure if necessary? Investors in plantations considered recruitment by incentive, whether bonuses or high wages, expensive and thus detrimental to profits. They lobbied for state mobilization of workers under indenture or from Europe with assisted passage to shift cost from the private sector to taxpayers. Class interests and struggles, racializations and resistance, and reformatting of patterns of thought on "the human condition" impacted decisions to migrate.[4]

## Forced Migration in the Black Atlantic

After two centuries of transatlantic slave migrations, mulattoes and Negroes in French Saint-Domingue / Haiti cast off their yoke once, in the interactive white and black Atlantics, concepts of government by

social contract were discussed in pre-revolutionary France, and concepts of self-determined lives were discussed by enslaved Africans.
Ideas, carried by travelers and migrants from France, brought class
distinctions between *grands blancs, petits blancs,* and *gens de couleur* to
a crisis. Together the three groups accounted for less than 10 percent of
the population. Segments of the other 90 percent, the approximately
half a million slaves of African birth or origin, held distinct views.
Slaves who as servants lived at the interface between white and black
spheres were conversant with both discourses and could negotiate between them. Men and women recently force-migrated from Africa
knew of lifeways other than those imposed by the slave regime.
Whites, resident or migrant, opposed the extension of human rights
to the colonies; mulattoes demanded it, with the support of the French
*Amis des Noirs*—a group that Paul Gilroy overlooked in his book
*Black Atlantic*. Slaves began self-liberation in August 1791; France's
National Assembly liberated chattel slaves only in 1793. When Napoleon, under the influence of the French-Caribbean mixed-ancestry
transatlantically mobile planter class, reinstituted slavery, the force-
migrated and self-freed Africans defeated the force-migrated forty
thousand soldiers of the invading French army. After Haiti's independence, many of the free families left the plantations to pursue subsistence agriculture and self-determined lives. The resulting collapse of
the sugar-plantation-based economy gave a competitive advantage to
British-controlled Jamaica, where slave imports increased and slave labor continued to the 1830s.[5]

Planters, fearful of losing their purchased labor force, and thus
their investments, almost frantically tried to recruit labor wherever
possible: poor Europeans, Asians who could be indentured, free or
semibound Africans. Economically, it was the price of labor that
counted, not the color of skin. In the early 1800s, trial shipments of
indentured Chinese laborers from Portuguese Macao were sent to
British Trinidad and to Portuguese Brazil. More than half a century

later, planters in Hawai'i would also experiment, asking for shipments, alphabetically, of "fertilizer" and "Filipinos," and having poor Portuguese and poor Japanese migrants work alongside each other.

Although the slave trade was banned from 1807–1808 in Europe and the United States, and although enforcement of this ban by the British Navy began in 1815, Brazil accepted the policy only in the mid-1850s and the trade's de facto end came as late as the 1870s. In these decades some 1.9 million men and women—"pieces" in the Spanish expression—were force-migrated. It needs to be recalled that, up to the 1820s, more Africans than Europeans came to the Americas, and one-half to two-thirds of the Europeans came under indentures rather than as free persons. Black and white, men and women, carried their cultural and spiritual practices with them. Often of Animist or Islamic faith, they continuously added African elements to the Afro-Euro-American Creole cultures. In mid-nineteenth-century Rio de Janeiro, some eighty thousand slaves accounted for almost 40 percent of the population, and two-thirds of these had been born in Africa. In the United States, on the other hand, where slave imports did end and population increase came by procreation, African-Americans were the most creolized in culture.

The British imperial government abolished slavery in 1834 but—to satisfy planters' demands—tacked on a four-year "apprenticeship"; in the French colonies abolition came in 1846. Latecomers as regards to ending slavery were the Dutch colonies (1873), the remnants of the Spanish colonies (Cuba in 1880 with a six-year "apprenticeship" added on), and the two largest independent slaveholding states, the United States and Brazil. Their slavery regimes lasted to 1863–1865 and 1888, respectively—some 85 to 110 years after the Declaration of Human Rights in France and later than the tsarist empire's abolition of serfdom in 1861. As early as 1776, the classic exposition of new middle-class—not capitalist—economic doctrines, Adam Smith's *The Wealth of Nations,* had called slavery an economic anachronism not competi-

tive with free labor. Afro- and Euro-Creoles understood the plantation regime's economy of theft of the rewards of labor. US slaves called
flight "stealing oneself," and French planters described a slave's purchase of his or her own freedom as "vendre un nègre à lui-même."

In the Caribbean, where marginal agricultural land was accessible
by short-distance migration, many of the freed Afro-Caribbean families refused wage labor. To replace slaves, planters in the British Empire hired African-origin men and women migrating within the
Americas or freed from slave ships, European "free" labor migrants
who left home societies that did not provide sustenance, and Asian
contract labor migrants bound for time. As regards African-origin
workers, Euro-Caribbean and mulatto planters first attempted to continue bondage in the form of apprenticeship or indenture. Next they
tried local—i.e., Caribbean—free labor, which, in terms of cost of migration, was cheapest. In Caribbean inter-island migrations, hundreds
of thousands moved according to wage levels, working conditions, and
legal status. In a third strategy, planters indentured Africans freed from
slave ships whom imperial authorities wanted to earn their keep. About
forty thousand were debarked in the Caribbean and British Guiana
before the mid-1860s. Many fled and joined free Afro-Caribbean communities. Planters also attempted to recruit free US Afro-Creoles, and
some did migrate to the less-racist island societies. Planters recruited
free Kru from West Africa, especially Sierra Leone, but once the first
migrants returned home and reported on working conditions, no further enlistments could be obtained.[6]

Planters' experiments with white labor began in the mid-1830s
and—like Asian indenture—assumed larger proportions in the 1840s:
Irish and English, French, Germans, Maltese, and Portuguese—many
of them "black" Cape Verdeans. Some workers abandoned plantation
labor as soon as possible and turned to small trading, often in competition and conflict with local Afro-Caribbeans. From Asia, some
270,000 Chinese reached Cuba, Peru, and other Latin American

economies, and about half a million South Asians came to the Caribbean colonies and the Guyanas. Yucatan Amerindian prisoners and their wives, as well as peons sold by Mexican Euro-Creole *hacendados,* were carried to Cuba before 1860. Polyglot interracial societies emerged, homogenized on each island, and divided into states that developed a regional sense of identity. Across color lines class solidarities were forged. The Caribbean segment of the black and white Atlantics became many-colored.[7]

The slave-labor regime immobilized workers at their destination for as long as their owners could use them profitably. However, as in European serfdom, involuntary mobility also continued. When the US cotton economy moved from the Atlantic seaboard to the Mississippi's riparian states, the free planter migrants forced their bound labor to follow. Slaves considered refractory were sold "down" the Mississippi River to regions where discipline was harsher and exploitation more brutal. In the Caribbean, the shift of the center of sugar production from Haiti to Jamaica to Cuba involved forced and voluntary mobility. In Brazil, the removal of plantation economies from the northeast to the southeast and the expansion of mining ever farther inland involved mobility of slave and free blacks. "Fugitives"—refugees from forced labor, manumitted slaves, and those who had purchased their freedom—were able to move according to their goals in the frames of economic and racialized constraints and options. With the end of slavery in the Atlantic world at the advance of industrialization, African-Americans' mobility, except in the United States, did increase—provided there were known options for earning a living elsewhere and provided racism did not prevent self-determined lives. In Brazil, African-origin men and women could and did move, as others did in the Caribbean inter-island migrations. In the United States, out-migration from the South was delayed until after 1900 and the "Great Migration" began only during World War I.[8]

## Asian Migrations and the Regime of Indenture

In terms of culture, economics, and migration, the eastern part of the tricontinental European-African-Asian world consisted of macroregions distinct to a degree that it makes no analytical sense to aggregate all data and discussions into a generic Asia or to construct generic "Asians" as migrants. We will deal with South Asia (British India and Ceylon / Sri Lanka), with Southeast Asia from Burma to Sumatra and beyond, with China, and with Japan. Although for a long time the Atlantic and Pacific Oceans were separating expanses, the Indian Ocean and the Strait of Malacca connected the many littorals to the seas eastward between the islands and northward along the coast of the mainland and the Japanese isles.[9]

The intrusion of tiny numbers of Europeans into the vibrant, multidirectional, and intensely traveled routes of the Indian Ocean trade emporia and into the Southeast and East Asian seas changed labor demands—on a modest scale at first, in larger proportions once plantation economies were institutionalized, and massively under nineteenth-century imperialism. Steamships, introduced since the 1830s, and the Suez Canal, opened in 1869, changed the region's accessibility from the world economy's core. In the 1850s, when Western European capitals established Łódź in Russian Poland as a textile center, a first cotton mill opened in Mumbai (Bombay)—in both cases sizable regional labor migration networks developed. Distant politics and warfare impacted on local economies globally: During the American Civil War, Britain's Manchester mills substituted Indian for American cotton imports. Thus, for five years laborers in India's plantations were in great demand, then after the end of war none were hired. In terms of family economies, a boom in one segment of the global economy and a related bust in another, often distant, segment translates into employment or underemployment, overwork or undernourishment, and, often, migration and dislocation.

## African Slavery in the Indian Ocean World

In most of the Asian societies, resident local people or short-distance and interregional migrants formed the labor forces. Bound and free East African men and women came or were brought to the Indies, the Malay Peninsula, and the Southeast Asian islands as sailors or as servants for ruling, merchant, or noble families. In the worlds of the Eastern Mediterranean and the Indian Ocean, slaves came from a wide variety of regions and cultural origins: Africans, Turks, Circassians. In extended merchant families, slaves became a kind of non-related kin varying in position from menial service in households, laborers on business premises, to educated and highly placed clerks. In contractual labor arrangements, slaves kept part of their incomes, and if successful could in turn own slaves, become substantial property owners, and purchase their freedom. Slave and free women might intermingle in the same household or court as wives and concubines. Children of a free father—including those by a master of a domestic slave from exploitative sexual relations—assumed his status and were of equal standing with the children of free wives. By giving birth, their slave mothers improved their status and could no longer be sold or alienated by the master-husband. Dependency relationships that placed restrictions on sale and bondage were part of everyday social life rather than a marker of segregation. The impossibility of return as well as the comparatively benign nature of the system of slavery in this region, enjoined by the Koran, legitimized the system to a degree that flight and revolt were rare. Cultures merged and slave mothers or nannies might tell children bedside stories about free lives in their culture of origin, their (forced) migration trajectory, and the culture of residence. Hierarchical mixed societies rather than regimes of segregation emerged.[10]

## Migrations in South Asia

The many societies on the South Asian subcontinent and in Ceylon have been described as sedentary by British imperial scholars, Kingsley Davis in particular. This culturally insensitive view overlooks the fact that Hindu views of kinship consider people in a village community as related and thus prohibited from marrying each other. Brides had to translocate in short-distance migration to a neighboring community. Courts and wealthy households attracted teachers, artists, and artisans in long-distance moves. To mitigate land shortages, people of the plains migrated into hilly regions, thereby displacing men and women from the "hill tribes." The many-cultured port cities were nodes of interurban circulation.

The London-based East India Company, a multinational or global player in modern terms, and the British Empire as the period's "superpower" restructured many of South Asia's societies, and the global cotton economy restructured local producing families' lives. Imperial regulations of the 1790s affected Bengal, Bihar, and Orissa in the north, regulations of the 1810s affected societies the south and, after its annexation in the later 1840s, the Punjab. These regulations and subsequent legislation introduced new land revenue systems, which grafted the role of English landlords onto Indian societies, made men from local elites tax collectors, and permitted alienation of village lands. As a result, a new class of landlords as well as middlemen, moneylenders, and tax farmers *(zamindars)* emerged, dependent on and allied with the temporarily resident colonial administrator-overlord migrants. Within a few decades these measures destroyed the traditional village community, with its precarious balance between population, agriculture, and handicrafts. A report to the British Parliament admitted that massive distress forced families to migrate or become vagrants.

In Punjab, a region of stable population and balanced economy, the British administrators expanded the irrigation system, made land a transferable asset, and required taxes to be paid in cash. The extension of cultivation and land sales drew or forced villagers into a money and market economy. Peasant families who perceived opportunities needed loans for investments, and good crops encouraged, just as poor harvests necessitated, borrowing. Rural indebtedness grew fast. Then the new railways brought cheap factory goods, displacing the rural peasant-artisan families. Out-migration became a necessity. Punjabi men became British "colonial auxiliaries"—clerks, policemen, soldiers—and labor migrants. Sikh men might be stationed locally or sent to Hong Kong, Singapore, and Malaya. They thus came to know other parts of India and of the empire—white Australia and Canada, for example—and initiated self-sustaining migrations. The railroads carried off men for wage work as far as the port of Calcutta (Kolkata), from where they could leave for Malaya or even North America. Women had no similar options.

Indian cloths, family-produced, enchanted European consumers by their colors and moderate price. In India's southeast such families owned land and thus derived income from two sources. This traditional risk diversification permitted flexible income substitution in unpredictable markets. When European purchasers increased demand, the weavers' decision to increase returns implied longer daily working hours and increased family labor. It alienated the families from their land. Food purchases and wages paid to hired labor necessitated larger cash flows. The artisan-farmer families entered debt relationships. At the same time, in Britain the mechanization of spinning and weaving began to permit production at a cost below that of family labor in India. Capitalist and state forces combined: policies levied prohibitive taxes on export of India's artisanal products but permitted free entry of British goods. Until 1800 London's Spitalfields weavers had suffered from Indian imports; by 1850 Indian village production had been destroyed. Single women, appropriately called "spinsters," could no longer gain subsistence; whole families starved to death. This deindustrialization of village handicrafts and the parallel refeudalization of land ownership and tax farming pauperized whole regions' populations, which, as "agricultural proletariats," were forced to migrate to wherever subsistence was available. Just at this time the empire-wide plantocracy needed semibound labor.[11]

## Southeast Asia, China, and the Chinese Diaspora

In the spice-producing and resource-rich Malaya and Southeast Asian islands, the European state-supported armed colonizer merchants, investors, and power-wielding administrators had long relied on forced local labor. Because "locals" could use their resources—knowledge of the terrain and supportive networks—to refuse waged labor and to resist force, bound labor was imported and immobilized at the point of arrival. The Spanish colonizers of the Philippines had carried enslaved laborers across the Pacific as far as New Spain in the Americas. The Dutch intruders' regional system of forced labor became globalized under the British Empire's expansion. Existing local migration systems were intensified and new ones created.

In the societies farther north, China's and Japan's imperial courts had prohibited emigration since the fifteenth century. In the case of China, mobile merchants, artisans, and laborers in particular from the southern provinces of Fujian and Guangdong had traditionally resided temporarily in outposts along the sea-lanes. Over time the "overseas Chinese"—a modern term—became a settled diasporic network extending to Manila, Bantam, and Malacca. A second network involved the "western ocean" connecting to Japan and Korea; a third one emerged in the "eastern ocean" in response to invitations by Siamese rulers to assume positions as foreign traders under royal monopoly. In Siam's capital, Chinese from the east and Muslims from the west lived in distinct quarters; others—Portuguese, Javanese, Malays, Makassa-rese, and Pegu—lived outside of the walls, each group administered by a speaker of its own choosing. Such communal living and self-administration was the practice in most of the Indian Ocean's port cities.

The community in Manila, Philippines, formed the second-largest overseas community after the Siam-Chinese. Like that of the Spanish, the Chinese community was almost exclusively male. Informal unions or marriages with native women initiated a process of ethnogenesis: a mestizo population emerged. The diasporic Chinese became cultural mediators and economic middlemen for the European in-migrants who lacked languages, cultural skills, and capability for intercultural exchange. In the mixed society of Luzon, Hispanicized *indio* culture, to use the Spanish term for local people, ranked lowest, and Chinese and Spanish competed for status, because both considered themselves as originating in a high culture. Over time, the Chinese-Philippine mestizo population assumed economic leadership, provided natives with credit, and—seizing land in case of defaults—expanded their urban-based economy to landholder status. By 1850, when the Spanish once again restricted Chinese migrants' activities, it was this native-born mestizo elite, rather than the marginal European elite, who profited.[12]

Given the high quality of Chinese goods and the vast array of goods produced, British and other foreign merchants had little to sell for whatever they wanted to buy. Opium sales would rectify their balance of trade—and opium could be mass-produced in India. When a regional Chinese administrator seized the cargos and burned them in 1839, the British Empire went to war. The resulting reintroduction of opium into the trade would also impoverish large numbers of Chinese, who were then sold, or had to sell themselves or their children or wives, into indentured labor. Parallel to peasant pauperization in India, the policy created the Chinese segment of a labor reservoir for work across the colonized world. To the migrants' image of being "heathens"—that is, of a different religion—the image of "opium dens" was added. As indemnity for the cost of the aggression, the British Empire extracted from imperial China territorial rights to Hong Kong. Rural-to-urban and interurban migrants increased the city's population from four thousand in 1842 to about two hundred thousand by 1900—colonizer entrepôts were poles of attraction.[13]

Within China, where many-directional migrations were of long tradition, several factors increased mobility in the mid-nineteenth century. As in Europe, population growth was fast, from 300 million in 1790 to 420 million in 1850. While the price of rice, the main food staple, increased tenfold, inflation reduced incomes; the government's devaluation of copper, the circulating medium, in regard to silver as the taxpaying medium further undercut peasant families' precarious living conditions. From about 1860 on, a policy of increasing production in industries created jobs but was hampered by inefficiencies of bureaucratic control. Widespread social discontent, political unrest, and ethnic antagonisms, some of them fused with issues of religion, caused large-scale dislocations. Uprisings throughout the 1840s, the Taiping and Muslim rebellions and their repression 1851–1864 and 1855–1873, and warlordism sent people fleeing to search for subsistence elsewhere.[14]

Chinese overseas migrants traditionally came from the coastal provinces of Guangdong and Fujian (including from Chaozhou and Amoy and surroundings, and Hokkien-speakers), as well as from the island of Hainan and from among the internally migrant Hakka. The provinces' population density reached one person per quarter acre. The British Empire tapped this reservoir when, in 1860, it imposed the principle of "free emigration" on the Chinese state. Middlemen sent indentured and free migrants far beyond the limits of the traditional diaspora. In reaction, in 1868 the Chinese government ended its policy of disregard for emigrants, regulated the "coolie" trade, opened consulates, and sought ties to Chinese overseas merchants whose social capital as middlemen it had shunned while all Western powers had benefited from it. Diaspora Chinese sent remittances to their "emigrant communities" of origin, in many of which only women, children, and the elderly remained. Sequential migration led Chinese, like all migrants, to clusters of kin and friends at particular locations in the three main destinations: Southeast Asia as the easiest migration route; Latin America, particularly Cuba and Peru; and the United States and Canada as the most costly destinations.[15]

## Migration in and out of Japan

Japan's government, after closing the society to foreigners in the 1640s, had always kept Deshima (an island in the port of Nagasaki) open to Dutch traders to acquire knowledge and products deemed useful. A squadron of US gunboats forced admission of American and European merchants in 1854. In contrast to China's entrenched bureaucrats, Japan's new Meiji era administration (1868–1912) embarked on a program of "restoration" of the nation to economic and military power. To finance this urban modernization, the regime taxed and uprooted agrarian populations. Increasingly powerful, Japan succeeded by the 1890s in abrogating the unequal treaties, granting extraterritorial rights to Western merchants. The government hired influential "guest workers" from the West: advisory British military officers replaced the samurai warrior class with a soldiery of commoners; US engineers and missionaries, by providing technical assistance, opened entryways for industry; German- and Harvard-trained men helped develop a strategy of imperialist expansion undergirded by a doctrine of Japanese genetic superiority and a xenophobic chauvinism. Dislocated peasant men and women in turn migrated to Hawai'i and the Americas.[16]

## The Institutionalization of Indentured Servitude

When colonizer governments abolished the African slave migration system between 1807 and the 1870s, planters from Java via Réunion to Trinidad and Cuba, mine owners in Malaya and South Africa, guano pit entrepreneurs in Peru, and others demanded from these governments new manageable workers with low reproduction costs. Attempts to recruit Europeans foundered because these shunned semibondage and selected destinations in temperate zones with free wage labor and democratic-capitalist institutions.

Succumbing to planters' interests, the British and newly imperial[17] French colonizer states imposed a regime of indentured labor, a "second slavery," on men and women in their Asian territories. Beginning informally in the 1820s, British imperial legislation buttressed the system in 1834, the year of abolition of slavery. Indigenous forms began earlier and lasted longer in the Chinese realm. The French recruited workers in Indochina, and slavers kidnapped men and women from Pacific islands, Fiji in particular. The term *coolie,* which symbolized cheap and despised laborers among Western white capitalists and working-class organizations alike, meant "bitter strength" in Chinese and "wage for menial work" in Tamil. Recruits came from impoverished rural families and urban underclasses. In transoceanic migrations, free or "passenger" migrants moved along the circuits of the indentured workers and established supply networks for food and clothing. Larger numbers moved internally to regions of mining and factory work with the help, or under the tutelage, of labor recruiters.

Recruitment involved deception and force: idealized descriptions of working conditions, deliberate tricking into debt bondage, agent-induced gambling in China, self-pawning, or clan fighting. To be "shanghaied," a term used by sailors when enlisted against their will, derives from this practice of kidnapping. In southern China, middlemen

or "snakes" controlled recruitment; in India, the colonizing British mobilized migrants and, only after much abuse, appointed "protectors of
emigrants." In Meiji Japan the government attempted to recruit suit-
able workers and prevent exploitation by distant employers.

Travel to destinations across the Asian seas took a few days or
weeks, whereas the Calcutta-to-Caribbean trip lasted about six months.
Before the 1850s, America-bound Chinese on British and Spanish
vessels suffered mortality rates of up to 12 percent. The introduction
of steamships in about 1865 lowered mortality, and the reduction of
fares and travel time resulted in vastly larger numbers of migrants.
During the sea voyage from India, involuntary rites of passage replaced
village and family social ties with labor agents' control. This partial de-
culturation, in the eyes of Europeans, turned people of many specific
regional cultures into generic bound workers. While caste, class, and
custom lost some validity, faith remained a marker—Hindu, Muslim,
Sikh, Jain, Christian. And the multilingual composition—Urdu, Hindi,
Bengali, Tamil, Telugu, Punjabi, Gujarati, and others—necessitated
the development of a South Asian creole, usage of a non–South Asian
lingua franca, or assimilation into the largest language group at a particular destination. Similarly, Chinese laborers spoke mutually unintelligible dialects and had to develop a language of cross-cultural
communication.

Of the 2.5 million Chinese who left for Asian destinations in the
nineteenth century, no more than one-eighth were indentured laborers in the literal sense. A second group, under the "credit-ticket system," owed travel cost to kin, previous migrants, or merchants. Free
migrants relied on diasporic networks for selection of destinations—
within the limitations imposed by economic constraints: Burma, Malaya, the Dutch East Indies, Siam, French Indochina, the Philippines,
and the Pacific islands. Less than a million Chinese, most of whom
paid their own way, left the Asian orbit for Australia, Latin American
economies, and North America.[18]

The mass of India's transoceanic migrants—only 10 percent of whom were indentured—came from a northern belt extending from Bengal through Bihar to Uttar Pradesh and from a southeastern coastal belt from Orissa to Madras (Chennai). To the mid-1850s, recruiters targeted mainly non-Hindu aboriginal people, the poor of the ports, and the lowest castes. Many were famine victims with no prospects of reinsertion into labor markets or social positions. Recruitment followed patterns of ethnoculture and skills. In Burma, Bengalis provided clerical workers; sweepers came from Nellore; middle-class Tamils worked as clerks; Telugus from the Coromandel coast provided the labor for mills and other factories. The first of four outbound routes, to Burma, Malaya, and Ceylon, involved an estimated six million, most of whom returned. On the second route, small numbers of merchants, often with families, migrated to traditional centers of trade in East Africa and to new contract worker settlements. On the third route, the British brought Indians as "imperial auxiliaries" to Malaya as administrators, to Hong Kong as policemen, and to other possessions. Finally, on the fourth route, about 1.5 million contract workers were transported to destinations outside of Asia: one-third each to Mauritius and the Caribbean, one-tenth to Natal, the others to East Africa, the Indian Ocean, or the Pacific islands. After 1870, long-distance moves increased.

Most contract migrants were healthy young men, exploitable in the prime of their strength. Migration of women depended on restrictions in societies of origin as well as at the destination. The ratio of women was lowest among Chinese; among migrants destined for Latin America, a mere 1 percent were women. To counter the low rate among Indian migrants, the British government set a quota of 25 percent women among outbound workers. The actual percentage grew to just over 30 percent in the early 1890s. All societies of departure placed restrictions on women's migration. Among employers in the receiving economies, attitudes to women depended on labor force requirements and gendered role ascriptions. Where men were encouraged to stay, as in Trinidad, women were viewed as a stabilizing factor. The Australian government, expecting male workers to leave at the end of their contract, excluded women and children from entry to prevent permanent settlement. The slow pace of community formation among indentured laborers was related to the low rate of women. Transoceanic family lives impacted on gender roles and the raising and education of children.

Migration under indenture as well as of credit-ticket and free passenger migrants to the Pacific coast of the Americas began in the mid-1840s. Free Chinese came with the California and Fraser River gold rushes. Though free Chinese laborers were in great demand for railroad construction to the 1870s or 1880s, anti-Asian racism in North America led to unsuccessful attempts to restrict the hiring of Chinese workers. The period from the 1870s to the 1920s, from the introduction of steamship transport to the stepwise end of the Indian variant of the regime of indentured servitude, would form the apogee of this labor migration regime.[19]

## Transatlantic Connections

Migrations to the Americas, usually viewed as transatlantic, also involved transpacific crossings. Within Europe internal migrations preceded and accompanied the emigration, and within the Americas intracontinental moves contributed to settlement patterns—for example, northbound in New Spain to the regions that were to become the US Southwest. Colonization from California to the Bering Strait had been undertaken, in terms of empires, by Creoles and Spanish from New Spain, by British coming via the Pacific from East Asia, and by Russians from Siberia. The northern Pacific coast was Amerindian in culture and so were California and the Greater Southwest before the latter became Hispanic (Spanish-Indian mestizo) and before the first English- or French-speaking migrants arrived. Immigrants from New Spain reached New Mexico decades earlier than religious migrants settled in what they called New England.

On the West Coast of North America, Russian and Siberian fur traders, entrepreneurs, and fishermen, accompanied by Aleut hunters, came as far south as San Francisco Bay. Thousands of Chinese settled in Hawai'i, a few dozen sailors and skilled workers reached Vancouver Island in the 1790s. The latter were employees of the British East India Company engaged in a global competition with both Spanish transpacific shipping and its rival megacorporation, the Hudson's Bay Company, whose migrant traders came across the Atlantic. The first transpacific arrivals remained few, but from the mid-1840s the second phase of the Pacific migration system—after the sixteenth- and seventeenth-century connection from Spanish Manila to New Spain—brought Chinese and, later, Japanese settlers and workers. Their eastbound mobility and their labor helped build the transcontinental railroads that would facilitate European-origin westbound migrations in the 1870s and 1880s.[20]

The Atlantic world's age of revolution impacted deeply on migrations in Europe. Changes in societies and, more so, two decades of warfare interrupted goal-directed migrations within Europe and to the Americas. The contrast between the new republican United States and the reimposed dynastic rule in Europe created a dual discourse of hope: Individuals and families began to consider improving their personal life chances by transatlantic migration; and collectively, reformers and, later, reform parties struggled for better conditions and called upon people to stay. Finally, a new emphasis on ethnic-national cultures, a democratizing move challenging the nobilities' trans-European culture, began to make "the people," often constructed as families tilling the soil, the *referent* for statewide national cultures. The "nationalization" of the largest and most powerful ethnocultural group in a particular region often forced smaller groups of different cultures living in the same territory to consider emigration. The European war commenced in 1792 with the revolutionary attempt to export France's republican model into neighboring dynasties' realms and the counterrevolutionary old order's aggression to contain the French Revolution; it continued with Napoleon's imperialist expansion as far as Egypt and Moscow, his plantocracy-induced attempt to recapture Haiti, and the intra-European wars of "liberation" from French-Napoleonic rule. Large numbers of men and women were displaced; more than half a million soldiers were marched into Russia; defeated units, disabled men, and stragglers were left behind. Soldiers, depopulating fertile countrysides, might return as settlers with their families after the war. When in 1815 a backward-looking dynastic order was reestablished, defeated revolutionaries and reformers turned to the United States. Arrivals would skyrocket in the 1870s and 1880s.

Before independence of thirteen of the British colonies, European immigration to colonial North America peaked with some 15,000 arriving annually in the fifteen years before 1775: Protestant Irish, Scots, English, and German-speakers were the main groups. About three-fifths of these, under indentures, had to work off the cost of the ocean passage by three to seven years of bound labor. However, the largest group of newcomers were 85,000 enslaved Africans. Given the imperial structures of rule and shipping connections as well as language affinity, migrants from the Western and Northern European cultures moved to the northern regions from the St. Lawrence Valley to the Carolinas. Few French-speakers migrated because, the society's Catholicity notwithstanding, couples traditionally limited their fertility to two children and thus no surplus rural population without land emerged. Those from the Iberian Peninsula moved to Florida, New Spain, or Brazil. Portugal's global reach influenced its migrants' destinations: By 1800, 1.8 million European-born and Creole-born Portuguese lived in Brazil, as compared to 400,000 on the Atlantic islands, 80,000 to 100,000 in Equatorial Africa, and 120,000 or fewer in Asia. To the

1870s, the Atlantic migration system remained a dual one, from Western and Northern Europe to North America and from Iberian and Mediterranean Europe to South America, with some interaction in the Caribbean.

From the Atlantic world's two major revolutionary societies, the United States and France, supporters of the old order departed by their own choice or had to flee. Nobles and segments of the clergy spread to courts and monasteries in neighboring dynastic states. From the new United States, supporters of the Crown (loyalists) left for British North America (Canada) or moved to Britain and other parts of the empire. The French Revolution, which, from a guillotine-centered view, was far more violent than the American, displaced only the small nobility and clergy. The split in American society divided the urban and rural middle classes and sent hundreds of thousands fleeing.

Interregional migrations made colonial and revolutionary North America a mobile society: circuits to sell redemptioners (indentured servants who would redeem their liberty), migration from New England to Nova Scotia or westward to the Ohio Valley, sale and forced migration of slaves, deportation and return of Acadians, the mass flight or emigration of loyalists. Of the German-language soldiers (Hessians), traded by their sovereigns to the British for service in North America, some deserters and many of those taken as prisoners of war decided to stay and settle. Like voluntary migrants they took advantage of the local options. With those who returned to Hessia came about two hundred African-Americans who had enlisted in the Hessian regiments.[21]

In the new United States and in the reestablished multiple German states, farming families could not settle all of their children on the parents' land. Wherever a family on a subsistence farm raised more than two children into adulthood, the "surplus" had to migrate. From the southwestern German states people had migrated eastward down the Danube to the fertile south Russian plains from which previous Ottoman-ruled peoples had been sent fleeing. From the 1820s, they changed destination: via the Rhine River and Dutch ports to North America. There, a perceived shortage of land east of the Allegheny Mountains had led to demands that the British government open the Ohio Valley, protected by the Proclamation of 1763 as native people's (Indian) territory. Speculators and settlers moved into the region, annexed to the United States without the consent of the native people living there. Americans' and Europeans' settlement migrations generated refugee migrations of agricultural and hunting families and whole societies of Native Americans, who, from the late 1860s to the 1890s, were either killed or confined to reservations.

At its founding the United States had a population of 3.9 million, consisting of English (49 percent), enslaved and a small number of free African people (20 percent), Germans and Scots (7 percent each), Scots-Irish and Irish, Walloons and Dutch, French, Swedish and other Scandinavians, and Spanish. Men and women from Minorca, Livorno, and Greece settled in Florida. Religious refugees included Pietists, Moravians, Huguenots, Mennonites, and Old Order Amish. The society, later constructed as a homogeneous "Anglo America," had heterogeneous origins and was multicultural from the start. From 1790 to 1820, just under a quarter million migrants arrived; from 1820 to 1840, three-quarters of a million; in 1841–1850, 1.7 million; and in the last decade before the American Civil War, 2.6 million. Because US government statisticians counted only arrivals, these gross figures need to be adjusted for return migration to Europe. Actual return was low in times of sailing vessels, but after steamships came into use in the 1870s, rates of return increased to one-third of the arrivals.[22]

In bicultural English- and French-language British North America (Canada after 1867), migration followed similar patterns. Its prairie West, inaccessible across the Canadian Shield, was settled from the 1870s. The third North American country, Spanish-language Mexico (independent since 1821), attracted few migrants: given the large haciendas, no "free" land was available for peasant settlers; the laws of the 1850s deprived the sizable native population of much of their land and created a mobile reservoir of wage laborers. An insurgency by those loyal to Spanish rule in the late 1820s and a European French-led invasion in the 1860s resulted in strong antiforeigner sentiments. The whole of the North American migration region achieved its final territorial and political-social shape in 1867. British North America became the Dominion of Canada. The United States—after annexation of almost half of Mexico in 1848 and 1853—purchased Alaska and began its post–Civil War Reconstruction. Mexico defeated the European invaders and began a period of reform under President Juarez in the 1870s.[23]

In postrevolutionary Europe, a changing and expanding economic order demanded flexible labor. As a result, states began to emancipate their agrarian serf families from bondage between 1762 (Savoy) and 1861 (Russia). The former serfs, with few or no means, had to compensate their former lords for the loss of *corvée* labor and fees. Like Mexican native peoples deprived of their land, and like freed US slaves without compensation for the labor of generations, reduced landholdings and cash payments forced emancipated—and emaciated—peasants and their children to migrate within Europe or, if they could afford it, to the four frontier societies of the Americas: Canada, the United States, Brazil, or Argentina. The portrayal of their settlement as one broad and continuous westward movement across North America or into South America's interior glosses over the multidirectional nineteenth-century internal migrations. The Euro-American creoles' and immigrants' advance required the construction of roads, railroads, and, in the northern part, canals. Such earthworks mobilized unskilled labor locally and from afar and, after completion, facilitated travel of further migrants—from the 1870s the transcontinental railroads were completed.

Internal migrations in North America included mobility across the US-Canada and US-Mexico borders both into and out of the United States. In New England, newcomers from old England introduced textile machinery. Mills, requiring waterpower, were located in places with no previous settlement and attracted farm families' daughters, whose brothers often migrated west to lands more fertile than the local hills. From the 1840s on, factory owners replaced the "girls" migrating within the region by transatlantically mobile Irish families whom British colonialism and famine forced to leave and by Catholic French-Canadian families from the St. Lawrence Valley, where high numbers of children, slow industrialization, and a backward-looking regime of the Catholic Church hindered the development of job opportunities. In the southern United States, the cotton plantation economy—free owners and enslaved workers—shifted from exhausted soils along the tidewater via the piedmont of the Alleghenies to lands east of the Mississippi. From the late 1860s, high urban demand for labor induced an east- or northbound migration of supernumerary farm children to Pittsburgh, Chicago, and the many other industrial, commercial, and transportation nodes.[24]

Among the South American receiving societies, Brazil, as the largest, experienced a first post-independence phase of European migration from the 1820s to the 1860s, a period during which African slaves continued to be imported. German, Italian, and Polish settlers came to the coffee plantations of Rio Grande do Sul on the southern border, where investors had relocated because of soil exhaustion north of Rio de Janeiro. A second phase with vastly increased in-migration, departures, and transatlantic circular migrations began in the 1870s. In Argentina, too, the takeoff of in-migration came in the last third of the nineteenth century.[25]

To put into perspective the hopes for a better life in the Americas and the volume of migration, we have to remind ourselves that in the European context, Vienna was viewed as an El Dorado, Paris as a city of freedom, the German Ruhr district and London as providing multiple opportunities. Regardless of continent and destination, migrants valued the increase in choice when wages were paid in cash rather than in kind. The transatlantic migrations, beginning after 1815 and accelerating from Western and Northern Europe in the 1840s, created the frame and the ethnocultural neighborhoods and transatlantic family branches that, from the 1870s on, provided the proletarian mass migrants with first anchor points.

## The Russo-Siberian Migration System

European Russia and its Siberian and Central Asian regions were arenas of several migration orbits: southern Russia, Siberia, and the Amur borderlands, northwestern European Russia. In a long struggle with the Ottoman Empire, tsarist armies expanded the state's territory to the Black Sea, subdued local Asian peoples, and opened the region for settlement of Ukrainian peasant families, and then also, from 1763 on, for southwest German-language peasants and religious refugees, Mennonites in particular. A kind of homestead law provided the migrants with land. These West Central Europeans could keep their faith and language and establish their own schools. Five decades later, authorities ended the admission of German-speakers because southeast European and Slavic migrants appeared to integrate better. Then potential eastbound migrants turned westward; from the 1880s, with revocation of privileges, Russian Mennonite and other German-language families would move in secondary migrations to North America.

Its huge distance away and its harsh living conditions made Siberia, in the view of tsarist authorities, ideal for penal colonies: An estimated hundred thousand Polish "rebels," fifty thousand Russian political exiles, and forty thousand criminals were sent there before 1914. About five thousand women, some with children, joined their deported husbands. To the contested border with China, the government sent troops and settlers. Peasants moved to southern Siberia on their own because of "free" land from which native people had been displaced and because thereby—turning distance to their advantage—they (almost) left the reach of tax collectors and other government officials.[26]

European Russia (which since the late eighteenth century included one-third of Poland as well as the Baltic peoples) had attracted or even invited Western European migrants for investment, technical expertise, commercial connections, and artisanal skills, as well as for military service. Because the Russian nobility owned the enserfed peasants and looked down on commercial activities, no indigenous middle and proletarian classes could develop: Migrants became an "inserted" middle class of different cultures and languages. For this very reason, Polish rulers had invited persecuted Jews from Western Europe to settle in their realms centuries earlier. The Ashkenazi Jewish culture had emerged from both these invitations and the West European pogroms.

From the early nineteenth century, the range of activities and regions of settlement open to Jews became ever more restricted. In 1804, Jews were designated as an urban people and ordered to leave the countryside—half a million men, women, and children were affected. In the mid-nineteenth century, further restrictions followed and the "May Laws" of 1882 prohibited settlement in rural areas altogether. From 1835 they were limited to a "pale of settlement": the traditional communities in Poland, Belorussia-Lithuania, and Ukraine, as well as areas in the Baltic provinces and regions of southern "New Russia." In the Kingdom of Poland, where the Jewish population almost tripled from 1816 to 1865, exclusionary legislation prevented Jews from living in many of the larger cities. The enforced and yet restricted mobility contributed to their concentration in stagnating small towns. In all of Russia, the Jewish population increased by 156 percent the three decades before 1867, a vast reservoir for outbound migrations. The pogroms of the 1880s provided the trigger.

In the early decades of industrialization, before the emancipation of serfs in 1861, common laborers and workers for the new industries needed to be recruited from among serfs. In the northern *obrok* system, serf duties had been monetized. Serfs paid their owners an annual sum from income obtained by sale of crops, cottage production, or labor migration. Some owners even helped their serfs to find city labor. Cottage production and seasonal migration resulted in higher literacy rates. In the south central belt with fertile soils and sufficient rain, the lords needed servile labor throughout the year and, under the *barschina* system, immobilized serfs by means of high work obligations. In St. Petersburg, founded in 1703 with the help of in-migrating Dutch drainage experts and German-language artisans, the temporary migrating servile labor force accounted for one-third of the 450,000 inhabitants around 1840. Such mobile rural people lost their utility once industrial production in the 1860s and 1870s began to require training and skills. The government first initiated programs to train local labor with the help of in-migrating foreign experts, and then it adjusted the structure of society in order to reduce the need for foreigners. Toward the end of the nineteenth century, due to the nobility, who were jealous of the position of West European migrants with social and human capital, and to Russian nationalism, immigrant foreigners lost their protected status. At the same time exchanges with Western Europe, French culture in particular, remained intense.

Late nineteenth-century European Russia was an industrializing society. Land shortages and cash crises were exacerbated by a near-doubling of the population of 68.5 million in 1850 to 126 million in all of Russia in 1897. Families' adjustment of child-bearing patterns to new socioeconomic circumstances achieved results only a generation later. Relative rural overpopulation resulted in migration and proletarianization, voluntary for those who desired wage incomes, involuntary for those who would have preferred to remain on the land. Romanov Russia, like the Hohenzollern territories east of the Elbe and the Danubian sections of the Habsburg monarchy, was characterized by a feudal-bourgeois type of socioeconomic development that contrasted with the bourgeois-capitalist ways of Western Europe and North America. These vast agrarian regions in the three semifeudal empires became reservoirs of labor through internal migration to Russian industry, through seasonal migration to German and Austrian agriculture and industry, and through emigration for other parts of Europe and North America.[27]

Peasant emancipation did not make men and women independent. Each village commune *(mir)* held land collectively, reallocated this commonwealth among its male "souls" annually, and was collectively responsible for payment of taxes, for redemption payments to former lords, and for sending recruits to the army. Out-migrating men remained part of the community, needed passes for seasonal or multiannual absence, and were expected to return for spring sowing or harvest work. Such seasonal migrants had to be fed in the village in winter, and they also returned during slumps in employment. Later, men who renounced their rights to land could leave permanently, but with no urban social security system in place, few chose this option. In the decade after emancipation (1861–1870), some thirteen million men migrated for one year or less. In the next decades migration increased continuously.[28]

In terms of mobility across the globe, the completion of networks of railroad lines with port cities and the introduction of steamships in the 1870s vastly increased the speed and volume of travel, though in view of the population growth not necessarily the rates of mobility. The improved means of transport and communication affected the outbound mass movements from Europe as well as return migration from the Americas—the "proletarian mass migration" began. Similarly, there was a quick growth in the mass migration of bound proletarianized men and women in the Indian Ocean and the Plantation Belt under a regime of temporary bondage imposed mainly by the

British Empire. The ending of permanent bondage of serfs in Europe between the early 1800s and the 1860s, and of slaves in the Americas by the 1880s, permitted mobility, but it was constrained by color of skin: white Europeans could move regionally across Europe, transatlantically, or worldwide, but people of black African origin could move only regionally within the Americas. Population growth in almost all regions of the world sent people searching for "free"—that is, less densely settled—land and, far more so, for wage work. In East Asia, the same migratory potential also resulted in mass outbound mobility. Most African peoples' mobility remained constrained or controlled by the European colonizer states and the investor migrants or their personnel.

CHAPTER TWO

# The Global and the Local

The outline of migrations before the beginning of industrialization and transformation demonstrates that the movement of people as much as of goods was global then, and in fact even earlier. "Globalization" has a far longer history than the early twenty-first-century catchword suggests. To analyze movement of people, we need an understanding of the scope of regions across the globe that migrants connected, and a differentiation of categories of migration. We also need to understand systematically how migrant agency developed in the context of the society of birth, and how migrants developed belongings and identifications or—in an earlier interpretation—had national identities. Finally, we need to ask how migrants inserted themselves at their destination, if there was only one, or during the several layovers and at multiple points of arrival.

The approach of an older migration historiography involved a "progress of history" perspective, which usually neglected allegedly backward societies of departure, began at the port of entry, and assumed that only highly developed societies attract migrants. Most historical writing was generated in receiving countries, especially those of the Atlantic world, so a self-congratulatory tone emerged. Migrations within Europe, with few exceptions, began to attract interest only in the 1980s. Migrations elsewhere were studied in separate historiographical slots. The US Ellis Island approach to migration history saw "free" Europeans arrive with cultural baggage to be deposited before entering a melting pot. It subsumed other migrants under the labels *coolie* and *slave,* designations that connote passivity and even

European immigrants arriving in North America at Ellis Island Immigration Station in New York Harbor, ca. 1904. Ellis Island, an entry gate for immigrants from Europe since 1892, was considered both an "island of hope" and an "island of tears." Very few immigrants were rejected, because European officials had already refused departure to those deemed not admissible. But while waiting for inspection, immigrants still felt fear that they might be excluded. (Library of Congress)

inferiority. No comparative approach or scholarly exchange with historians of the Chinese diaspora and its migrations or those of the Indian Ocean emerged.[1]

## Spaces of Mobility

In the above survey, geographic denominations, whether continents or oceans, have been reconfigured as major socioeconomic regions with locational references such as the Atlantic economies, the Plantation Belt, and the several distinct cultural regions of Asia. Physical geography, except as hindering or facilitating mobility, has little meaning for migrants. What is important is how particular locations are imbued with meaning, "home" or "better opportunities," and how societies experienced as constraining are being connected with others assumed or known to provide better options. Geographic *places* thus become lived social *spaces* and, in Arjun Appadurai's term, *scapes*. Beyond the spatialization of physical geography by social and economic life, a land-scape or a sea-scape is lived space imbued with meaning, is a fixed geography in flexible frames of interpretation. Migrants' writings show how a person leaving his or her space of birth and socialization appropriates new landscapes or sea-lanes into the familiar frame of reference for geographies or, if they do not fit, may label them "strange," "alien," or "exotic" rather than expand or change the frame of reference.

An Italian or Chinese migrant, for example, leaving a family plot far inland from the emigration port will experience the first leg of the route—on foot, cart, or carrier animal—as slow, the landscape as familiar. The bustle of the port will seem unfamiliar, hectic, difficult to decipher. The voyage across the Atlantic or the China Seas will be short, at least in memory, because nothing of interest is being recorded. What for mariners is a sea-lane, for a rural or urban migrant is an empty expanse. If arriving from Genoa in New York, he or she will see the El-trains and report back to friends and family that trains are going over the roofs of houses. Among the recipients, such a piece of information is difficult to place within the customary frame of reference: "at home," only birds fly over roofs. If arriving from Guangdong in Manila, merchants would have mental maps connecting the trading ports, artisans would concern themselves with similarities and differences between their neighborhoods. Geographies and their social usages are developed in people's minds and emerge as comprehensive scapes. Because such mental understanding and appropriation of spaces changes constantly, scholars have introduced the concept of "processual geographies" to counter the traditional notion of fixed place.[2]

For historians of migration, as for those of the movement of goods, the transport connections between different spaces matter as much as to migrants and traders. Such connectivity was overlooked in bordered nation-state approaches to history from top down, from nonmigrating statesmen's and historians' viewpoints. State approaches add fixed territorial boundaries to fixed geographies and, in the nation-state version, add national-cultural boundaries as a third fixed dividing line. Nation-state historiographies separate themselves from neighboring communities and societies or distant linked ones. If some 150 million men and women migrated in the three major migration systems quantified by McKeown, 320 million across international border from the 1840s to the 1940s, and additional hundreds of millions moved medium distance across international borders, nation-state historiography would need to incorporate them as much into their narratives as economic sectors extending across the world. Where was the cotton, necessary to clothe statesmen and commoners alike, grown, how was it transported, where was it processed? How did plantation, mining, and factory workers and investors and their overseers, clerks, and technicians move to satisfy the demand for cloth or, at courts, for luxury goods?[3]

To understand interconnectedness, scholars have criticized the reification of dividing borders, the vagueness of "global" expanses, the simplification of a "global village." People are socialized during in-fancy, childhood, and adolescence into the space and value systems of their locality of birth in family, local society, and regional or statewide educational institutions. Separating themselves from the parental household in their late teens, they tend to search for jobs (or tillable land) or professional options in the region familiar to them or in oth-ers accessible through information feedback. They may have to take into account statewide labor markets and regulations. Thus, the local, the regional, and the statewide form three sequential layers of social-ization and experience. The economic sphere, in which they search for an income-providing occupation, does not necessarily stop at the bor-ders of their state of birth. Meso- or macroregions, the interconnected Caribbean islands or Europe's landmass, for example, are accessible through road, rail, and shipping connections. Thus, scholars need to establish empirically the extent of migrant geographies, spaces, and scapes. For 1870 as a specific point in time, for example, it makes no sense to speak of generic "European" migrants: Those from the western and west-central regions of Europe had moved for generations to par-ticular destinations afar and had connected them in mental maps; those from southern segments had moved to different locations and had established their specific information flows; those from northern regions were relative newcomers to transoceanic expanses. Similarly, the regions of recruitment of indentured laborers and the regions of departure of migrants in India shifted over time, expanded and con-tracted as did the destinations. For each period, spaces of migration and their micro-, meso-, or macroregional extent need to be delin-eated, because social geographies are in flux.[4]

Conceptually, research distinguishes between *inter*-state and *trans*-border moves: the "inter" posits two distinct entities, usually polities, as in "international;" the "trans" emphasizes continuities and overlapping spaces. The validity of the recent conceptualization of "transnational" needs to be questioned. In its original formulation it was applied to migrants since the 1990s, a period in which nation-states lost some of their hold on societal developments and much of their hold over economies. In the later nineteenth century, most migrants originated not in nation-states but in empires—the Qing, Romanov, Habsburg, Hohenzollern, and Windsor realms, the labels of which were being nationalized into China, Russia, Austria-Hungary, Germany, Britain—though every one of them contained many peoples and the Habsburg empire called itself a "state of many peoples" *(Vielvölkerstaat)*.

The term *transcultural* provides a comprehensive meaning for movements between societies, regardless of geographic distance traversed: translocal, transregional, transnational or trans-state, transoceanic. Although ideologues of the nation-state, historians included, posited migration as occurring from nation to ethnic enclave in another nation, 94 percent of the European-origin migrants arriving in the United States in the early twentieth century traveled from their place of birth or a previous migration destination to friends and kin in a particular locality in the United States. They migrated in family and friendship networks between urban neighborhoods or villages and, in the frame of family economies as well as individual aspirations, between mesoregional or national economies. Self-determined migrations and recruitment of indentured workers also connected specific regions of India or China to particular regions and localities in the Plantation Belt. A recent approach calls such migrations "glocal"—connecting local social spaces in one society with specific spaces in another across the globe. Family economies may thus connect individuals and constraining frames with opportunity structures across locations in several continents or macroregions. An early twentieth-century southern Chinese peasant family might thus establish a second base on Canada's Pacific coast and perhaps branch out to inland cities. People sought options on the basis of information provided by reliable members of their network at destinations to which possibilities of travel existed. Only in some states' overblown mythologies did they reach for "unlimited opportunities."[5]

## A Typology of Migrations

Both everyday language and scholarly terminologies aggregate multiple migrations into undifferentiated, often implicitly value-laden catch-all terms. Views of migrants common in the United States and the neo-Europes saw hardy men (without mention of hardy women) colonize assumedly virgin rural regions and bequeath the land to generations of children: white-skinned Europeans as cultivators of wooded wilderness and prairie grasslands. The earlier residents held different views of such intrusions, which often turned them into refugees. The designation "proletarian mass migration" for the Atlantic world's decades from the 1870s to 1914 implies that all migrants were urban workers.

A comprehensive approach analyzes migrants' decisions and trajectories—within institutional frames—in a spectrum from free to forced, from local to intercontinental, from seasonal to permanent, as well as in terms of the range of goals to be achieved at the destination. Within each and every type, gendering is required: men and women are assigned different roles, have different experiences and different goals. Intergenerational aspects also need to be included. A classification along the free/unfree or self-willed/bound axis yields the following categories:

- free migrants who decide when to depart and where to go according to their own desires and life-projects on the basis of trustworthy information available within the frames societies and states impose;
- labor migrants, the "free" transatlantic migrants of the late nineteenth century and of the late twentieth-century South-to-North migrations,

who, however, live under often severe economic constraints and thus decide to depart "self-willed" under duress;

- bound-labor migrants who have to sell their labor for a number of years because of poverty (European and Asian indentured servants and credit-ticket migrants);
- forced-labor migrants who are enslaved for menial work for life (Africans in the Atlantic world), who are enslaved for service or intellectual labor (Africans in the Indian Ocean world and people elsewhere), who are bound for a certain period of their life against their will (South Africa under apartheid), or who are corralled by force and interned for an indeterminate period (Nazi Germany, imperialist Japan, the Stalinist Soviet Union);
- involuntary migrants displaced by political intolerance (exiles), by religious intolerance (religious refugees), or by other causes like ethnocultural or gender-based inequalities;
- refugees from war and other violence;
- persons displaced by ecological disasters whether natural or human-made, the latter meaning *men*-made.[6]

Transatlantic and transpacific migrants of the turn of the twentieth century—like Third-to-First-World migrants of the turn of the twenty-first century—made and make decisions "free" *under the constraints of economic conditions* that leave no room for life-projects or even survival. Their "home" may be a society that is unfair and unsupportable, that does not permit sustainable lives. Institutionalized restrictions of colonialism, imperialism, and racism constrained decisions; gendered restrictions and sexism were intended to prevent women from making their own decisions. Children have to follow parents even though they may resent being separated from friends and other family. On the other hand, parents may migrate and accept a downward move during their own lifetime to improve, in a middle-range perspective, the life chances of their children; men may migrate to better provide for their wives. "Free" decisions are framed, in the double meaning, by systems of reference at best and massive constraints at worst. Involuntary migrants, refugees and exiles, depart under political, ethnoracial, gender, or other persecution; because of warfare within or between states; social ostracism or fundamentalist religious pressures; tradition-bound stagnation or other. Usually refugees hope to return if conditions improve in their society of birth. Forced migrants are torn out of their social environments by military, police, or private entrepreneurs, whether raiders for forced laborers, slave catchers, or traffickers in the sex trade.

Distance of migration may be short, medium, or long. Migration of long geographic distances may lead to similar occupations and cultural environments: Indian Ocean port cities were part of transoceanic commercial and migration networks with similar labor practices and trading protocols; rural young men heading for work on another continent often remained in earthwork and lived among migrant compatriots. Similarly, geographic proximity does not necessarily imply cultural proximity. Young peasant women moving to domestic labor in middle-class households of nearby towns and cities face transitions across class and status lines. In the past, greater distance often involved higher travel cost in terms of both transportation and time. Cost also depends on means of transport; land-bound voyaging was usually more expensive than water-borne ship travel. Patterns of travel became time-compressed in the 1870s with the introduction of steamships and again from the mid-1950s with air travel.

As regards intended duration, migration might be seasonal, annual, multi-annual, for working life, or permanent. In agricultural societies across the globe, men and women, sometimes with their children, migrated and migrate seasonally to harvest work or to food processing, temporarily to mines or factories, or multi-annually to a distant branch of an internationally active company, whether a multinational textile company of the late nineteenth century or a 1920s automobile firm, or to domestic service and caregiving work. People might leave for a number of years to gain additional experience in a craft or at a university, to set up a branch of a family business, or for income-generating reasons. Migrants often plan to stay for only a number of years, but both poor labor markets "at home" and adjustment to the receiving society may induce them to extend their sojourn. Thus some, wanting to return, become unwillingly permanent migrants. Others adjust and stay as unintentionally permanent migrants.

From the 1870s to the 1930s, about one-third of the migrants to the United States, labeled "immigrants" in public and in research terminologies, returned to Europe, more to Asia. They were temporary or, to use a modern problem-laden term, "guest" workers. Most of the indentured servants from Asian societies returned to their respective regions of departure, but some—jointly with free passenger migrants—formed communities at the destinations, whether Indians in Natal and the Caribbean or Chinese in Malaya and the Americas. In the Atlantic migrations, two-fifths of the migrants were women; after 1930 women accounted for just over 50 percent. In migrations within the Indian Ocean and the seas of East and Southeast Asia their share was lower. However, when men decided to stay and form communities and, because of racial and ethnic hierarchies, could not marry women from the resident cultural groups, marriage migration increased the ratio of women, and families began to be formed through transoceanic correspondence.[7]

In the three-quarters of a century from 1870 to 1945, inter-state agricultural settlement migrations remained limited; inter-state bound and free labor migrations accounted for the majority of the long-distance moves; migrations of professionals were small in number. *Intra*-state migrations related to urbanization and industrialization were far larger in volume than *inter*-state ones. In many cities across the urbanizing segments of the globe, more than half of the population had not been born there. Small, but extremely powerful, were the migrations of white men (and some women) from the European to the colonized segments of the globe. Their armed political and economic domination resulted in intensification of colonial penetration and of mobilization of working men and women of colors other than white for the plantations and mines across the subtropical and tropical segments of the globe.

## A Systems Approach to Migration

To understand the complexity of migrant men and women's agency in local and society-wide frames as well as during their trajectories between societies, historians have developed a systems approach. This comprehensive theoretical-methodological frame incorporates causational and incidental factors and outcomes as well as multiple rationalities. Specifically, it connects migration patterns and decisions in terms of (1) the society of departure in local, regional, statewide, and global frames; (2) the actual move across distance given an era's means of transportation and communication; (3) the society or societies of destination again in micro-, meso-, and macroregional perspectives; and (4) linkages between the communities in which migrants spent or spend part of their lives. Its interdisciplinary and transcultural character permits analyses of the structures and institutions—which constantly evolve and thus could be called processual structures and structured processes. It also permits analytical inclusion of the discursive frames of migration in the societies of origin and of arrival in particular local or regional variants. It deals with all aspects, including industrialization, urbanization, social stratification, gender roles and family economies, demographic characteristics, political situation and developments, educational institutions, religious or other belief systems, ethnocultural composition, and traditions of short- and long-distance migrations. The approach emphasizes lived culture and indicates how the interrelated economic, social, political, and technological forces converge into migrants' cultural "habitus" and whole way of life.[8] The systems approach analyzes societies as they reshape within the global hierarchy of domination, dependency, and development. Societies and economies have been and are linked globally through families spread across several countries.

The systems approach analyzes the impact of out-migration on families and societies of departure and of in-migration on receiving societies and specific communities. What did out-migration mean for agricultural villages, whole agrarian regions, or urban neighborhoods, whether in China or in Europe? The decisions of millions of men and women to depart change communities and societies of origin as much as those in which they establish transitory or permanent homes. This agency approach needs to be modified in the cases of forced, indentured, or enslaved workers, as well as refugee migrants who are deprived of agency at the time of departure. But their postmigration survival and insertion depends on choices, even if under severely constraining conditions. Slave acculturation resulted in African-origin cultures in the Americas, and refugees impacted on labor markets and social customs, whether Koreans under Japan's occupation or German Jews in 1930s Turkey. People act in their own perceived best interest but do so under conditions not of their own making but imposed by historical developments and power structures.

Precipitating and facilitating factors for migration include rigid stratification and class structures that prevent upward mobility or choice of economic activity. Established patterns of mobility ease departures because potential migrants may rely on information and, often, on guides. People traveling from Hong Kong to San Francisco or Vancouver, from rural village communities to St. Petersburg, or from small towns to Buenos Aires, follow clearly, if often orally, demarcated routes. The self-reinforcing attractiveness of migration systems emerges from information generated and easily accessible. Distances to be traversed, cultural affinities, possibilities (and cost) of regular return, congruence of skills and job openings inform migration decisions rather than imagined future wealth.

Societal arrangements and processes always impact on migration, but states' roles changed dramatically from emigration regulation or prohibition, until the mid-nineteenth century in many dynastic states, to immigration controls in the late nineteenth and early twentieth-century Atlantic world and subsequently elsewhere. The introduction of state-issued passports changed a travel document from a permit to pass a port of entry into an instrument to exclude those of other cultures, colors of skin, or class. It took decades for states to fully enforce such controls. Asians—women at first—were restricted from North America in the mid-1870s; for Europeans, regulations were tightened but near-exclusion came only in the 1920s; along the US-Mexican border, patrols initiated in the mid-1920s were meant to limit the movement of "brown" people out of Mexico but several economic sectors in the United States depended on their labor. In Europe, passport laws were operationalized faster. In a side effect, they made 1930s flight from fascist states difficult as states denied entry to refugees without papers. Under national chauvinism, especially under fascism, and in cases of corrupt political elites, whole states have become refugee-generating apparatuses. Oppressive and self-enriching political elites lose the trust of large segments of the society.

High rates of out-migration change states and societies. In phases of demographic transition, emigration might decrease pressure on labor markets and permit wages to rise and standards of living to improve. Thus, societies might become more stable. But out-migration may also reduce the need to create jobs or to reform constraining structures and thus exacerbate tensions. Policy makers and administrators feared loss of tax revenues and army recruits as well as loss of women able to bear children for the state's armies; others wanted to rid their polity of what they considered surplus populations. Only recently has the social cost of emigration been conceptualized: Families and societies "invest" in raising and educating (as yet unproductive) children. These, as adults, "repay" intrafamily and intrasocietal investment by intergenerational transfer of the cost of caring for the "dependent" young and old. This "compact between generations" is broken when people withdraw from the obligation by emigrating. Working-age migrants take their accumulated individual and social capital with them. States of birth cannot recover social costs, and states of destination, getting trained and educated men and women "for free," benefit from their productivity and taxes. This has been called "development aid" given by poorer societies to more-developed societies.

Out-migration deprives societies of departure of part of the human capital that, given the respective state's economic stage of development, often cannot be used there. Emigrants may send back remittances and thus contribute both to their family's budget and to the state's foreign currency reserves. The budgets of some sending states, such as late nineteenth-century Italy, have depended and still depend on individual migrants' remittances. Though some economists and politicians have extolled investment opportunities provided by such transfers, the recipient families often need such funds to prevent their daily lives from sliding below subsistence level. Migrants may also transfer ideas through communication or return in person. Such innovation may improve stagnant economies, but elites benefiting from the old state of affairs often impede or prevent change and reform.

The actual process of transition to a location in another society may be extended over time, compressed into a few days, or delayed if, for example, refugees are stacked away in camps rather than being able to restructure their lives. Obstacles to departure include cost of travel, which needs to be related to the days, months, or years of work it takes to procure the sum necessary. During the period of voyaging, formerly extended, no income may be earned. Emigration regulations may pose barriers; the barriers posed by immigration restrictions might be almost insurmountable. Racial barriers erected in the Anglo-American and European societies against "people of color" made entry difficult. Inducements include prepaid tickets sent by earlier migrants or, in the case of indentured migrants, contractually guaranteed return fare. Even more so, they include accurate information on the trip and the availability of income-generating positions after arrival.

Arrangements for travel are made on the basis of information sent by prior migrants, with the help of guides from the community, or by labor recruiters. For centuries, "travel agencies" arranged package tours: medieval Christian pilgrims destined for Jerusalem or Muslim Hajj pilgrims are examples. From the mid-nineteenth century, migrants across Europe contracted with the local representative of a reliable agency connected to the distant shipping and railroad companies; contract laborers in India or China would approach a recruiting office that would also take charge of the trip. Change of trains and embarkation was done under supervision of the agencies' personnel—the voyage was as organized like modern group tourism.

Some migrants move stepwise, first as far as their limited funds take them—perhaps to a job-providing city, ideally the port (in the present: the airport) of future departure. For some, the need to earn money for the next leg of the trip was an unwelcome delay, for others a welcome stopover for a first adjustment. Travel experiences and emotional coping vary from person to person. To gauge the capabilities required of migrants, we need to be aware that many nineteenth-century emigrants had never seen a train or a ship before they stepped aboard one. Accounts reflect both easygoing confidence and bewilderment. From the imposition of immigration controls, admission procedures were fraught with fears of rejection. Even the US rules, liberal for migrants from Asia to the mid-1870s and for those from Europe to 1917, were difficult to negotiate because of frequent administrative changes, lack of precise information, and sometimes abusive treatment. Such regulations had a gendered impact: women faced more administrative harassment than men.

Migrants live and, if self-willed, decide at both ends of their trajectory, comparing labor markets and other income-generating options. They select perceived increased options in a place accessible given their means and where they expect to be able to communicate, given their language. Far more migrants moved to a neighboring city or job-providing mine, plantation, or other site than crossed oceans. The intercontinental connections directed them to communities of previous migrants of the same language. Job-providing economies of destination for the period of imperialism—as for other periods—need to be placed in the global as well as mesoregional hierarchies of political and economic power relations. The sociopolitical frames of the receiving societies need to be analyzed with the same comprehensiveness as those of the societies of departure.[9]

## National Identities, Societal Belongings, Identifications

If territorially bordered states or culturally bordered nations were not the primary identification of migrants, two questions demand answers: Why has a nation-state approach been so dominant in migration history? Why do receiving societies refer to migrants by labeling them according to national origin? States do have an impact on research because they collect data on mobility, but often only at international borders and not about internal migrations. Such data lump together people of different regions, dialects, and social attributes, aggregate those of majority with those of minority cultures, and often do not count women separately. Important as they are, the data provide only a skewed image of the composition of migrant populations and of overall mobility. Scholars using nation-state-produced data necessarily use nation-state terminologies for the people they are analyzing. In public discourse in receiving societies, the variety of cultures within states-of-origin is usually not known: migrants from India became generic "Hindoos," those from a particular region in China generic "Chinese," and German-speakers from the many different regions generic "Germans" or, misnamed, "Dutch." Such naming implies ascription of national identities. It emerged in the nineteenth-century climate of opinion: first, in the emergence of (middle-class) national consciousness in juxtaposition to status-centered nobility's cultures and dynastic interests; second, in the self-organization of the middle classes in the national revolutions of 1848–1849; and third, in the aggressive national chauvinisms. National descriptors are further complicated by the development of the Russian, German, Austrian, and English descriptors within empires that comprised many peoples. In the colonized regions the colonizer/colonized or white/colored dichotomies were the main demarcation lines.

In much writing the *early* nineteenth-century national consciousness, a pride in group culture, has been conflated with the *late* nineteenth-century nations' chauvinism and the self-assertion of "minority" cultures. Such authors saw imperial structures as given and depicted struggles for self-rule as disruptive and responsible for the refugee-generating warfare of the early twentieth century. Legitimate affirmation of group culture (internally differentiated by gender, generation, age, class, and region) became oppressive when a polity's largest ethnic group not only designated itself "nation" but also denigrated all other cultures in the same territory as "minorities." The creation of such cultural hierarchies stood diametrically opposed to the age of revolution's political human-rights concept of each and every human being as equal before the law. The contradiction notwithstanding, political practice and political theory merged the concepts into the nation-state construct in which citizens were equal before the law—unless they were of non-national culture, of lower-class status, or of female gender. Equal rights were extended to lower-class men from the turn of the twentieth century, to women from the 1920s. In the same period, men and women from marginalized cultural groups migrated to states granting, if not equal, then at least better, status.

Migrants depart with regional cultural practices. In the later nineteenth century these did become homogenized to some degree within nation-states, but national chauvinism in Europe's empires exacerbated ethnocultural differentiations. In their society of destination, migrants would cherish the language, food habits, and other practices of everyday life they brought with them. But they would discard the society of origin's emperor worship, class hierarchies, or, if women, gender hierarchies. Migrants thus show both cultural affinities to previous ways of life and clear dislikes of the unacceptable aspects. Rather than arriving with a national identity, they came with cultural practices and with goals for life-projects that they could not realize "at home." (This is similar for migrants at the turn of the twenty-first century from, for example, Indonesia or West African states, who migrate to neighboring states, Europe, or North America.)

Recent scholarship avoids the term *national identity* as an analytical category but continues to analyze its ascriptive functions. It asks how people identify themselves and discusses multiple identifications. It explores how migrants relate to new structures, institutions, communities, and ways of life: it studies *belongings* rather than identities. Migrant self-organization validates this approach: migrants from the Qing Empire might have been labeled "Chinese," but they organized themselves by home region and family group; migrants from Europe might have been labeled Hungarians, but they organized themselves by regional cultural affinity. Faith and class or status also played a role in postmigration self-organization. The receiving society's institutions, once said to demand unconditional surrender of previous culture or "assimilation" to a new national identity, provide embeddedness (or marginalization). Newcomers are not "in limbo" or even "uprooted" (unless refugees or forced migrants), but they acquire knowledge of the new changeable structures, cultural practices, and institutional processes only gradually. Once the concepts of a fixed "identity" and the paradigm of nation-to-ethnic-enclave migrations are abandoned, steps toward participation may be empirically observed and analyzed. Acculturation is the process of selectively fusing old and new ways of life, coming to terms with societal structures and political institutions, and thus developing new identifications and belongings.

Transitions are facilitated by supportive migrant or ethnocultural patterns of self-help in mutual aid associations or by cultural clustering in ethnocultural neighborhoods. The formerly used term "ethnic ghetto" implied nation-rooted genetic or bloodline identity and suggested a self-segregation of migrants incapable of dealing with the "new world" around them. "Ghetto" may also be a reference, more empirically grounded, to segregation into slots of inferiority by the receiving society. Ethnocultural communities rarely achieve "institutional completeness," because its adult members leave its confines daily for their workplaces and the younger ones for schools. Individuals and families constantly negotiate the demands of their life-projects in the frame of both new structures and options and cherished aspects of pre-migration ways of life. They negotiate between community cohesion and the political strength it may provide and openness to the many options the receiving society at large provides. No "New England" or "New Spain," no "Chinatown," "Little Italy," or "Little Manila" ever replicated the society of departure. All emerged from negotiation and compromises with the new environment. Outside observers saw ethnic enclaves emerge, segregation of migrants by the receiving society was frequent, and self-segregation into neighborhoods and communities facilitated acculturation. However, as data for Chicago show in detail, the perceived mono-ethnic communities were, in fact, on the street level, areas of geographically mixed settlement where such mixing implied contact but not integrated social networks.[10]

Some groups have been said to form diasporic consciousnesses, a conceptualization that originates from the historic Greek and Jewish dispersions. Ancient Greek migrations, however, involved a fusion of several cultures, with the Persian and Egyptian cultures in particular. Hellenism thus was an Eastern Mediterranean syncretic culture and as such original rather than Greek-diasporic. From the Jews' expulsions, migrations, and persecutions an ideal-type "diaspora" may be deduced if also differentiated: People defined by religion, everyday practices, cultural ways of expression (high literacy), and—perhaps—genetic similarity because of intermarriage migrate under duress (destruction of the Second Temple by the in-migrant Roman rulers): westward to southern Europe and northern Africa, eastward to the Indian Ocean littorals. As diaspora they were defined by a shared memory of a cultural-geographic homeland and by communication between the different communities in the many regions of arrival. This connectedness differentiates diasporas from ethnic enclaves. However, rather than coalesce into a single diaspora, migrants of Jewish faith differentiated into a Sephardic community and an Ashkenazi community, as well as into distinct other groups in Asia and elsewhere. Distinctiveness, including different dialects, may overshadow connectedness. Most nineteenth-century migrant communities did not develop strong global connectedness. Italian, Polish, and Scottish migrants spread worldwide but did not always remain connected. Imperial administrative channels rather than diasporic community formation connected the worldwide British and French colonizer personnel. The multidirectional migration of southern Chinese is better analyzed by region of destination—Nanyang (southeast insular Asia), Australia, the Latin American and Anglo-American Pacific coasts.[11]

The late nineteenth-century intensification of nationalism, in the two complementary variants of armed nation-states and expansionist chauvinist ideologies, has had major consequences as regards emigration (release from membership, expulsion) and immigration (admission, imposed assimilation). Many states with a relative surplus population, that is, men and women who would not find jobs to support themselves, were happy to see the departure of such potential for militant change. Some placed obstacles in the way of men who, it was posited, should be available to die for their country in military service. European states with resident "minority" cultures increased emigration of these by reducing educational opportunities in other than the majority language, by disadvantaging economic development in peripheral regions, and by not providing equal access to state institutions and labor markets. Furthermore, with increasing demands for self-rule among peoples of the Balkans, of divided Poland, and of the western tsarist empire, people of unwanted religions, like Jews in Russia, or of unwanted cultures, like Slovaks in Hungary, began to be persecuted or, in the case of the Habsburg-Ottoman military frontier, to be deported: Populations that did not fit the construct of monocultural nation-states had to be eliminated. Such state violence has been called "ethnic cleansing" of a national home, though there is no reason to assume monocultural nations to be cleaner than many-cultured societies. Some states, reaching beyond their territorial borders, began to use "their" emigrant nationals as a bridgehead for economic and cultural penetration of receiving societies. Such instrumentalized people became "enemy aliens" to be interned or deported in wartime. "The growth of the modern nation-state implied not only the naming of certain peoples as enemies of the nation, but also the expulsion of significant groups for whom the state would or could not assume responsibility." The First World War "schooled the new masters" of nation-state apparatuses: "Civilians could become dangerous enemies . . . , it was best to eject unwanted [groups]." Under such conditions proactive departure as "free" migrants helped people survive.[12]

In receiving societies, too, migrants considered to be of different status under dynastic rule began to be treated as Other and marginalized. An exception is the treatment of newcomers from Europe in Latin America, where they were considered racially more desirable than resident native people, and in Australia, where they were needed to make the country economically viable. Admission restrictions first excluded those who could be identified by color of skin and who were genetically constructed as "race," that is, as inferior. Jewish ghettoization and Asian exclusion became the prototypes. Next, Anglo-Saxon and Teutonic ideologues, buttressed by so-called scientific racism, agitated for exclusion of the darker or olive "races" of Europe, East and South Europeans as well as the Irish, who, colonized and Catholic, were less than "white." From the 1880s newcomers and resident "minorities" were subject to acculturation pressures, whether in America, Canada, Germany, Russia, or Austria. The Welsh and Scots had been Anglicized centuries earlier. Such pressures induced earlier migrants who, under the eighteenth century's different incorporation regime, had been granted the privilege to practice their religion and speak their language—groups like Mennonites in the tsarist realm, for example—to depart in secondary migrations to more flexible societies. At the apogee of nationalism, democratic-republican states' attempts to enforce assimilation replaced absolutist dynastic societies' acceptance of pluralism among a ruler's subjects.[13]

Cultural and racial hierarchies—but no nation-state ideology—also existed in other segments of the world. In the many South Asian societies, lighter color of skin was considered a mark of status; in parts of China the migrant Hakka people suffered from marginalization; imperialist Japan pursued a policy of superiority that relegated Koreans, Manchurians, and Chinese to an inferior position. At the turn of the twentieth century, racialized identity politics became instruments of refugee-generation and of in-migrant segregation. In a complex interaction, migrant-generating nation-state policies were paralleled by migrant-segregating or exclusionist policies of migrant-receiving nation-states. Across the world, but in the Atlantic economies in particular, labor migrants became a segregated underclass with no equal access to the institutions of the state to which their taxes contributed. Around 1900, Jews, Slavs, or Mediterraneans who did not find acceptance could blend in only over generations. As residents after migration, they remained "foreigners," were subject to "alien laws," and could be deported. Under earlier societal frameworks, migrants had been able to find a slot or be granted a status that permitted economic activities and, often, cultural expression. The most-cited cases are Huguenots in Europe and Chinese in Southeast Asia. Policies that marginalized migrants as Other made insertion, acculturation, and belonging difficult. Although in the 1920s some criticism of exclusion, (scientific) racism, and discrimination was voiced, the onset of the Great Depression increased support for restrictions. New attitudes would emerge in reaction to the racism of fascist European and corporatist Japanese expansion and its immense refugee generation and death toll.[14]

It needs to be added that the transition to nation-states also could have positive implications for belongings. Societies could provide for, at first, limited participation in policy making that did create "belongings." People did develop an affinity to their nation of birth if cultural-structural practices changed to provide increased options and more equality. The in-migrant receiving societies, in particular the Anglo–North American societies, many countries in Latin America, and Australia, pursued integrative policies for white men and their female and child-age dependents. After decolonization from the 1950s on, Western political scientists and political advisers would transport the analytically untenable nation-state concept to the newly independent states, most of which combined peoples of many cultures.

## Color-Coded Colonials and Bound Bodies

Debates about citizenship and belonging had their counterpart in a body-parts approach to migrants. The calls for additional "hands," "muscles," or "braceros" indicates as much, and so does the sexual exploitation of women and, perhaps, men. The emaciated bodies of "coolies" attest to the physical aspects of migration, and European workingmen brutalized by company thugs in the United States felt they had been "raped" and noted that they were forced to sell their bodies on a "flesh market." In contrast, British middle-class "boys" in their twenties or even thirties migrated to the white Dominions where outdoor physical labor would "make a man" out of them. Furthermore, all exclusionist movements argued by color of skin, genes, and bloodlines. Men and women were reduced to bodies in oppressive migration regimes.

While "at home" the Western colonizer societies denied or, under the impact of both workers' and women's militancy across borders, debated the political and human rights of workers and women, discrimination was exacerbated in the colonized segments of the world where skin or the color of it entered into the establishment of hierarchies. Colonizer personnel, predominantly male, in Senegal, India, or Indochina, for example, had to construct all indigenous people as inferior and unfit for inclusion. The construction of nationals and colonials was inextricably entwined. Strong men from self-styled advanced nations were ruling weak colonized peoples, the imperial ideologues asserted. The subalterns, trained to observe the masters so as not to incur their wrath, did observe them. They saw men without the knowledge of the society's language of communication; men who extolled their own culture but totally lacked understanding of the culture into which they had been sent; men with sexuality but without women; men who could not or would not do their own housework. The colonizer migrants were caught in many contradictions, as Ann Stoler and others have pointed out—that is why firepower was so important to their sending states.[15]

Earlier historiography written in terms of empire overlooked the construction of masculinity and gender roles. The strong men knew that they lacked stamina for plantation or mining work or even the will to make their own tea. Because women from their own culture, in the everyday sexism of the times that considered women the weaker sex and fit only for service tasks, were not available, men from the indigenous people had to be ordered or forced do such work. To fit this role ascription they had to be demasculinized and constructed as weak, as effeminate, as unable to act by and speak for themselves. The "manly Englishman" (and any other colonizer man) constructed the "effeminate Bengali" (or any other colonial man), to use Mrinalini Sinha's felicitous phrase.[16]

British officials, for example, in Burma, considered the empire to be engaged in a "human experiment to sweep away the cowardly, the inefficient, the weak." Colonial men had to become "strong," able to confront the world, if necessary "savage" and ready to destroy: "He must learn to be a man." That was what seasoned army officers and administrators in the colonies also told their younger countrymen who, sent off from their familiar surroundings by their families and the state to do duty in contexts alien to them, were deprived of emotional comfort and embeddedness. When colonial men did struggle to push others aside, as in the First Indian War for Independence (the "Mutiny" of 1857, in British parlance), they were gunned down. A future US president, Theodore Roosevelt, went out as Rough Rider to gain Cuba for US planters. Japanese officers in 1930s China saw the Chinese as weaklings to be shunted aside to make room for the more manly and ruthless conquering men. Imperial and capitalist strategists, like those of Latin American mestizo ruling classes, relied on constructions of men's bodies.

If colonizer countries exported young men, young women could not marry. British population planners sent off "surplus women," those who would not find husbands "at home," to become "imperial mothers" in the colonies. Other women migrated by their own choice and for their own purposes. Wives of ranking colonizer administrators were part of the ritual display of power in many subjugated regions. Depending on empire or period, the imperial planners of colonial rule at first encouraged men's unions with native women. Concubinage was considered medically less dangerous than consorting with prostitutes. The bodies of colonized women were to be available for colonizing men. Japanese military planners drafted Korean women as prostitutes for soldiers.

However, consensual relationships between migrant men and resident women of different skin colors were not to the liking of white Church authorities. Imperial Christian missionaries insisted on white-to-white monogamous church-celebrated marriage and underpinned their dogma by stigmatizing women of colors other than white as squaws, as promiscuous and dirty. They did not interfere when plantation owners and their overseers refused to assume the wage expense of 1:1 ratios of productive to reproductive labor by excluding women from labor recruitment. In view of the low wages, men could not afford to bring unemployed wives. Some policy makers, in Australia for example, admitted that such separating of husband and wife by admission of male laborers only was inhumane. But they did not change the system, because "colored" children born to "coolie" couples on Australian soil would be British citizens, and it was feared that, if they were boys, when they grew up they would partner with white women. Exclusion based on skin color as a phenotypic marker was treated like it was a necessity for the white race's existence. It was not sex but the potential life-giving consequences that caused racial exclusion. Individual identifications and identity ascriptions were contingent on global power relations mediated by migrating colonizer personnel.[17]

The "anthropology of empire" involves analysis of the construction of Others in gendered and sexualized terms—sexual violence and exploitation included. However, the relationships also involve consensual unions and the concomitant cultural exchanges, "tender ties" on the "intimate frontiers of empire," as Sylvia Van Kirk noted. The regime of bound-labor migration, which deprived the predominantly male labor force of the option to develop cultural and, through family procreation, intergenerational communities, was the reverse side of nation-building processes based on families in which mothers inculcated national virtues into children. Neither Polish harvest laborers in imperial Germany nor Indian plantation laborers in the British Empire could migrate as families. Nation-states' regimes of migrant admission and exclusion, both to the metropole and to the colonies, were deeply gendered and racialized.[18]

To summarize, the comprehensive or systems approach to migration requires that the society of origin, as a frame of state and nation, as a region, and as a locality of origin, is studied in its whole layered complexity to understand the individual and social capital migrants have at departure and the networks in which they act. This society needs to be placed in global perspective as regards job and income opportunities as well as racial and ethnic hierarchies and inter-state power relations. Within each group, gender roles and relations determine both options to migrate as well as discriminations and income differentials. In some societies children and young adolescents have to migrate and need to be studied separately. Only a gendered approach can explain the formation of intergenerational communities. In a second step, the trajectory to the society of destination sets frames for subsequent insertion and acculturation. Migrants departing by their own choice in a frame of information flows and established migration corridors have a better chance to adjust to the demands of the receiving economy than those sent under contract or by force. Again power relations are highly important, and even "free" migrants move under constraints. Finally, the receiving societies need to be studied in the same comprehensiveness and same differentiation between statewide, regional, and local. If migration occurs within or into colonies, hierarchies of color of skin ("race") and colonizer views of the bodies of the colonized impact on degrees of exploitation or of agency. Migrations question the "container" view of states, and unlike nonmoving residents, migrants acquire familiarity with more than one way of life.

CHAPTER THREE

# Migrations, Free and Bound

Migratory developments followed different time lines in the major cultural macroregions, but in the 1860s and 1870s they coalesced in both new coherence in some regions and accelerated change in others. Transoceanic migratory movements expanded rapidly with the introduction of steamships in the 1870s. Industrial development, urbanization, and increased production in the Plantation Belt's "factories in the field" (as Carey McWilliams and Eric Wolf pointedly called plantations) accelerated demand for labor. "Taylorization"—the breaking down of factory manufacturing processes into simple, repetitive tasks—changed the character of many tasks from skilled to semi- or unskilled, and thus labor migrants with different predispositions were in demand and regions of recruitment changed accordingly.[1]

The Atlantic world's political economy consolidated. In Europe, industrialization extended to East Central regions and European Russia. As latecomers, the fragmented Italies and Germanies embarked on industrial expansion and unified as nation-states, though the German-language peoples, due to the German-Hohenzollern and Austrian-Habsburg rivalry, became two nations. The continental empires ceded neither to middle-class-driven nation building nor to their internally subjected peoples' demands for self-administration. Instead, they engaged in the all-out warfare of 1914–1918 and, outdated as their structures were, self-destroyed. Vast refugee migrations accompanied their disintegration. In North America, the three continental states consolidated while the Caribbean societies remained colonized. The American Civil War—only twelve years after the war of aggression

against Mexico—cemented unity and abolished the old-style plantation regime. As early as the 1840s, when settlement of the western regions accelerated, only one-third of the immigrants were settlers; artisans and skilled workers accounted for another third, and unskilled
workers, agrarian laborers, and domestics for the last third. Canada,
achieving Dominion status in 1867, extended its territory from coast
to coast and attracted both agricultural settlers and urban workers.
Immigration of farm families ended in the United States in the 1890s,
in Canada in the 1920s. The Estados Unidos Mexicanos, having lost
half its territory to the United States of America in 1848 and 1853, re-
pelled a European French-led invasion and, under President Benito
Juarez, embarked on a policy of (limited) social reform. The deprivation of the *indios* of much of their land forced them into internal cityward migrations, and thus no need for working-class in-migration
arose. Immigrant or absentee European and US investors took advantage of the surplus labor force, but from the end of the nineteenth
century ever larger numbers of Mexicans would migrate northward.[2]

In the many Caribbean societies, European influence declined
while that of the United States grew, in particular in consequence of
the war against Spain in 1898 and the resulting annexation of Puerto
Rico and the establishment of a protectorate over Cuba. After the abolition of slavery in the British Empire in the 1830s, sugar production
had shifted from Jamaica to Cuba's slave-worked, partly US-owned
plantations. Steam-powered sugar mills turned Cuba into one of the
foremost industrializing and urbanized countries in the world, and it
became the sixth-largest receiver of immigrants from Europe and the
largest receiver of Cantonese bound workers after the abolition of
slavery.

Central and South America's states and societies experienced uneven development. The Pacific coast and Andean regions stagnated,
the Atlantic seaboards and the accessible interiors, with plantation

and mining regions, expanded rapidly, with Brazil and Argentina at the forefront. Iberian, but in particular Italian, as well as some West and East Central European migrants provided man- and womanpower as well as technical and cultural expertise. Urban growth relied mainly on European migration. Liberated ex-slaves, native peoples, and earlier immigrant rural settlers stayed put and thus, in relative terms, declined. When they did move to the cities later, they—like natives in Central America and Mexico—arrived as latecomers and formed a social stratum below the recent European migrants. Because much of the investment came first from Britain and then the United States, economic decision making did not necessarily have societal and country-wide development at its center. Thus, in the long run these countries underwent a relative decline in comparison to the economies and polities of the northern Atlantic. Migration declined accordingly.[3]

Africa, often overlooked as part of the Atlantic world, became the object of the continuing British, new French, and late Belgian and German imperialist greed. The new rulers and their labor demands for new extractive economies replaced slave catching and slave export with displacement and involuntary migration. In French North Africa, British Kenya, and the British Dominion of South Africa, immigrant European agricultural settlers displaced resident peasant populations. The investors and intruders established regionally varying regimes of forced labor that mobilized or immobilized men and women according to decisions made in the European and, again later, US cores.

Across the Plantation Belt the demand for labor, whether temporarily bound, permanently bound through debt peonage, or free and cheap, had resulted both in recruitment drives in impoverished segments of Europe—Ireland, Poland, and southern Italy, for example—and in the imposition of the indenture system on Asian populations. The latter were transported westward as far as East Africa and the Caribbean, within the Indian Ocean to the plantation islands and littorals, eastward to Malaya and Australia, and transpacifically as far as the Americas.

In West Asia and Egypt, the Ottoman Empire and its formerly well-structured cohabitation of many peoples was challenged by unsuccessful demands for self-rule and successful imposition of British or French zones of influence: Egyptian cotton and Iraqi oil were annexed to the North Atlantic's industrial economy. In British-ruled South Asia, demands for independence increased. Concentration of production and intensification of mining spurred vast migrations. These followed patterns of imperial rule and investment as much as local cultural and economic exigencies. Japan pursued its own distinct political economy, a dynastic-corporate regime of Western-style modernization, which forced overtaxed peasants into internal and outbound migration. From southern China a transpacific migratory connection emerged from the mid-1840s on and, expanding to additional regions of origin, accelerated from the 1870s.

In the northern Asian segments of China and Russia, as well as in European Russia, there developed internal patterns of migration as well as some transoceanic out-migrations. Mainly laboring men and women of peasant background moved. In addition, rural families migrated from European Russia to southern Siberia, and a new mass migration from northern China to Manchuria continued earlier traditions of rural-to-rural migrations. Urbanization, especially of the Harbin region, made distinctions between agricultural and industrial migrations fluid. Elsewhere, small numbers of peasants still moved to farming regions, and some states and ideologues of white people's expansion as late as the 1920s advocated colonization migrations of Europe's and North America's surplus farming families (labeled peasant "stock") to ever more marginal farming regions—but such schemes remained rhetoric.[4]

The havoc and destruction of World War I temporarily ended transatlantic migrations. They resumed after 1918, the increasing US restrictions notwithstanding, but were cut short by the Great Depression after 1929. In the black Atlantic, small-scale reverse migrations from the Americas to Africa began. The 1930s also witnessed the first arrival of West and North African sailors and workers in France, as well as educational migrations of the sons of upper-class families from the colonies to France and Great Britain. The Plantation Belt's labor regime changed with the gradual abolition of indentured servitude in the 1920s and the collapse of world markets in the 1930s. Thus, depending on macroregion, the period of mass labor migrations lasted into the mid-1910s or into the 1930s. All bound as well as self-willed labor migrations were accompanied by numerically smaller free migrations of middle-class men and women.

## A Mobility Transition?

During the so-called demographic transition, when population growth and economic growth do not match, families and unmarried young people have to depart. Infant survival rates and life expectancy of adults increase, but birth rates have not yet declined nor have labor markets expanded. This, if called a "mobility transition," implies lower mobility in earlier decades and centuries. Recent research indicates that rather than a vague "modernization" in some regions, improvements in transport routes and speed accelerated mobility. Demographic expansion occurred in Europe and China from the mid-eighteenth to the late nineteenth century. Only France, where couples had limited their number of children far earlier, remained an exception.[5] (This demographic change is occurring in many Arab, African, and Asian societies in the present.) In 150 years after 1750, Europe's population tripled to 430 million and its share of the world's population grew from one-sixth to one-quarter. People in family units, particularly adolescents ready to leave the parental household, correct such demographic-economic imbalances by migrating from spaces with a surplus of livelihood-seeking men and women to spaces with a demand for additional workers or thinly settled land, often constructed as "free land." In the late nineteenth century, demand for labor was limited in the European cities of the societies of their birth but high in societies a continent away. Patterns of migration usually begin interregionally and as rural-to-urban moves within a language region before they become long-distance and international. Migration is a learning process, and routes need to be established and extended. Once a society's labor markets expand to provide sufficient options for wage work, departure rates decline. This was the case in Western Europe from the 1890s; in Italy and Eastern Europe, migration began in the 1880s and continued to the caesura of World War I.[6]

The conceptual shift from textile and food production to the steel and iron industries as indicators of a modernization in nation-states and their economies has obscured the causes and effects of migration as well as the gendered divisions of labor. Work and consumption in the home are little affected by tons of steel produced. But imports of cheap grains mass-produced by immigrant farmers and laborers, whether wheat in Europe or rice in Asia, wrought havoc on family farm economies. The resulting agricultural crisis of the 1880s and 1890s forced millions of small peasant families to depart from their plots and head for jobs in the new industries. This "proletarian" mass migration involved rural men and women with little or no land, the towns' lower classes, and urban workers—it was a proletarianizing rather than a proletarian migration.[7]

The transition-by-migration from rural to industrial tasks was facilitated by the initial stage of industrial mass production in food and garments: mills for cane sugar in the Caribbean and for beet sugar in East Central Europe, sewing machines for producing clothing—for which most women had the skills. The conveyor belt began as a disassembly line in the slaughterhouses from Chicago to Kansas City. Rural men and women who had done their own food conservation and slaughtering on small farms moved to seasonal canning and year-round meatpacking in large firms. On a small family farm, slaughtering a pig provided a feast and food for the winter, but slaughtering on a production line was gruesome work. Such mass production in the fields of the plains and in the factories of new metropoles reduced food prices worldwide and caused more and more families to depart from marginal lands. Similarly, investment in cotton plantations in the southern United States, Egypt, Uganda, India, and elsewhere, and investment in cloth factories, whether in Manchester or Mumbai, Lowell or Łódź, demanded quick and permanent changes in allocation of family labor, whether Irish, Dutch, Egyptian, Tamil, or Burmese. Men and women, from adolescence on, responded with myriads of back-and-forth, circular, temporary, and permanent moves.

## The Proletarianizing Mass Migrations

With the concentration of production in hand-powered manufacture and machine-powered factories, the protoindustrial period's transfer of raw materials or semifinished goods to sedentary cottage dwellers with spare time and a need for cash income reversed to self-transfer of such working families to centralized job locations. In addition, rural men moved to work in local infrastructural improvements, and women continued their migration to domestic labor in nearby towns and cities. Railroads and steamships permitted such workers to move intercontinentally: Some twenty million from Europe to the United States from 1880 to 1914, of which about six million returned to Europe. These migrants, considered "unskilled," were skilled agriculturalists and household managers in the economies they left and inexperienced only in the factory production they entered.[8]

The mass migrations to farm and factory labor targeted the mass-producing plains from southern Russia to North America and from Argentina to Australia as well as the mass-producing factories from

Men and women on a transatlantic vessel's crowded lower deck, mid-ocean, ca. 1890. Sharing expectations as well as uncertainties about their destination, passengers often banded together as "ship sisters" or "ship brothers." Images like this one, however, are not always what they seem. Joseph Stieglitz's famous photo "The Steerage," for example, shows migrants returning to Europe from the United States. Around 1900, about one-third of all migrants to the New World returned. (Library of Congress)

St. Petersburg to Chicago to Buenos Aires. When East German landlords converted to machinery, drove out their tenants, and imported Polish seasonal laborers, North American second-generation immigrant farming families hired these displaced tenants-turned-migrant laborers, and industrial employers, also descended from earlier immigrants, hired them for Taylorized (simplified) tasks in machine-driven production. In the societies of departure, home and subsistence producers, usually women, became dramatically aware of the futility of their labors when factory-produced cloth came to be available cheaply in a nearby store. To supply a family with cloth demanded a winter's work—but its purchase required cash at the very time when the agricultural crisis of the 1880s reduced family incomes. The crisis of "free" time and empty tables forced individuals and whole regional populations to reorient their lifestyles and their attitudes to migration.

The combination of human agency and socioeconomic frames may be illustrated by migration from Italy. The almost fourteen million men and women who departed from 1876 to 1914, and the further four million from 1915 to 1930, selected as destinations Western Europe (44 percent), North America (30 percent), Brazil and Argentina (22 percent), and other places (4 percent). Craftsmen followed traditional routes to France and Germany; rural migrants compared work offered by East Elbian and Argentinian landowners and found working conditions in Germany's East worse and train fare over the Alps more expensive than transatlantic fares. The latter were cheapest to the United States, but those who could afford it went to Latin America because there, comparatively, prospects were better, language problems smaller, cultural adjustment easier, upward mobility higher. From North America one-third of the migrants returned to Italy—they came as temporary workers, not as immigrants. "Unskilled" men and women skillfully evaluated life chances in several regions of the Atlantic world. Migrants' remittances—through deposit in banks—funded industrialization of the Milan-Turin-Genoa triangle. Family economies in villages were "glocal," and remittances supported mesoregional development.[9]

In the society/economy of destination, migrants faced complex stratified and segmented labor markets. Jobs in the primary growing, capital-intensive, concentrated sector offered relatively high wages, good working conditions, and stable employment. Only a few migrants, like skilled German workers and English mechanics, could reach for such jobs, whether in Budapest or Chicago. In the secondary stagnating, competitive sector with irregular employment, low pay, and unpleasant working conditions, migrants were hired regardless of cultural origin or nationality. A tertiary marginal or ghetto sector demanded and provided high flexibility. Migrants could enter only those labor market segments commensurate with their skills or lack thereof, their communication capabilities or problems, and their cultural Otherness. Furthermore, labor markets were segregated by gender, ethnicity, color of skin, and sometimes religion. Only some segments offered transatlantic internationalized access—the labor markets were heavily racialized.[10]

Jobs provided migrants with the initial income and basis for survival. Culture provided links to others—permitted community formation and expansion of individual human capital by development of social capital. Contrary to Karl Marx's assumption, migrant men and women had more to lose than chains: To avoid the loss of regionally specific ethno-class or race-class cultures, and thereby individual practices of belonging, they based their support organizations and material life on transferable aspects of the culture of origin within the frame of the receiving society. Adjustment to new societies and labor movements involved multiple and gendered negotiations and compromises. The working-class migrants were transculturally mobile, but they were not necessarily a conscious internationally minded proletariat.[11]

## Europe's Cores and Peripheries

The oft-repeated juxtaposition of labor-exporting European (emigration) and labor-importing North American (immigration) countries skews the evidence. Europe itself was divided into a labor-importing core and a labor-exporting periphery. Industrialized England, the Netherlands and Belgium, France, the west and central German regions, lower Austria, Bohemia, and Switzerland attracted migrants first from surrounding agricultural regions, then from Europe's periphery. Great Britain and the Germanies as well Belgium and sections of Austria exported settlers and workers at the same time. England drew workers mainly from its Irish colony, Switzerland from Italy (earlier from Germany), France from most of its neighboring countries and Poland, and Germany from Poland and Italy. The peripheral societies of Ireland, Portugal and Spain, Italy and southeastern Europe, the Polish and Jewish territories, as well as the Scandinavian countries supplied labor. People's identifications, rather than being based on membership in a nation, emerged from a search for options to earn a living.[12]

State-propounded ideologies of national identity notwithstanding, some population planners attempted to rid their country of "undesirables," including political or religious dissidents, "the poor" in general, underemployed proletarians, and people considered deficient for other reasons: deportation of dissidents and criminals from Russia to Siberia; of paupers and criminals from Western Europe to America and Australia; Great Britain's program of shipping off unmarried women, orphaned children, and lightly disabled soldiers; US deportations of alleged socialists and revolutionaries during the "Red Scare" (or "white fear") around 1920. Nationalist economic elites forced people to depart because institutionalized relations between capital and labor did not provide for sustainable lives, and people of minority cultures were deprived of access to societal resources by cultural elites.

Intra-European labor migrations were vastly larger than outbound ones: At the height of the transatlantic migrations, only 5 percent of all Austro-Hungarian migrants left the empire for other European economies or North America; 95 percent moved internally, with Prague and Vienna being the largest receivers. Many of the expanding manufacturing towns in Europe still resembled industrial islands in an agrarian world and thus drew on work-age populations from the countryside: ethnoculturally similar but economically distant peasant people. In the ethnoculturally stratified eastern cities, ethnically distinct from local peasants, multilingual working classes emerged.[13]

Regions of industrial investment, like Lancashire in England or the Ruhr district in Germany, or investment-attracting rural towns, like Łódź, attracted people in transition from rural to industrial patterns of earning a livelihood. Capital cities, because of political linkages, the nobility's consumption patterns, and bourgeois investments, attracted heterogeneous migrants. Vienna, linked by railroads to the Germanies and by Danube shipping to the Black Sea, exerted its pull over Bohemia, Moravia, Slovakia, the Hungarian lands, Polish-Ukrainian-Jewish Galicia, and Bukowina. Greek traders, Italian merchants, and Jewish families lived in distinct quarters. The tantalizing facades of aristocratic and bourgeois quarters suggested riches to be made, while the harsh working conditions of the factories and the poverty, pneumonia, and prostitution of the drab working-class quarters were invisible from the locations where migrants developed their expectations. Many workers came seasonally, and ethnic associations registered a membership turnover of up to 100 percent per year, as did Germany's labor unions. The proletarianizing migrations involved high mobility in a particular stage of the life cycle rather than a single and unidirectional emigration.[14]

Even though most cities were dependent on in-migration for their growth, newcomers experienced segregation and hostility from the increasingly nationalistic host societies. In Austria and Germany, assimilation pressures undercut the viability of immigrant cultures. Exclusions and, in the case of people of Jewish faith, racializations were common to all of Europe's states. In urban societies, whether London, Paris, or Berlin, racialization targeted in-migrating Italian and Eastern European workers. The development of nations and national economies depended on migrant workers of other cultures and on their Otherization.

## North America from Canada to the Caribbean

The popular adage "Go to *America*" refers to the United States, but migrants went to two states, the United States and Canada, and to several linguistic regions: French Canada, the Spanish-English US Southwest, and the creole regions of Louisiana. Mexico and the societies of the Caribbean islands, positioned as a connecting region of the Americas by patterns of migration since the 1880s as well as by patterns of US political interference and economic penetration, are best considered part of North America.

Most migrants to North America had originated in Western and Northern Europe—they were white. From the 1870s and more so from the mid-1880s, migrants originated from Eastern Europe, southern Italy, and as well as the southeastern European societies. The racial ideologies of Anglo or Teutonic whites color-coded them as dark, swarthy, or olive. The ideology of US racial identity, and to a lesser degree Anglo-Canadian racial identity, led to restrictions against inmigration of "yellow races" from Asia and, after 1924, of nonwhite Europeans. Lynch violence (sometimes called "lynch law" in the peculiar parlance of national discourse) and lack of migration traditions kept black African-Americans tied to the southern states into the 1880s. "Brown" migration from Mexico remained limited before 1900 and was hardly discussed in public. Canada, with its demand for prairie settlers and urban workers, kept its doors open for Europeans through the 1920s.[15]

In the United States, nineteenth-century economic and demographic development was characterized by a sequence of large-volume internal migrations. Westward migrations did not serve as a safety valve that defused class conflict; instead urbanization attracted young surplus rural people, as it did in Europe. From the early 1900s, "bonanza farms" or corporate *latifundia* displaced settler families, and flight from the land accelerated in the 1930s during the Great Depression.

A Chinese poem carved into the wall of the Angel Island Immigration Station in San Francisco Bay. Angel Island, the Ellis Island of the Pacific coast, often served more as an interrogation station and a detention center than as an entry gate. Asian immigrants arriving at Angel Island were frequently detained upon arrival, the victims of exclusionary and discriminatory policies. Many of the migrants expressed their sorrow and anger by carving elaborate poems into the wooden walls of the station. (Carol M. Highsmith's America, Library of Congress, Prints and Photographs Division)

Pushed by pogroms and disenfranchisement, the southern ex-slaves' children began to migrate to northern urban jobs, about one hundred thousand net in the decade before 1900. When immigration from Europe came to an involuntary stop in 1914, the African-Americans' "Great Migration" became a proletarianizing mass movement involving about one million men and women from 1916 to 1920, or almost 10 percent of the 10.4 million black citizens.[16]

In addition to the multicultural cities, rural regions were made bicultural by the presence of migrants, and the international northern and southern borderlines became borderlands in which people moved back and forth. From the St. Lawrence Valley, Canadian French-speakers came to New England's Anglo-owned textile mills. English-Canadians settled in Michigan, the Prairies, and Washington State; US farmers accounted for the largest number of in-migrants in Canada's prairies. The border along the 49th parallel was permeable, it was but an imaginary line. A German-Scandinavian belt with distinct linguistic practices and with Ukrainians on the Canadian side emerged, as did a Hispanic Spanish-English belt along the Mexican border.[17]

The United States of Mexico, while part of the Atlantic economies and cultures, remained distinct as regards migration. Not only were few labor migrants needed, due to the government's disenfranchisement of the *indios,* but the incursions of Spanish royalists in the 1820s, of US armies in the mid-1840s, of French-led European troops in the 1860s, and since then of powerful British, US, French, and German investors, created an antiforeigner sentiment that, for the Americas, was singular. The mid-nineteenth-century urbanization and land "reform" (dispossession of native peoples) accelerated the internal cityward migrations of the dispossessed but segregated them by racialization. Capital influx from the United States, accompanied by investors and migrants with technical skills, also mobilized dispossessed rural Mexicans. Increasing numbers headed for the United States during the disturbances of the anti-Porfiriato revolution after 1910 and during the burgeoning US labor demands of World War I. From the 1940s on, the United States recruited large numbers of *braceros.* Already by the 1920s Mexican and Canadian migrants entered the same labor markets in Detroit factories and Michigan mining.[18]

From the 1890s to the 1930s, a North American migration region emerged. Borders were porous, and when European migration was being reduced, the "backdoor" for Mexicans—a "front door" for them—was left ajar. American planters with capital moved to Cuba, Mexico, and elsewhere. Railroad and transportation impresarios developed the Mexican and Isthmus of Panama railroads, not always based on sound engineering expertise. Canada, in addition to being a country of immigration, became a transit country for Europeans: 2.6 million moved to the United States between 1871 and 1930. Only a tiny percentage of both US- and Canada-bound migrants crossed the Pacific from Asia.

In the 1920s, low cotton prices pushed white families out of the US South's rural economy. Most headed for California and became migrant agricultural laborers. In the 1920s, mechanization beyond the scope of family investments, exacerbated in some regions by drought, displaced people from family farms. During the Great Depression, first-generation European and Mexican migrants returned to their societies of birth. Because of continuing racism, a small but vocal "Back to Africa" movement emerged from the United States as well as from Brazil and the Caribbean. Along the Pacific coast—as in Mexico, Peru, and eastern Siberia—Chinese migrant or immigrant workers had become part of the respective proletariats. The working-class diasporas from Europe and Asia overlapped in North and South America, where they joined forces or competed with free black and white labor.

Framed by such global connections, the Caribbean served as a hinge region between North, Central, and northern South America. Several of its societies, Cuba and Trinidad in particular, received Cantonese and Indian indentured workers and free migrants. After the end of slavery, African-Caribbeans' migration was at first limited to the Caribbean area. US-bound migration grew parallel to US investment in the island economies. In the early twentieth century, the Panama Canal's construction sites became a major destination, attracting several tens of thousands of free and contracted Barbadian, Jamaican, Guadeloupean, and Martinican migrants. US investments in plantations increased seasonal mobility and expanded the catchment area to Costa Rica and Nicaragua. By the 1930s the Caribbean plantation regimes had become political regimes—"banana republics" under the remote control of multinational corporations. Caribbean migrants in the United States developed a cosmopolitan cultural expressiveness, centered on New York's Harlem and connected to Paris, France. African-American and African-Caribbean music began to attract white audiences; cultural fusion was a consequence of migration.[19]

## South America

About one-fifth of the fifty to fifty-five million transatlantic migrants headed for South America.[20] Their numbers grew after 1850, rose rapidly from 1885 to 1914, stagnated in the interwar years, and resumed for a decade after 1945. Most originated in the Mediterranean cultures, especially Italy, Spain, and Portugal. Argentina and Brazil received almost four-fifths of the newcomers, Cuba 14 percent—in all three of these societies the patterns and composition of migration and the labor regimes changed after the abolition of slavery. Around 1900, Italian migrants modified the Euro-Atlantic migration patterns and increasingly selected North American destinations. Thus, the Mediterranean- and Atlantic-European departure areas and the several receiving areas in the Americas became integrated. Self-selection of migrants channeled people to destinations according to their social profiles and the receiving society's economies.

Migrations internal to Latin America increased when ex-slave families left plantations, first in a process of moving to or forming villages, and then in medium-distance cityward migrations. Plantation owners and the governments they dominated experimented with various labor recruitment schemes before they settled on free migrants from Europe. In the Latin American scheme of skin color gradation, European working-class immigrants held a competitive advantage over local workers of mixed origin, and these over African-origin workers. However, no US-style segregation into black and white ever developed or, given the many-colored *castas,* could develop. The societies of the Guyanas and the Pacific coast, like those of the Caribbean, also included contract laborers and free migrants from Asia. After exclusion

An oil-drilling team of Portuguese immigrants in Patagonia, Argentina, 1907. Most photographs of immigrants show men, but women accounted for about 40 percent of the Atlantic crossings. Communities of immigrant men and women, often with children, emerged throughout the Americas from Patagonia to Alaska. (Patagonia Mosaic Project, Dickinson College)

from North America, Japanese immigrants came to Brazil and Peru, often as families. Internal migration to states and migration between states involved women moving independently to domestic service. Although economic growth had been high for more than half a century after the independences, migrants at the turn of the twentieth century reached economies of "expansion without development," societies experiencing urbanization without further industrialization. Still, wages compared favorably to transportation cost and to living expenses in the cultures of origin, but harsh working conditions on plantations resulted in high rates of secondary rural-to-urban migrations and of return.[21]

In Argentina, which pursued a policy of encouraging in-migration of both agricultural and industrial labor, about 6 million Europeans arrived from 1869 to 1914, and 2.7 million returned; by 1914 the Argentinian population had more than quadrupled to 7.9 million, 58 percent of whom were foreign-born or the children of immigrants. Agrarian settlement resembled that of plains across the world, with railways constructed by private companies using British capital, government subsidies, and immigrant labor. After the mid-1890s it was no longer possible, even for hardworking families, to advance to independent landownership. Argentina had no frontier of settlement. Its only city, Buenos Aires, had a Spanish elite, Italian bourgeois and lower middle-classes, and multiethnic shantytowns. In the latter the tango and *lunfardo* developed, to become popular across the Western world. For six decades, 70 percent or more of the city's residents were foreign-born, a percentage twice as high as was ever reached in the United States. Half of the migrants were Italians, one-third were Spanish, 5 percent were French. Steamship fares as low as fifty dollars from Italy to Buenos Aires made the trip profitable even for seasonally commuting harvest laborers, who, because of the inverse season, could thus achieve year-round employment. In contrast to rural settlers, urban immigrant families experienced intergenerational upward mobility and immigrants could participate easily in political life.[22]

In Brazil, the post-independence phase of European migration up to the 1860s had brought German, Italian, and Polish settlers to the coffee plantations of Rio Grande do Sul, where planters had relocated because of soil exhaustion farther north. In secondary migrations many fled the miserable—literally "unsettling"—working conditions. The second phase, from 1870 to 1920, brought a total of 3.4 million, of whom 860,000 returned to Europe or moved elsewhere. Given Brazil's population size, the ratio of immigrants to native-born was always lower than in other receiving states in the Americas. African-Brazilians, as part of the multicolored population, migrated to jobs or sharecropping. In prospering cities European labor displaced free Africans, who had to migrate to stagnating regions or take the most menial jobs. The Brazilian Euro-Creole elites engaged in a nation-building process conceived in European terms and relying on contemporary concepts of race to prevent *indio* and black peoples from accessing political or economic resources. Notions of improving the "population stock" by "crossbreeding" and "whitening" emerged. Belonging, in the minds of elites, was predicated on color.

For African-Brazilians, belonging was predicated on culture. In brotherhoods and through socioreligious practices of *candomblé* they struggled against alienation and displacement as well as the slave traders' insidious "witchcraft" that had transformed them into forced labor "across the water." The importation of slaves into the 1860s kept the institutions closely related to African multidivinity. They organized by nation, color, gender, and status to pursue material as well as spiritual goals. Portuguese-origin Brazilians were aware of cultural differences between groups of different African origins, such as the Savaru, Ardas, Hausa, Tapa, Jejé, DaGome, and Nagô. Such diversity of origin demanded search for a common language. The African languages also impacted on the official European language; some twenty-five hundred Brazilian-Portuguese words are of sub-Saharan African origin. Ethnically based working-class organizations combined slave and freed workers and organized strikes, resisted government interference, controlled quality of work, and asserted self-governance. Many members were African-born, others internal migrants from the declining sugar regions. Some, in old age, reembarked for Africa, like European-origin workers in North America who at retirement returned to their societies of birth.[23]

Migration to the Americas and the establishment of Euro-domination there has been discussed in terms of white over black and the annihilation or displacement of red people. If the imposition of a white-topped racial hierarchy was indeed a major goal, skewed sex ratios—expressed in sexual attraction as well as violence—brought forth new mixed peoples. In all of the Americas, including the northern self-labeled "white" societies, racial mixing resulted in ethnogenesis, the development of new mestizo peoples in new ecological environments. While gatekeeper ideologues of the Anglo-Protestant societies invented a myth of racial purity and whiteness, in Latin Catholic societies the hierarchized *castas* remained porous and wealth could override color. In 1920s Mexico, partly in a reaction to the arrogance of neighboring Yankees, a self-identification of *mestizaje* emerged, a blending of Europeans, Native Americas, Africans, and even some Asians. An extreme version, countering Yankee superiority fantasies, made Mexicans a "cosmic race." All migrations involve mixing, *métissage,* or *mestizaje,* and they involve new self-arrogated or ascribed hierarchies by phenotype or genes.[24]

## Intercolonial Migrations

Parallel to the free-under-constraints migrations in and between the Atlantic economies, free-under-massive-constraints and unfree mass migrations occurred within the Atlantic imperial powers and were imposed by those states on people in the colonized tropical and subtropical extractive economies circling the globe.

From the Atlantic world, numerically small migrations of investors, plantation owners or inheritors, their personnel, and support personnel for such imperialist economic penetration, whether administrators, soldiers, or governing elites, converged onto the vast colonized territories and peoples and diverged into the region's many different locations and spaces. For the resulting mobilization—as well as immobilization—of labor forces, exact quantitative data are difficult to compile, given the many different recruitment regions, routes, and destinations in extended societies as well as specific economic regions. Recent scholarship indicates that the volume of intercolonial long-distance migrations equaled those of the Atlantic world and, through political and economic power relations, were intricately connected to them. Migrations within the colonies, like those within Europe and North America, come in addition—though the borderlines between free and unfree, internal and external, locally induced and colonizer-mandated are fuzzy.[25]

Again, it is necessary to reflect on images and connotations framing the thought on colonial worlds, the Plantation Belt, and nodes of mineral extraction or wood "harvesting." Geographically accurate maps of continents and territories reflect neither the economic importance nor the size of demand for labor. From a socioeconomic perspective, such maps are inaccurate and misleading. Territorially small islands like Saint-Domingue, Jamaica, and Cuba demanded more workers and, through European white planters' appropriation of the surplus of such black African labor, produced more wealth than the whole of colonial continental North America taken together. In the Indian Ocean, the islands of Mauritius and Réunion and, in the Southeast Asian seas, the so-called Spice Islands as well as Java and Sumatra had become the core of wealth production in the interest of the colonizers. In all of these, the small resident populations did not meet the intruder-investors' demand for labor. Muscled laboring bodies—there was little interest in minds and emotions—were imported like fertilizer for fields or luxury goods for the colonizer elites' homes.

Agricultural production units in the Plantation Belt, the "factories in the fields," required (and for centuries of colonization had required) as much labor, designated as unskilled, as the new factories in the cities of the Atlantic economies. Again: "unskilled" refers to repetitive tasks at the destination. Migrants, in their societies of birth, had led lives with skills that enabled them to cope with adverse conditions.

That they were forced to migrate was usually due to local socioeconomic frames and imperialist impositions rather than to a lack of survival skills, although mismanagement of land and other assets could also be the cause of individuals' self-indenture or of the indenturing of family members.

In addition to the regions of the plantation regime, locations of mineral deposits and other types of extraction, like forest clear-cutting, guano digging, or rubber collecting, required labor forces from afar in order to become economically viable and profitable. *Labor force* is a neutral, production-oriented term for men and women, and often children, who wanted to lead whole lives but whose concentration in camps at centers of investment and of natural resources often involved brutal exploitation. Camp regimes need to be analyzed on a continuum from those inhabited by voluntary migrants (under economic constraints) for woodcutting or placer mining, for example, to those with forced migrants like the plantation camps in the Caribbean and the factory barracks in fascist states—both with extremely high death rates. The distinctions between a colonized region and an independent region were not always clearly defined. One region with a long tradition of voluntary migrations, North America's "Greater Southwest," from Arizona and New Mexico to Sonora and Zacatecas, underwent rapid expansion of mining in the later nineteenth century. US investors and the pliant Mexican ruler Porfirio Diaz set the frame; white US personnel exploited often skilled but brown Mexican laborers to dig silver and copper. Protesting workers were subdued by armed military units (as at the Cananea mine in 1906) or deported and dumped in the desert without water (as happened at the Bisbee mine in 1917). Cananea, at the time, also housed several thousand imported or migrant Chinese workers.[26]

Both the plantation and the mining/extracting labor forces were predominantly male, but when the male reservoir of labor for European and, later, US investments was insufficient, women were imported. Male nodes of in-migration usually became gendered communities if their sex ratios were skewed. Even where only men were employed, reproductive work needed to be done: cooking, washing of clothes, mending. Some migrating men did such work for themselves, and in isolated labor camps across the world men were hired as cooks. Elsewhere women came on their own or were brought in to do the "household" work where no households existed: mass production of food in cantinas, washing of endless piles of dirty work clothes. Women might also be brought in for sex labor or, as small businesswomen, migrate on their own account to sell provisions or their bodies (like men sold theirs to exploiters).

The plantation regions and the centers of mineral extraction, often distant from towns and transportation facilities, needed connections to centers of processing and consumption. Thus, further workers were mobilized to build dirt roads, paved roads, railroads, or waterways and the necessary hardware, carts, wagons, or rail cars. Once transportation routes were completed, the carters, canal men, and railroad men created further demand for reproduction labor. Thus, isolated productions sites, barracks for plantation and mining laborers, and solitary hostels became gendered communities. Women followed their husbands; families separated by migration were reunited, single women came to work and often to marry. Women's patterns of migration involved independent moves, sequential ones with prepaid tickets, or transport under contracts. Only the birth of children and multigenerational communities ensured continuity. Given the gendered allocation of tasks, men did often move first. The "women who stayed behind" did become a topos of public debate (as well as, belatedly, of migration research). It needs to be reemphasized that women did form their own migration connections and, when such decisions were open to them, searched for independent incomes. The labor regimes entwined the categories of class, gender, and race-ethnicity.[27]

By the last decades of the nineteenth century, the plantation, mining, and transportation complexes were becoming ever more integrated. The increasing use of machinery created a fast-growing demand for lubricating palm oil; caoutchouc plantations provided the rubber for transmission belts and tires. Capitalists and state agents sought control over territories, partly for their "natural" resources, like fertile soils or minerals, and partly to reduce resident populations to mobile labor forces. Depending on location and demand, people were immobilized for work locally, were forced to move over short or medium distances individually or in family units, or were sent into long-distance migrations—at the end of which they were immobilized again. This, too, involved a balancing of labor demand and labor supply, but it imposed the interests of investors and employers.

The consumption demands of Europe's rapidly increasing populations and the speedup of transportation through steamships and new canal connections, the Suez Canal in particular, intensified production in the extractive industries. Because neither the British- nor the French-controlled areas (nor, for that matter, the remaining Dutch and new German colonies) could be kept under control by the migrant soldiers and administrators sent from the cores, some ethnocultural groups, voluntarily or by coercion, joined the repressive apparatus of the colonizer powers. Sikh police from Punjab and Gurkha soldiers from Nepal or, in French-controlled regions, the *tirailleurs sénégalais,* are examples; Bengali administrators in Burma form another category. In the French Empire of 1930, there were 76,900 colonizer personnel controlling sixty million colonized people with the help of "colonial auxiliaries" transported about. When, in the First World War, which was predominantly a European or Euro-Atlantic war, labor forces in Britain and France shrunk through draft and death, hundreds of thousands of colonial contract laborers and soldiers were transported to Europe and to battlefields in those colonies that were drawn into the Euro-centric interimperial conflict.

Chinese indentured laborers carrying shells at an ammunition depot in France, 1917. During World War I, Indians, Vietnamese, Chinese, and West Africans were recruited or forced to enlist by the British and French imperial governments to support the Allied war effort. Some, like the *tirailleurs sénégalais,* served on active duty. (Private Collection / Peter Newark Pictures / The Bridgeman Art Library)

They labored, fought, and died for the Allied cause. Given the skewed thinking of national ideologues, demands for acceptable living conditions by indentured workers (or native working classes) had never been tolerated. But the argument that "colonials" had fought and many had died for the nation (which was not theirs) induced colonizer governments after the war to reconsider the regime of indenture.

## Indentured, Credit-Ticket, and Self-Paying Migrants

With the establishment of the indenture system in British India, in Imperial China in the period of the Unequal Treaties, and in Fiji, as well as in other specific regions, workers, like the free-under-constraints European migrants, had been socialized in particular cultural systems of meaning, languages or dialects, and socio-scapes. Those leaving through ports have been counted; those walking or being walked on land have not necessarily been counted—thus quantitative data are inaccurate. For terminological clarity and empirical soundness, forced migrant labor in Africa will be discussed below.

By status, three major categories of migrants in the colonial circuits need to be discerned: (1) those coming under indenture or contractual debt relationships, (2) those coming on loans for their fare, and (3) self-paying (passenger) migrants. Indentures of Indians from the eastern coastal regions, of Chinese from the southern provinces and later the northeastern provinces, as well as of those recruited or kidnapped from Fiji and other Pacific islands, lasted usually five years with no option to change the contract. Not all arrangements guaranteed return fare. Lack of funds for return, exploitative pay conditions, overcharging by company or plantation stores, nonwork because of illness or pregnancy, all might contribute to involuntary reindenture. A new contract could also be signed voluntarily, either because working life in all its aspects was acceptable or because conditions in the place of origin, "home," were unacceptable. Reindenture might also be a strategy to accumulate savings and establish a small business within the region of indenture or a nearby town. Second, in a different arrangement, people without means could migrate by taking a loan for the cost of their passage. Such "credit-ticket migrants" worked off the loan at the destination. Repayment usually involved a three-year period but could be achieved faster or under exploitative conditions might take longer. Finally, self-paying individuals or families decided on their destination and intended to establish themselves in business. The term *passenger migrant* for people from India differentiates them from "coolies" who, on the same boats, were treated like cattle. The term *merchants* for Chinese reflects the long tradition of diasporic trader migrations. Such migrants, often with wife and children, could be large merchants with wide-ranging import and export connections. They could also be artisans or small traders, migrating singly or with family labor. Some migrated in family networks in which travel costs were advanced without debt relationships but with an obligation to contribute to the family economy.[28]

Once shipping routes and regular traffic had been established, free migrants from other cultural origins could take advantage of them. Free men and, with some delay, women from Meiji Japan began to migrate in the late 1860s, and Filipinos did so after their country became a US colony in 1898. Within the orbit of Dutch colonialism in Southeast Asia, workers were recruited in Java for work on other islands. In some Pacific islands, where at first small populations were depleted by forced migration and then indentured Indians were imported, societies underwent traumatic changes.

Calculations and estimates of total numbers of migrants have varied widely. Adam McKeown's reassessment suggests a total of 48 to 52 million, divided between some 29 million Indians and 19 million Chinese as well as people from other cultures but excluding Dutch Indonesia, which was neither part of the regime of indenture nor an arena of forced long-distance outbound migrations. Less than 10 percent of the migrants came under formal indenture, but much of it occurred with financial assistance from colonial authorities or under debt obligations in the *kangani* recruitment system, under which employers sent one trusted and capable laborer, the *kangani* or *maistry,* to his home region to hire additional workers among acquaintances and dependents. More than 2 million Indians migrated as "passengers." Of Chinese from Guangdong and Fujian, less than a million indentured themselves to European employers but large numbers were bound to Chinese employers, who might be subcontractors for Europeans. Other types of contracts involved wage labor or profit sharing.

Asian destinations for migrants from India included Burma (15 million), Ceylon (8 million), Malaya/Malaysia (4 million), other ports in Southeast Asia, as well as islands in the Indian and Pacific Oceans. From among southern Chinese, up to 11 million traveled to the Straits Settlements (Penang, Singapore, and Malacca)—but one-third or more used the port only for transshipment to the Dutch Indies, Borneo, Burma, and elsewhere. Nearly 4 million headed directly for Siam, 2 to 3 million to French Indochina, over 1 million to the Dutch Indies, less than 1 million to the Philippines, and more than half a million to Australia, New Zealand, Hawaiʻi, and other islands in the Pacific and Indian Oceans. Destinations in Africa and the Americas included 1 million Indians to South and East Africa, and hundreds of thousands of Chinese to Latin American and the Caribbean. Contract laborers in Cuba, some 270,000, and Peru became de facto slaves. After 1900, indentured laborers for South Africa, and for Europe during World War One, came mostly from northern China's new recruitment region. For most destinations, 80 to 90 percent of the migrants returned; of Europe's transatlantic migrants, only one-third returned around 1900.[29]

In 1917–1920, British India's national leaders used the contribution of more than one million Indian soldiers and indentured workers in Britain's armies and behind the front to the 1914–1918 war effort to negotiate the end of the indenture regime. However, through voluntary or involuntary reindenture it lasted in some regions into the 1920s or even 1930s. From China, in contrast, departures almost tripled between 1901–1905 and 1926–1930 to 3.3 million. The decisive break in

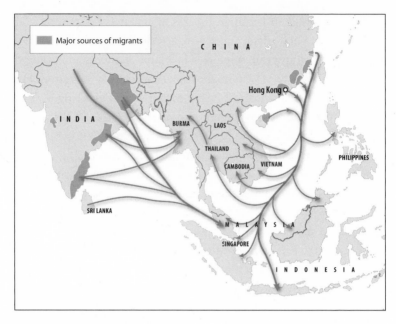

Migration to Southeast Asia, 1850–1914.

patterns of migration in the East Asian, Southeast Asian, and Pacific macroregions came with Japan's aggression against China in July 1937.

## South Africa, Mauritius, and the Malay Peninsula

Destinations within Asia included Burma, Siam, Malaya including the Straits Settlements, some Pacific islands, as well as "white Asia," Australia and New Zealand. Westward travel across the Indian Ocean reached for East and South Africa, Natal in particular. Across the Pacific or around Africa's cape, specific locations along the West Coast of the Americas and in the Caribbean could be reached. Migrants could take advantage of long-existing trading connections of Gujarati merchants to East Africa and of Malabar Coast merchants to Siam and the Malay Peninsula. Capitalists took advantage of short-term global changes. Plantation owners in Mauritius observed the collapse of Antillean sugar production following slave revolts and the abolition of slavery in the early nineteenth century, saw the marketing opportunities in continental Europe, and expanded production by importing coerced Indian labor. Migrations, trade, and investments were of oceanic, hemispheric, and global extent. Mauritius, Natal, and the Malay Peninsula will serve as examples for migrant insertion.

The Mauritian plantocracy, under the postslavery global realignments, changed its traditional voluntary contract labor to brutal exploitation of forced labor. Of the 450,000 Indians who came from 1834 to 1907, less than one-third returned. The planter-administrator complex had designed legislation, regulation, and taxation to force migrant workers to reindenture and to bar them from moving to opportunities outside of the plantation economy. They used vagrancy laws and licensing regulations that the British upper classes had applied for centuries to English working classes. This labor regime, consolidated in the "slave code" of 1867, remained in effect until 1922. However, economic changes, especially the centralization of sugar milling in the 1880s, provided job options in rural towns, to which many workers migrated. Labor militancy was punishable; labor combinations were outlawed until 1937. In Mauritius, the indenture regime was a "new system of slavery," to use Hugh Tinker's term.[30]

Conditions and structures were different in the South African colonies, especially in Natal, where some two hundred thousand South Asian men and women arrived in 1860–1911. About 75 percent stayed permanently, nearly two-fifths of them women. In 1911, when 44 percent of the community of 150,000 was African-born, only 10,000 had been able to enter commerce and a mere 729 the professions. When, after 1911, exclusion legislation ended the old-world influx and constant cultural renewal, acculturation proceeded rapidly. Some sixty-four thousand Chinese were brought to Transvaal mining under the

Labor Importation Ordinance of 1903 and the Anglo-Chinese Labour Convention of 1904 as "captive" workers before abrogation of the scheme in 1906. Europeans' prejudices against "primitive" tribal people and African men's and women's sophisticated resistance combined to retard the development of an indigenous labor force. The plan was for Europeans to control the economy, an inserted and partially bound Indian laboring class to do the plantation and railway work, and Africans to be culturally and geographically marginalized.

Pursuing their own agenda, Indian migrants in Natal developed a full-fledged community. At first laborers were brought in for the newly established sugarcane economy. When early returnees' complaints about abusive treatment reduced further recruitment, a "Coolie Commission" in 1872 improved living conditions, if only minimally. Planters briefly turned to hiring free and slave Africans from Zanzibar but then again recruited Indians because they needed experienced workers. Though early migrants originated from Madras, in the 1870s most sailed from Calcutta. The volume of labor imports depended on the sugar industry's economic cycles, on particular railway construction projects, and on general depressions like that of 1866–1874. Arriving men and women were distributed along the coastal belt according to employer demand—similar, in one scholar's words, to Virginia and South Carolina in times of slavery but with a British "sugarocracy" at the top. When the British government imposed a quota of about 30 percent women migrants, planters paid the women only half the men's wages and food rations. Children were paid according to age. Women (and children) had to endure multiple abuses: women were allocated no food when no labor was available for them or when pregnancy or child care prevented them from working; employers sexually harassed them, and jealous husbands mistreated or murdered them; some women committed suicide after being sexually abused. Some resisted exploitation by "desertion"—by joining African communities. From the 1880s on, Indians also worked in coal mining and in railway construction from Witwatersrand to the coast of Natal. Railway workers often came with skills acquired in construction work in India and, after their time expired, moved to similar work in the Belgian Congo and Portuguese Angola.

Free Indians came as traders, and plantation owners had to rely on them to supply the migrant workers with food and fabrics. Shopkeepers dispersed and settled in coastal cities, plantation camps, and country towns and villages. The government culled the immigrant community of nonproductive as well as politically active members. In Durban and Pietermaritzburg the free Indian population, including independent women, survived in economic niches. Free Indian mechanics, masons, blacksmiths, and carpenters were brought in from Mauritius. In Durban's vicinity ex-indentured servants and enterprising immigrant families established truck farming and began to operate small tea or sugarcane plantations. During economic depressions the community suffered and return migration increased, but a lasting presence was established.[31]

In the other South African colonies, in contrast, African labor had been mobilized or immobilized for almost a century before Indian and Chinese contract laborers were introduced. In Transvaal the gold-mining capital, supported by a pliant government, refused to offer wages that would attract African labor from the local competitive labor market and instead tapped four other reservoirs: Africans from Portuguese Mozambique, convicts, unskilled whites, and Asian contract workers. The latter were recruited by a firm that also supplied coolie labor to Russian employers in Vladivostok. Health inspection before departure permitted selection of the fittest, and to achieve maximum exploitation the government criminalized leaving the job ("desertion"), slow work ("loafing"), and inefficient work. Racism ended recruitment of Chinese coolies after only three years, and the government decided to repatriate all.[32]

In the Malay Peninsula, which from 1870 was integrated under British rule, as well as in Burma and Siam, migrants arrived from both India and China to take advantage of mining, agricultural, trading, and imperial opportunities. The resident Malays, Thai, and Burmese, and the large numbers of multiply ethnoculturally differentiated Indians and Chinese sojourners and immigrants, with a European and Eurasian superstratification, developed new societies. In the process, the Chinese and Indian migrants expanded the economy and created jobs, often establishing themselves above the resident peoples.

When the segments of the Indic world, fragmented by three centuries of rule by competing European powers, were reintegrated into the new whole of the British Empire, comparative labor costs induced capitalists and administrators to move labor from the colonized population core, India, to other locations. Singapore's population, for example, increased eightfold to 90,700 in the four decades before 1864: 58,000 Chinese, 13,500 Malays, and 12,700 Indians. Chinese came on their own to work in tin mining or in commercial agriculture; Chinese entrepreneurs provided the capital. Depending on economic cycles, demand, and productivity, the size of this population fluctuated greatly. The contracts bound men to work off the cost of passage within a year, but overtime pay went into their own pockets. The short contracts and the large number of small employers permitted workers to use their own discretion in finding the most remunerative job. European plantation owners had intended to use Malay people as a labor force, but these were able to live off their land and had refused the indignities of wage work under foreign masters. Chinese investors were able to attract workers without government support, but European capitalists demanded public support to import labor. From among the Indian migrants, 90 percent originated from southern Tamil-speaking people, the rest from Telugu districts and the Malayalam districts of the Malabar coast. They were used in the production of coffee, sugar, tapioca, and coconut, and when, after 1900, rubber plantations expanded and oil palm cultivation increased, labor demand skyrocketed. The whole region from British Burma's Irrawaddy Delta via Siam's central plain to the French Indochinese Mekong Delta became a mass

Immigrants on board a junk, Singapore, ca. 1900. Singapore was the main transit port for migrants from China and India from the 1890s to the beginning of the First World War. Several hundred thousand arrived each year to work locally or to continue their journey to the Malay Peninsula or other islands in Southeast Asia. (National Archives of Singapore)

producer of rice to feed the rice-eating labor forces transported by the British across the globe.

In 1921 the multiethnic populations of Singapore and Malaya of 3.3 million included 1.6 million Malays, 1.2 million Chinese, five hundred thousand Indians, and some sixty thousand others. Ethnic ascription was as common as in other parts of the world. Malays often considered Chinese dangerous and looked upon Indians as "small people." In contrast, in the Burmese construction of foreigners, Chinese, of whom few came, were "cousins," Indians and British were "black men." The British viewed the Burmese as "happy-go-lucky people" or as the Irish of the East, and the Chinese as the Jews of the East. After 1929, over-production of natural rubber and the worldwide depression induced British administrators to reduce Indian in-migration by quota and to ship about a hundred thousand workers back to India within a year. The colonized laborers were expendable human beings.[33]

In distinction to the South Asian diaspora of colonial auxiliaries, free migrants, and contract workers, the Chinese diaspora never became an integral part of British or other colonial empires. Its experience in Southeast Asia varied from ghetto life in Batavia and Manila to easy intermarriage and emergence of the Philippine mestizos and Indonesian *peranakan*. When the presence of women increased, community formation and a re-Sinicization began in the Nanyang, and return migration decreased. The role of the ethnic Chinese as middlemen, and their complete control over particular sectors of the economy, eventually resulted in anti-Sinicism and repeated violence.

## Trade Connections and Migrations in South, Southeast, and East Asia

The presence of colonizers, and their creation of the Plantation Belt, which was powerfully imposed and established by the second half of the nineteenth century, in the Indian Ocean and the East and Southeast Asia seas, impacted on regions that had millennia-long traditions of seafaring mobility. It changed such traditions, permitted or enforced new labor and merchant migrations during the regime of indenture, and remolded directions of regional mobilities. To understand agency in and historical frames of the societies, it is useful to discuss some of the many intra- and interregional moves separately. Examples will be selected from the western Indian Ocean via insular Southeast Asia to Japan. Migrations and influences emanating from this macroregion extended westward to East Africa and eastward across the Pacific to the Americas.

Colonizer penetration might intensify existing local migration practices and systems; the sojourning or settling European powerful investor and administrator migrants might also induce emergence of new ones. Resident people could and did refuse to enter wage- or bound-labor relationships. They used their resources— knowledge of the terrain and supportive networks—for resistance. Imported bound laborers, lacking such resources, were more easily controlled.[34] In British India, investment and labor demand or job opportunities did not necessarily result in mobilization of resident rural people. New and growing economic sectors or locations remained unattractive; agriculture, village crafts, the caste system, early marriage, and joint family living arrangements supported sedentary ways of life.

From northwestern India, Gujarati merchants had traded with and settled in East Africa for centuries. From the southeastern Malabar coast merchants had connected to Siam and the Malay Peninsula for a millennium and a half. Because voyaging is costly in terms of both time and conveyance, merchants often establish branch firms and communities at distant places of exchange. Trade voyaging thus turns into migration, and once a trading community has been established the migrant traders begin to bring in personnel, circular migrations develop, and communities emerge and grow.[35]

The Western trade had, for example, led to settlement of merchants from the Gulf of Kutch and from Jamnagar in Zanzibar. In view of local hostility to intermingling, the merchants brought in wives and a community emerged by 1860. Its five to six thousand Hindus and Muslims fragmented, however, along ethnoreligious and occupational lines: Baluchi as soldiers of the Omani sultan, Memons from Sind in shipping and fishing, Parsi merchants, Hindu trading castes—Baniyas, Bhatias, Lohanas, and Shia Muslims, as well as Daudi Bohoras, Ismaili Khojas, Isthnasteris, and Goan Catholics. Ethnoreligious-professional traditions framed agency: Hindus usually returned when they had accumulated savings or wealth, whereas Muslims stayed and formed families. Return also depended on the world economy. It grew when American cloth undersold Indian cloth and when the British enforced the ban on Indian Ocean slave trading after 1873. In the frame of dependencies between colonizer and colonies, the Gujarati enclave, protected by the Omani sultanate, did in the 1870s become a conduit for British influence and, over time, for colonizer ascendancy. Distinct vertical links of each of the South Asian ethnoreligious groups to the British in Mumbai hindered horizontal Indian-cultured homogenization in the community. Mumbai's commercial expansion resulted in increased Gujarati in-migration, and Gujarati became the community's lingua franca. The privileged and thus distinct status granted by the Omani sultanate prevented indigenization. The immigrants remained an outpost of the Gujarat in East Africa and in the later nineteenth century pursued a strategy of Westernization to improve their position toward the power-wielding colonizer and to enlarge their commercial circuits.[36]

In most of the littoral societies of the Indian Ocean, in the interior of Africa, Arabia, and India, and in China, long-extant bondage continued. In many African societies rights-in-person slavery kept dependents within a family, yet deteriorating economic circumstances might always result in transfer to a creditor or sale to a trader. In most of

India's family economies and hierarchies parents might alienate children, and the larger socioeconomic power structures implied servitude of poorer social groups. In Bihar, loans to the poor gave lenders the right to their services. Children born into such service relationships could be sold, leased, mortgaged, or transferred with land until debts were repaid. In Madras, rural laborers and servants became virtual serfs of landlords when unable to repay loans. Such practices intensified under British rule. In Southeast Asia and the Indonesian archipelago, customs of slavery, debt bondage, and forced labor of war captives were as varied as the societies. All involved involuntary mobility under slavery-like conditions or as members of a restricted underclass.[37]

In South Asia, including British India, middle- and long-distance internal free and contract migration was, it has been argued, small in proportion to total population if compared to Western Europe, European Russia, or North America. According to the 1891 census, which, it must be emphasized, did not include international migrations, 89 percent of the population resided in the district of birth, 97 percent in the province of birth. Such data underestimate intraprovincial long-distance moves—the subcontinent is as large as West, South, and East Central Europe taken together. The data also exclude women's marriage migrations and marriage-ancillary migrations of servants who accompanied brides from wealthy families or of needy female kin who accompanied brides from poor families. Birthing migration, the custom of women in many South Asian cultures to return to their parents' home for the first child's birth, added to sojourning mobility. If men migrated to distant jobs, marriage migration could follow the routes of labor migration.

Under the distinct but related Indian and British economic developments, four major internal migration systems emerged: (1) medium-distance northeastward migrations to Calcutta's jute mills and other industries, to Bengal's coal mines, to Assam's tea plantations, and to

Bihar's indigo plantations and factories; (2) migration to urban Mumbai from a circle stretching some 300 kilometers (180 miles) in each direction; (3) in-migration from surrounding areas to Delhi, and from the same areas of the United Provinces westward to newly irrigated lands of the Punjab; (4) northward migrations from Madras into Mysore and Hyderabad as well as westward into the estate agriculture of the Ghats. In addition, numerous smaller movements crisscrossed the subcontinent and others targeted plantations in Ceylon.

Four socioeconomic types of migration may be discerned: family agricultural, to plantation labor, to mining, and cityward. Peasants, often in family units, migrated to Assam and the Canal colonies. The valleys of Assam offered fertile land, but local people resented the arrival of hundreds of thousands of Bengalis after 1900. Migrant families clustered according to faith and caste (rather than ethnicity). In-migration of young couples meant high birth rates and population increase. Indentured estate laborers migrated to tea, coffee, rubber, and cardamom plantations, especially to the tea estates of Assam, Jalpaiguri, and Darjeeling. Tea cultivation, introduced in 1840, required importation of labor beginning in the 1850s. In the single decade after 1911, Assam became the destination for 770,000 coolies. Many organized and fought for better conditions. A slump in the market in the early 1920s, due to declining exports to civil-war-torn Russia, reduced the number of workers. This migration took many forms: individual migrations for seasonal labor, migrations of entire working families, granting of small plots to in-migrating families as an inducement to stay. By the 1930s, immigrants constituted one-sixth of Assam's population. Mine workers for coalfields in West Bengal, for example, were recruited from the nearby hills since the 1870s. As long as women's underground labor was not prohibited, whole families migrated. Under the British *zamindary* system, owners of large mines acquired rights over people in neighboring villages. They created a semifeudal labor regime by combining land grants with an obligation to work a stipulated number of days in the mines.

In all of South Asia, rural-to-urban migrations, which involved larger distances than rural-to-rural migrations, accounted for nearly half of the internal moves in the early 1930s. The male-to-female ratio of 60 to 40 equaled that of transatlantic migrations. On average, 37 percent of urban residents were in-migrants, but in Mumbai their share reached 75 percent. Calcutta, which grew more slowly, counted 57 percent in-migrants in its population of 680,000 in 1891, and 64 percent of nearly 900,000 in 1911. Demand for labor was high, both because villagers had little predisposition to migrate and because people remained welded to caste-assigned trades. Once indenture declined and free migrations increased, information flows and voluntary departures replaced employer-dominated recruitment. By the early twentieth century, rural-to-urban moves integrated the northeast, Bihar, Bengal, and Arakan (coastal Burma) into one system of interconnected migrations. Elite migration involved families who wanted to be close to the British administration and have their children attend urban schools. Migrations of high and low became entwined when servants of elite migrants became anchor points for low-caste chain migrations. Internal migration occurred parallel to, not interlinked with, transoceanic migration.[38]

In Siam and the adjoining Dutch Southeast Asian islands, people traditionally followed multiple smaller intra- or inter-island migration routes. Because islanders could live off their agriculture, fishing, or local seafaring, Dutch-Javanese planters imported labor, but the colonizer authorities also forced Javanese to migrate to the "outer" islands, which from their point of view were undersupplied with labor, and even to Dutch possessions in the Caribbean. In Sumatra, tobacco cultivation relied on indentured workers. By 1934 more than half of the 1.25 million Chinese migrants lived in the outer islands; of the quarter million European immigrants, 80 percent lived in Java, where connections to the metropoles were best.[39]

Japan in the 1870s began a policy of expansion and industrialization. In a first step, the government established settlements on the near-empty and chilly island of Hokkaido in the north and on the southern, densely populated subtropical Ryukyu Islands, including Okinawa. Large-scale migrations from Japan's densely settled main island increased Hokkaido's Japanese population from 60,000 in 1860 to 2.4 million in 1920. Okinawans, on the other hand, migrated in small numbers to Japan proper and later to the new colonies. Imperial authorities did not consider the islands' natives as equal to "Japanese proper," nor did they consider the migrating Japanese as equal to those staying in the core island—just as American colonists had never been accepted as equals by the British or the Spanish cores. A second, aggressive move, also in the 1870s, opened long-secluded Korea to influence and migration from Japan. Japan annexed Korea in 1910 and invaded Manchuria in 1931. This colonization project involved a strategy to rid society of the ex-samurai warrior class, demoted to commoners, by sending them as soldiers to other countries.

Industrialization generated considerable internal migration, especially short-distance migration of rural people to towns and urban agglomerations. After liberalization of emigration regulations, migrants established themselves in Hawai'i and along the Pacific coast of the Americas. When anti-Asian hate campaigns and exclusionary regulations in the United States and Canada made entry and settlement difficult, Japanese migrants shifted their destination to Peru and Brazil. Only a small percentage moved as contract laborers; in contrast to imperial China, the government cared for Japanese laborers abroad and, if protection proved impossible, attempted to prevent their emigration. The volume of migration remained small. In 1937 there were 40,000 Japanese living in other noncolonized Asian states, 207,000 in Hawaii and North America, and 227,000 in Latin America. Japanese migrants became part of the government's project to extend Japan's influence abroad. Thus, self-willed migrations became an aspect of imperialist strategies.[40]

## Transpacific Distances, Connections, and Racializations

After the first phase of the Pacific migration system, which had connected the Philippines with New Spain from the 1570s to the mid-seventeenth century, commercial connections within the Spanish imperial sphere continued but, during a two-century-long hiatus, involved almost no migration. The distances of the Pacific Ocean were not easily traversed. Even though the Indian Ocean and the Southeast and East Asian seas were connecting waters, the Pacific remained a dividing ocean. Via well-traveled routes from the Indian Ocean to the Atlantic, a first few hundred indentured laborers had been shipped to Caribbean and Brazilian plantations in the early 1800s. The Pacific migration system's second phase evolved in connection with intra-Asian migrations. It thus resembled the emergence of the Atlantic system. Merchants, prospectors, and free laborers developed small communities in Hawai'i and along the Pacific coast of the Americas. Since the 1840s indentured Chinese and Indian laborers were transported to the Caribbean and South America, and free migrants and subsequently credit-ticket migrants came to North America. From the 1880s, Japanese, Koreans, and Filipinos also migrated—though at this time race-based exclusion began to hamper this mobility.

From around 1800, the Polynesian-settled Hawai'ian Islands, halfway across the Pacific, became the destination of migrants from continental Asia as well as of a few Europeans. Both Chinese and Western capital-owning migrants established plantations, but the demand for sugar in California gave US planters a competitive advantage after midcentury. This they buttressed by positioning themselves as advisors to the Hawai'ian rulers and thereby marginalizing Chinese planters.

Until the 1870s, Hawai'ians made up most of the plantation labor force. But from the 1850s on, indentured Chinese, including some women, labored alongside South Sea Islanders and Japanese, Norwegians, and Germans, as well Portuguese from Madeira. Because of harsh conditions, many of the latter moved on to the Macao- or Sino-Portuguese communities in California. After the United States annexed Hawai'i in 1898 and the extension of the Asian exclusion laws, migration declined and the two major communities stabilized. The Chinese community, numbering twenty to thirty thousand, had its own institutions and ethnic enterprises. From marriage with either Chinese or local women, a mixed second generation emerged. Its rice cultivation economy expanded to market gardening. The Japanese community grew and came to account for about 40 percent of the islands' population by 1930. Independent farming families leased land, and workers labored on European- and US-owned plantations. When these workers struck for better working conditions in 1909, the Chinese, Filipino, and Portuguese working-class diasporas did not yet support them; ethnocultural specifics still ranked over class solidarity. An internationally mixed labor force and a differently mixed entrepreneurial class had emerged.[41]

From the late 1830s, the Caribbean and circum-Caribbean mainland colonies became the destination of South Asians, indentured under the British Empire's labor allocation across the globe. French planters in Guadeloupe, Martinique, and French Guiana imported hundreds of laborers from colonized Asia; the Dutch recruited 33,000 workers from Java for Surinam. Such contract workers labored alongside African creoles and slaves from the Congo and East Africa liberated from slave ships but forced to "redeem" the cost of their liberation. A total of about 1.75 million voluntary and enslaved workers reached the Caribbean from 1811 to 1916: perhaps 800,000 Africans, 550,000 Asian Indians of whom fewer than one-third returned, and 270,000 Chinese who were sent to Spanish Cuba or Puerto Rico. In addition, 60,000 or fewer free African and 200,000 European migrants came. In the context of empire, 80 percent of the more than half a million laborers sent to Britain's island and mainland possessions came from India, and in British Guiana, Trinidad, and Jamaica, free communities emerged by the 1870s. Among the offspring of East Indians who had migrated to the West Indies, the salience of caste declined. Their chances for community formation were better than those of the Chinese because more women were present. South Asians, mobile within the region, became peasant proprietors, shopkeepers, or import-export merchants. An affluent urban elite emerged, and by the early twentieth century the first Indian-Caribbeans were elected to legislatures.

For Chaozhou, Hokkien-speaking, and Cantonese indentured workers, in contrast, options were few. Recruited for Cuba, Jamaica, Trinidad, and Guiana at below-subsistence wages, many were forced to reindenture. Those in Spanish Cuba were virtual slaves. Spanish merchants, engaged in contraband slave trading, attempted to cut their losses by shifting to the legal trade in coolies. Recruitment of families was considered desirable because children, like women, were contractually bound to work alongside the men in the family. Planters estimated mortality, including suicides, at a rate said to be the highest in the world, at 10 percent per year; others have estimated it to have been higher. An international French and American commission revealed forced recruitment, transport in prisonlike ships, and twelve-hour workdays. Without guaranteed return passage and without money to bribe officials for a passport permitting departure, the survivors became perpetual contract laborers. The few who gained freedom dispersed to wherever they perceived opportunities, sold their labor in self-organized work gangs, or became marginal retailers, artisans, and domestics. Some established themselves in vegetable farming and oyster fishing. A few elite men opened larger trading establishments or owned cocoa estates. In the early twentieth century, the Trinidad community and separately the Havana Chinese established contacts with California Chinese. Acculturation of Asian migrants to the Euro-African-Amerindian heterogeneity proceeded by gradual change of language, intermarriage or liaison, and emergence of a community of mixed ancestry.[42]

A few South American economies—Peru, Nicaragua, Brazil—also recruited Cantonese, Hawaiʻian, and Japanese laborers. In Peru, which attracted investors from Britain, America, Germany, and Italy, working conditions resembled those in Cuba. Hawaiʻian and Japanese workers on plantations, in internal improvement projects, and in the digging of bird manure (guano) for export died in large numbers. Hostility against Asians abated somewhat when Japanese men fought in the Peruvian army during a boundary dispute with Ecuador. Subsequently a thriving community emerged, but during the Great Depression in the 1930s, many of the descendants, especially of Brazilian Japanese, migrated back.[43]

In North America, the first Chinese arrived in the context of the early transatlantic US-China trade. When transpacific migrations of free Chinese began with the gold rushes—California in 1848, British Columbia in 1858, and Alaska later—a direct route connected Hong Kong to Vancouver. In California, racist legislators imposed a "foreign miners' head tax" on Chinese as well as on Mexican prospectors. These entrepreneurs, adventurers, and service workers formed a nucleus that attracted credit-ticket migrants and contract laborers for transcontinental railway construction. The migrants worked in industries, in independent market gardening, or as sharecroppers, and, along the coast and in the Rockies, as miners, in fishing, and in canneries, as well as in niches like abalone fishing. Some moved to Louisiana and Gulf of Mexico fisheries, others were hired for southern plantations after the end of slavery, and a few traveled to eastern factories before the depression of 1873. Because wealthy Chinese occupied positions as ethnic leaders and middlemen in the credit-ticket business, hierarchies were

Indian immigrants debarred from entry to Canada on board the *Komagata Maru,* Vancouver Bay, 1914. Though British subjects, regardless of skin color, were free to move throughout the British Empire, the Canadian government used bureaucratic subterfuge to prevent entry. The most famous case involved the 376 passengers of the *Komagata Maru.* Erroneously labeled "Hindoos," most of the would-be migrants were Sikhs. All but twenty were sent back. (Library and Archives of Canada, PA-034015)

strong and exploitation was frequent. The small US-Japanese community expanded after 1890, and Filipinos and East Indians became part of this migration. Total immigration from the Asian Rim to the Pacific Rim, in 1850–1920, amounted in the United States to 320,000 Chinese, 240,000 Japanese, 30,000 from "other Asia," 10,000 Pacific Islanders, and 44,000 Australians and New Zealanders. These gross figures include multiple migrations. In Canada, the census of 1921 listed 39,600 Chinese, 15,900 Japanese, and 10,500 "East Indians." Compared to European migration in the Atlantic system, in the Pacific system numbers were small. The demand for cheap labor in the United States remained high after the Asian restriction, which did not apply to the colony of the Philippines, but Filipinos continued to come and recruitment of Mexicans for work began around 1900.[44]

In all of the societies of the Americas, migrants from Asia kept diasporic ties to their cultures of origin. When racism in the Anglo-American societies was operationalized in restriction regulations beginning in 1875, migrants circumvented the bureaucrats' Great (paper) Walls. By creating "paper" sons and daughters, dependents migrating with false documents and assumed identities, the migrants breached the state-fabricated racist regulations. Such irregular migration, which lasted into the 1930s, permitted communities to remain stable. Racists demanded independence for the Philippines so that Filipinos and Filipinas might also be excluded. Once again nation-state ideologues refused to accept working-class human beings as equal. They did accept comradeship in arms, and in 1943 the United States relaxed restrictions against the Chinese because China had fought as an ally in the Second World War, which began in 1937 in Asia.

## Peasant Migrations and Mobility in China and Manchuria

The century-long traditions of outbound migration from Guangdong and Fujian provinces had involved the diaspora formation in Southeast Asia, or Nanyang, and the migration of indentured workers. The vast and differentiated inland regions had been arenas for peasant settlement migrations, refugee moves from famines and, from the mid-nineteenth century in particular, from internal warfare and rebellions. Early industrial development from the 1860s on did not achieve a scale that provided jobs in sufficient numbers. Increased trade, expansion of coal mining, and establishment of shipyards and factories induced internal migration of skilled laborers and technicians. Construction of railways and ports absorbed surplus labor, but once new transportation systems became operative the vast numbers of men previously engaged in porterage and barge pulling were thrown out of work. The introduction of steam power into a social economy based on human power caused immensely larger unemployment than economies based on animal-powered transport incurred. Furthermore, as in Europe, population growth was rapid. In European societies that were unwilling to undertake structural reforms, the possibility of emigrating provided people with options elsewhere; in contrast, except for the two southern provinces the Chinese had neither traditions of emigration nor, before the late 1890s, a railroad network connecting to port cities, nor a political and discursive frame that would encourage emigration. From the 1880s there developed a new northbound, mass-migration system from Shandong to Manchuria. In these very decades, the terms of trade imposed by the European colonizing powers dislocated large numbers of Chinese.

Toward the end of the nineteenth century, emigration began from the provinces of the northern littoral, first under indenture or credit-ticket practices. Men were recruited as contract laborers for Russian Siberia and for South African mining. Early twentieth-century railway construction in the northern plains increased information flows and provided outbound transportation in the impoverished agricultural provinces of Zhili, Shandong, and Henan. In Zhili, climatic conditions and short growing seasons prevented predictable crop yields; in Shandong, where better conditions prevailed, floods were a constant threat. An estimated nine to ten million people died or fled during the drought and famine of 1876–1879.[45]

In a macroregional context, Sakhalin, Korea, and Manchuria became contested territories after the Russian Empire incorporated the Far East into its territories: two competing powerful neighboring states and a northern Chinese peasant population with too little land even for mere subsistence. North of the Amur River, settlement of and interaction between Chinese and Russian migrants had developed over two centuries when eastbound migrations from European Russia extended to the Amur and the port of Vladivostok. Japan, seeking access to China's presumed markets, attacked in 1895, annexed Taiwan and the Pescadores Islands, and "leased" the northern territories (renamed Kantoshu) with Port Arthur (Lüshun) and Dalian in Liaoning Province. In 1905 it defeated Russia and annexed South Sakhalin (renamed Karafuto). Korea, at first a protectorate, was annexed in 1910 and Manchuria and Inner Mongolia became part of Japan's zone of influence. Under Japan's corporatist military-economic rule, mining and industrial production increased. Labor was needed, and in the view of Chinese peasants, land was but thinly settled.

The Treaty of Shimonoseki in 1895 opened China's northern ports to European and Japanese imports. Cheap machine-spun cotton cloth increased demand for cash while home production collapsed. Only those with the initial means to migrate could depart in family units or hope for a potential cash flow of individual emigrant remittances. As everywhere, the most impoverished could not move. The limited educational institutions of the villages and province were further reduced when students left temporarily and teachers and journalists joined the diasporic communities. Northbound transportation became cheaper and faster; Manchuria appeared closer. The whole northeastern Asian region, but Manchuria in particular, became the destination for 28 to 33 million Chinese, 2 million Koreans, but just over half a million Japanese—far fewer than the Japanese government's colonizing project had envisioned. Japanese migrants, under the empire's protection, took possession of Korea's cultivated agricultural land and allocated urban jobs to themselves. In consequence, especially in the 1930s, about 2.5 million Koreans migrated or were "induced" to migrate to militarizing and industrializing Japan as laborers of inferior status.

Chinese internal migration as well as emigration involved people speaking many different, often mutually unintelligible, local dialects.

In addition, about 10 percent of China's population were "minorities"—conceptualized as such only in 1930s China—of more than fifty nationalities: Muslim Turkic-speaking peoples from the Uighurs to the Kazakhs in Central Asia, Mongolian and Tibetan people in Mongolia and the Himalayas, Koreans and Manchu in the north. Through internal migration, Beijing accommodated small communities or seasonal populations of maritime Arab Muslim traders, Turkic Muslims from Samarkand, and nomad Mongol traders. Commercial connections reached deep into the interior; the Muslims of Inner Mongolia, for example, grew tobacco for the British American Tobacco Company. Mongolia was targeted by the Chinese government's colonization policies. Men with limited means migrated for seasonal labor, younger sons of peasant families moved, whole peasant families resettled. As everywhere, families with limited means were separated because some members, usually the male head of the household, departed to earn cash income afar. Alienation, experience of mobility, and bilingualism induced younger men to remain in towns as interpreters. Markets and new railways connected the nomad and pioneer economies to the core.

Migration to Manchuria, vastly larger, began in the mid-nineteenth century when northern Chinese had settled in the Liao River valley, then moved to regions north of Mukden and Harbin. Construction of railroads, eastbound from Beijing to Suiyuan and northbound to Harbin, provided mass transportation. Impoverished families, however, had to walk hundreds of miles and build homes out of sundried mud bricks with a mud roof on brush—similar to European newcomers' sod houses in North America's prairies. Manchuria's population doubled from fifteen million in 1911 to thirty million in 1931. Into the 1920s, China's government encouraged and assisted migration; private companies or administrative bodies held and sold land. To the mid-1920s, three-quarters of the half-million seasonal workers returned annually to their families in Shandong or Zhili.

Thereafter railway-stimulated in-migration increased to a million per year and permanent settlement grew through family migration. Most originated from Shandong Province and migrated voluntarily in the framework of continued droughts, famine, and internal war. The mass migration to "Manchukuo," the region's name under Japanese rule after March 1, 1932, provided Japanese-run coal mines, railway construction, and cities with workers via the Japan-controlled South Manchurian Railway from the port of Dairen to Mukden, Jilin, and Harbin.

In Mongolia, cultural interaction was the rule; in Manchuria, by sheer numbers the Chinese immigrants absorbed the local Manchu. The newcomers formed classic urban immigrant communities in which families from the same region or village of origin settled close to each other, founded mutual aid societies, banded together in vigilante-type groups to keep order under frontier conditions, and established credit arrangements to avoid moneylenders. Because settlement was compact, the frontier moved ahead slowly. New railroads, banks, and market crops facilitated settlement; Confucian concepts of family, of ancestral spirits related to land, and of sons' duties toward living and deceased parents retarded change. By 1940, Manchuria's population of 43.2 million consisted of 36.8 million Chinese, 2.7 million Manchu, 1.1 million Mongols, 1.45 million Koreans, 0.85 million Japanese, as well as Russians and others. The ubiquitous population planners estimated that Manchuria could still absorb a further 30 million immigrants. However, Japan's aggression against China in 1937, the beginning of World War II, turned mass labor into mass refugee migrations. The postwar change of regimes in China from nationalist to communist, as well as the need to rebuild the war-devastated country and resettle the internal refugees, ended the recent pattern of northward and the traditional pattern of southward migration.[46]

## Industrializing European Russia and Its Siberian Frontier

At the turn from the nineteenth to the twentieth century, the Russo-Siberian migration system involved (1) large-scale, mostly seasonal rural-to-urban migrations in European Russia of tens of millions; (2) increasing "internal emigration" of peasant families but also of workers to southern Siberia as far as the Amur River, the Sino-Russian border; and (3) from the 1880s, emigration to North America, predominantly of Jews, Poles, and Ukrainians.

Since emancipation in 1861, peasant families increasingly migrated to southern Siberian and trans-Caspian cultivable lands, and from the 1880s, parallel to the Canadian West, the mining frontier became a magnet. Transcontinental railroads facilitated movement since the 1880s. Similarities between the United States and imperial Russia were many: The "Great American Desert" had been considered as uninhabitable as Siberia. The US and Canadian governments encouraged migration through homestead acts, in 1862 and 1872, respectively, as did Russia from the mid-eighteenth century and again under Pyotr Stolypin's policies of 1906–1911. Migrants settled contiguous tracts of land and created social systems more equal and more dynamic than those of their home villages. In the United States, Mormons fled westward; in Russia, Old Believers moved eastward. Under Russification policies—as part of the Northern Hemisphere's nationalist surge in the latter nineteenth century—Russian Doukhobors, other religious dissenters, and south Russian German-language Mennonites migrated to Canada and the United States to escape religious persecution and national homogenization. Some 150,000 departed for North America from 1899 to 1914, and more left in the 1920s, fleeing policies of atheism and collectivism.

In the Russo-Siberian migration system, during the decades from 1880 to 1914 and into the 1920s, some ten million men and women individually or as families moved eastward and southward—the same period in which some twenty million Europeans, Jews and Ukrainians from Russia included, migrated westward. In the 1890s an average of forty-two thousand people arrived in Siberia annually; of these, less than 2 percent were deportees. Many of the political exiles were highly educated and socially responsible men and women who became teachers and nurses in Siberian villages and towns neglected by the distant government in Moscow. By 1911, First Peoples accounted for a mere 10 percent of the total Siberian population of 9.4 million. The immigrants and their descendants, mainly Russians, Ukrainians, and Ruthenians, concentrated along a belt of land six hundred kilometers wide in western and central Siberia. Settlement was easier for the estimated four million settlers in the trans-Caspian and trans-Aral regions and Kazakhstan. In Central and East Asia, Russian and Chinese migrants interacted with peasants living in interspersed but separate villages. The Amur River became a trade artery, Chinese merchants and artisans moved to Vladivostok, and Chinese migrants as unskilled laborers on the Trans-Siberian Railway worked alongside skilled workers from Germany and Italy in a labor force that was 25 percent foreign. In the Amur gold fields, Chinese contract workers made up 15 percent of the labor force in 1900, and 76 percent in 1915. By 1910, one hundred thousand Chinese, some skilled workers or urban artisans, lived in the Russian Far East. Like pidgin English in California gold prospecting, a Russo-Chinese pidgin became the lingua franca. Discrimination prevented Chinese from owning land or staking claims. Racism notwithstanding, intermarriage was widespread. While Russian administrators, of white mentality, attempted to restrict the "yellow peril," the whole regional economy depended on immigrants and became a meeting ground for Eurasian peoples.[47]

Internal rural-to-urban migration after emancipation in European Russia is well documented. The communities of origin, which shared responsibilities for taxes, kept detailed records of the temporarily absent. In the decade after 1870, almost forty million migration permits were issued—almost all for a year or less. At the time of the first empire-wide census in 1897, 9.4 million men and women (11.7 and 8.0 percent of their respective shares of the population) had moved away from their province of birth. The net figures do not reflect gross moves: multiple migrations, departure and return before the census date, emigration, rural-to-urban migration within the populous Moscow and St. Petersburg provinces, and other intraprovincial migration. The provinces of Moscow, the central industrial region, and St. Petersburg, as well as the four provinces of the Donbass and Urals industrial belt, received the bulk of the internal migrants. In 1897 almost three-quarters of Moscow's one million inhabitants and St. Petersburg's 1.25 million were migrants. All other provinces had negative migration balances. Low out-migration characterized the three Baltic provinces (subsequently Estonia and Latvia) because of the language differences. Many rural families followed the almost worldwide pattern of gender-specific allocation of labor resources: male wage labor at a distance and female double-load farm labor at home as an income-diversification strategy when cash rather than exchange came to characterize trade.

Temporary rural-to-urban mass migration influenced family relations as well as peasant, worker, and gendered mentalities, workloads, and self-organization. Men and women migrated jointly to the rural and mining zones of the Donbass and the Urals, but more than 80 percent of the urban migrants were men. Most families could not afford to or did not want to leave agriculture altogether, and women staying behind had to assume their absent husbands' workload. In contrast to work, independent decision making hardly grew in view of male relatives' roles and control. As in all regions of out-migration, children of such bifurcated households hardly ever saw their fathers. Women visiting their husbands in the cities got a glimpse of urban life and male working-class standards of living, the latter probably no inducement to follow. However, women who did migrate acculturated quickly to urban life, took factory jobs, and married late. Neighborhood support, shared traditions of everyday life, and festive customs eased the transition. In self-organized *arteli,* collective units of life, the men cooked together or hired one woman to do the work for many, elected a leader, and regulated their affairs. There were high levels of geographic, job, and residential fluctuation. Thirteen percent of Moscow's inhabitants of 1882 had arrived in the preceding year, requiring institutions similar to the village *mir,* and the *artel* was a democratic as well as a constraining frame.

Proletarianization occurred over generations. Serfs and emancipated peasants first became seasonal labor migrants, then, with longer sojourns in the factories, peasant-workers still bound to the village. When ties loosened, they changed to worker-peasants, and their urban-born sons and daughters would be urban workers, proletarians. However, due to the *mir* system and the bifurcated families, children were usually raised in the rural world, distant from urban working-class environments. They would have to begin the cycle again, with each generation of workers socialized anew into factory life, whether in Russia, North America, or Western Europe. Migrants who did not return to their village origins developed both craft skills and proletarian mentalities, and they or their children could enter skilled positions. More recent migrants had to take unskilled jobs that provided lower incomes.[48]

In a third movement Jews, Poles, Ukrainians, and Baltic peoples migrated westward into the Atlantic migration system. Jointly, Jewish and Polish migrants accounted for 68 percent of emigration from tsarist Russia to North America; others included Belorussians and Ukrainians (11 percent), Lithuanians (9 percent), Finns (7 percent), and Russian-Germans and Mennonites who left after their privileges were withdrawn (5 percent). From 1830 to 1860 only about thirty thousand of the tsar's subjects left the empire westbound; from 1860 to 1914, 4.5 million followed. Of special groups of migrants, the Polish political emigration ended with the last rebellion (struggle for independence)

A family of Jewish immigrant shoemakers in Paris, 1920. In the face of escalating violence and increasing social, political, and economic restriction, two million Jews emigrated from Russia between 1880 and 1914. Many settled in Europe's metropoles: Berlin, Paris, London. Others continued to North America. (Mémorial de la Shoah / CDJC)

in 1863–1864. Activists were sent to Siberia; some seven to eight thousand refugees headed for Paris and England. The émigrés became a nucleus for later Polish labor migrants. Russian reformers and revolutionaries also emigrated and emerged as a kind of society-in-exile, a "second Russia abroad." Militants who returned during the revolution of 1905 were soon forced into exile again; fleeing revolutionary Jewish workers increased the US-bound migrations. Of young Russian women, barred from universities, some five to six thousand migrated to Swiss universities from 1882 to 1913. Most planned to return and devote themselves to medical and charitable work among peasants and perhaps the urban poor.

Labor migrants from the Jewish Pale of Settlement, Russian-occupied Polish lands, and Ukraine headed to West European cities, Berlin, Paris, and London in particular, and to North American cities, from Montreal via New York to Pennsylvania. From Ukraine agricultural settler families also migrated to Canada's prairies. Of the world's Jewish population an estimated three-quarters lived in Eastern Europe. The 750,000 to 900,000 Jews of the late eighteenth century had increased to 5.2 million in Russia and 2 million in other parts of East and East Central Europe by the end of the nineteenth century. Early marriage, combined with large numbers of children, explains this increase, which was more than twice the empire's average population growth. Internal migrations from the stagnating northeastern borderlands of the former Polish-Lithuanian Commonwealth targeted Russia's southern provinces. Briefly, the government recruited Jewish families as settlers for agricultural regions. In contrast, some cities, such as Kiev, continued the medieval discrimination and barred inmigration. Again others, like the thriving, relatively new port of Odessa (founded in 1794), with a mere 250 Jewish inhabitants in 1795 but 152,000 in 1904, saw a vibrant Jewish culture emerge. Pogroms in the 1870s and severely restrictive legislation accelerated the mass exodus that transferred elements of the cultures of the small shtetl or urban

Odessa to North America. World War I brought all movement to a standstill, and the Russian Revolution of 1917 changed all parameters of action.[49]

## Mediterranean Africa, the Persian Gulf, and Sub-Saharan Africa

In the cultures of the Eastern Mediterranean, Mediterranean Africa, and the Persian Gulf (West Asia, North Africa, Arabia), the stability the Ottoman Empire was being challenged and the imperialist governments of Britain and France began to expand their influence into the region. In the core of the Ottoman Empire, multiethnic coexistence became more tenuous as administrators' inability or venality grew, as did aspirations for self-rule among Armenians and many other peoples.[50] In the Ottoman's former Mediterranean African realm, port and trading cities declined when the centuries-long ascent of Mediterranean Europe began, and subsequently economic activity shifted to the Atlantic. According to political-economic aspirations, imposed European domination, and migration patterns, four regions emerged: Egypt and the Omani state, Ethiopia, the Nilotic Sudan, and North Africa.

Egypt and the Omani state asserted influence over Arabia while, at mid-nineteenth century, British and French migrant entrepreneurs infused the Egyptian elites with concepts of Western-type modernization and inserted capital for construction of the Suez Canal. In the early 1870s, vast infrastructural projects as well as cotton cultivation—partly in response to the interruption of cotton supply from the secessionist US states in the 1860s—mobilized rural workers and marginal peasant families. A nationalist movement among the rising elites and antiforeigner riots among urban populations countered the impositions of the European immigrants and states. Ethiopia, coveted by the English and French, was militarily colonized by Italy after 1882. When the state, in a late colonizing attempt, planned to send Italian settler families, the millions of Italian migrants preferred the Americas and, in small numbers, destinations around the world. Even the fascist expansion of the 1920s and 1930s could not change this pattern. The Nilotic Sudan remained contested ground as a catchment area for slaves until, in the 1870s, the slave trade from the upper Nile region was abolished officially if not in practice.

In North Africa, the French state conquered Algeria and Tunisia after 1830, while Morocco remained independent until 1912. More than one hundred thousand agricultural settlers came. Labeled "French," they were of Spanish, Italian, Maltese, Swiss, Prussian, Bavarian, and Hessian background. The French government feared the mass in-migration of rural poor to Paris—some twenty-five thousand to thirty-five thousand added themselves to the one million Parisians annually. It planned to transport some hundred thousand of these *classes dangereuses* to Algeria, but only fifteen thousand could be corralled and shipped. The colonization process displaced resident Arab and Kabyl people. New regulations in the 1870s—when the tsarist government reclassified the position of Jews—reduced Muslim land rights and additional *colons,* including many French citizens of Jewish faith, came from Europe. Some 630,000 Europeans lived in Algeria by 1901. A Native Code serving the interests of the colonizers regulated and restricted local people's migration. Along with the long-term decline of the southern Mediterranean littoral and the impoverishment created by colonizer impositions, epidemics and famines reduced native North African populations.[51]

South Africa, the one other agricultural colony established by the Dutch, had been annexed by Britain in 1806. In contrast to the homogenization of immigrant settlers in Algeria, the Dutch and the British remained distinct and antagonistic. They fought over land and control of the native labor force. The resulting segmented and color-coded society provided a stark contrast to Latin American many-colored ethnogenesis. Against the Dutch-Afrikaners the British passed Aliens Expulsion and Aliens Immigration Restriction acts in the 1890s; the Transvaal Afrikaner (Boer) government in turn discriminated against British subjects. For the resulting war, the British Empire sent some 300,000 troops and, in the course of it, deported some 120,000 Afrikaner women and children to camps. Deportation as a British imperial strategy had been used against French-speaking Acadians in the North American colonies in the 1750s and was to be used against Kikuyu and Kabaka in East Africa in the 1950s.

Immigrant European farmers imposed restrictions on the resident Khoi, and by the mid-nineteenth century the government imposed segregation. From the 1860s the colonizers imported indentured workers from India and from China's northern provinces. With the discovery of diamonds in 1866 and of gold in 1886, the demand for mine labor, investment capital, and skilled gem cutters expanded massively. A niche economy connected the mines to Dutch-Jewish diamond experts in Amsterdam. Cities grew by leaps and bounds: Johannesburg's population, zero in 1886, by 1899 numbered one hundred thousand from across southern Africa and fifty thousand from across Europe. The diamond mines' migrant owners housed the migrant workers in closed compounds both for purposes of control and to permit them to carry wages home. At first the arrangement suited migrants to a degree that employers could rely on self-recruitment. In the last decades of the nineteenth century, African men from Portuguese Mozambique and other neighboring colonies joined the mine labor force. In these migrations ethnic identifications were reshaped by interaction, and male and female cultures—separated by migration and compound housing—evolved along distinct paths. By the 1930s the three hundred thousand mine workers formed a distinct ethnic class. It no longer included migrants from Asia, because the government of the

Union of South Africa, established in 1910, immediately excluded migrant labor from Asia. Australia, too, upon receiving Dominion status, had announced a white Australia policy in 1901.[52]

In East and West Africa, the actual end of the slave trade in the 1870s was paralleled by the British, French, Belgian, and German governments' quest for colonies. In the east the British government and merchants imposed their influence on Zanzibar, in part through the immigrants from India; Germans and British established mainland settler colonies. In the west, the French colonizers—after resistance from the Mandinka state and conquest in 1898—relied on traditional chiefs and on competition between them rather than on the integrative Islamic religious structures. The British government, in contrast, sent costly administrative personnel from the core. Both systems succeeded in dividing African peoples into frenchified or anglicized elites and traditional-culture urban lower classes and hinterland dwellers. Because labor was difficult to recruit, colonizer employers and colonizer missionaries combined forces to teach their values of work and to train skilled craftsmen and orderly housewives. Africans, however, adapted some of the Europeans' resources, like written languages, to their own purposes. Women missionaries, who migrated out of their home society's gender hierarchies, helped African women to undercut male authority. In some regions—among the Soninke, for example— itinerant traders, perceiving demand for labor, relayed information back to their communities and free migration ensued. The empires also extracted labor, and colonizer-appointed chiefs shifted the burden of compulsory labor to weaker members of a society. In the German and the Portuguese southwest, rulers and their male supporters, who traditionally had raided weaker peoples for cattle, held colonizers at some distance by becoming their extended arms. They raided villages for labor and delivered captive men and women to the colonizers. In West Africa, the British administrators—with regional variations— demanded compulsory work from men aged fifteen to fifty and women aged fifteen to forty-five. Wage incentives, if offered at all, were low—among East Africa's Kikuyu, for example, far lower than income from independent farming.

Regional patterns of migration depended on traditions, power impositions, and new patterns of mobility. In traditional market-oriented economies, like groundnut production in Senegal, migratory patterns existed previous to and independent of colonial rule. In the Ngoni and Ngonde societies of the Great Lakes area, gender hierarchies kept women in bondage, and in the 1880s and 1890s Bemba "entrepreneurial brigandage" captured women and children to be handed over to traders. Many such women fled to return to their people or to migrate independently. In Kenya, the British colonizers alienated Kikuyu land, and in consequence the number of migrant laborers grew from 5,000 in 1903 to 120,000 in 1923. Kikuyu and other people protected themselves by developing market agriculture in crops that did not lend themselves to economies of scale and thus remained outside of colonizer interest. Infrastructural projects like the building of the Uganda railway from Mombasa to Nairobi, begun in 1896, demanded large labor forces: in this case a mere 107 European technicians, overseers, and tavern keepers; 6,000 Indians, including 4,800 Punjabi Muslim coolies, 300 soldiers, and 1,100 Baluchi and Arab merchants; and 17,400 Swahili-speakers, comprising 14,600 free persons, 2,650 slaves, and 150 prisoners. Over the next years, some 35,000 indentured workers were imported, mainly from the commercially related villages and towns along the Gulf of Cambay. Asian immigrants to East Africa amounted to 54,400 by 1921. Denied the right to acquire land, they entered the trades.[53]

From Africa's many regions of fragile ecology, those impoverished by drought or other natural disasters migrated first. Caught in a web of power relationships between wage-appropriating local rulers and exploitative colonizers, by the 1920s people developed working-class militancy and collective action. Information about destinations permitted increased agency and migration over larger distances. In hinterlands, the coming of Asian-origin immigrant or traditional African traders created new expectations and a resulting need for cash. Wage incomes permitted escape from oppressive parents or societies, choice of marriage partners, and increase in prestige. On the other hand, centripetal forces remained strong. Women-and-child families remained behind; rural ways of life were stabilized by infusion of cash. Jobs within walking distance kept migrants in their own systems of orientation. African labor migration resembles migrations elsewhere in the world. Contact with European workers, often marred by racism, could also infuse European-style ethnic-class consciousness. French Guinean soldiers who fought in Europe in World War I carried back socialist ideas and organized the Conakry dockworkers' strikes in 1918 and 1919.

At the beginning of the twentieth century, the European presence in Africa was politically all-powerful, economically intrusive, culturally transformative as regards elites, but numerically weak. Settlement clusters were limited to 750,000 European immigrants and their descendants in Algeria (less than 14 percent of the population), 1.25 million in South Africa and Rhodesia (22 percent of the population), and 24,000 in Portuguese Angola and Mozambique. Unknown to contemporaries, decolonization was only a few decades away.

## Migrating Colonizers

Labor migrations have usually been discussed in terms of options or of exploitation. Migrations of agrarian settlers have been discussed in terms of soils to be cultivated. Migrations of imperial personnel were disregarded as comparatively small or, in an older version, endowed with a civilizing mission. However, colonizer personnel migrations are of particular importance in terms of interest groups, gender, and constructions of "white," not merely over "black" but over all "coloreds," in processes of racialization and categorization of peoples as Other.

Language needs to be used carefully: the white-over-black color scheme, from a different perspective, could read "pale trumps colorful" and connotations would change.

When the French state in the 1870s embarked on a new imperial strategy or "mission," its body politic—the middle classes—had just been humbled, forced into submission, by Prussia's victorious aggression. France's elite, unable to beat up the Teutons, turned to putting down the French working class (deportation of the Communards), French Jews (as in the Dreyfus affair), and peoples in Africa, Indochina, and Caledonia. Several wars later, in 1945, after five years of Fascist German occupation and considerable cooperation, collaborating French men turned against French women who had fallen in (carnal) love with German soldiers and humbled them: a ritual to regain their manhood. The aspects of maleness in British migration and statesmanship have been discussed in Chapter 2. Politics, warfare, and migration are bodied and gendered processes and involve strategies. This kind of manhood—both inside the nation and outside of it in the colonies—was conceived in terms not of humanity but of self-aggrandizement and bullying. Maleness implied the capability to put down weaker Others.

The white or paleface colonizer states' middle classes and ruling elites were internally segmented. Patterns of access to "national" state offices and specific cultural practices made hierarchies of class and gender as well as of ethnicity and race integral parts of "democratic" polities, whether called the "mother country" or the "fatherland." The constructed homogeneity of "the English," for example, was, as some contemporary and most recent scholarship of colonialism and imperialism has noted, intended for the benefit of a small group of profiteers, whether merchants and financiers in the metropole or Caribbean planters, South African mine owners, or Kenyan settlers. Implementing policies of imperial expansion, decided upon by statesmen, enormously increased state expenses for military men and equipment—all paid for with public funds. On the periphery, ambitious colonizer personnel generated their own expansive and enriching tactics. The Belgian king turned the Congo colony into his private fief; military officers did the same in French Sudan. It may be argued that, at the time, this colonial order was so entwined with the politics and economies of colonizer countries that its sudden abolition might have involved the collapse of imperial economies, regardless of the state involved.

Who gained advantages by or profited from which political stratagems depended on social customs and political processes in a particular state and society. The British gentry and nobility who could not provide for younger sons' lifestyles in keeping with the family name sent many of them into colonial service to live off government-paid, tax-funded incomes. Colonial administrations and armies, as James Mill, a Scottish Englightenment thinker, commented, provided "a vast system of outdoor relief" for the male children of the wealthy. Not having been brought up with business acumen, a trade, or professional expertise, most were unable to support themselves. The less competent were sent off by their families—just as Russian peasant communes rid themselves of their least productive members by detailing them into the decade-long army service. From the Netherlands, men with incomplete schooling and those labeled misfits by their families left. Such separation from or abandonment by birth families, as well as the life in all-male communities far from the world of childhood socialization, often involved emotional deprivation that was passed on as brutality against weaker subordinates and subalterns. For some family-sent colonizer migrants, mental disease resulted; the British in India hid their insane in asylums because their visibility to the colonized would have undercut the myth of the white man's superiority.

On the other hand, numerous military or administrative colonizer officials did come with education and what, in their own societies, were major capabilities. These, however, they had to put to use in societies they did not know, often did not understand, and usually made no effort to learn the language of. Their ethnological, geographical, botanical, or other studies have received acclaim and, in many ways, advanced knowledge. However, the cultural specimens they sent home were taken without the consent of the individual owners or social users. To take the statue of a Buddha or a Dogon mask for purposes of study and exhibition is like taking a Madonna from a Christian church. Thus the venerable British Museum contains "the loot" of British imperial expansion; a similar museum in Paris changed its original name, Musée Permanent des Colonies (opened in 1931), to Musée de la France d'outre-mer (1935) and then to Musée des Arts Africains et Océaniens (1960). Collecting material from and studying other, less powerful peoples has had a complex history—as critical anthropologists, like Michel Leiris in France and others elsewhere, pointed out as early as the 1930s.

Educated segments of the colonizer states' middle classes—university and school teachers, for example—showed great interest in other cultures and carved them into academic subjects. In the process they also provided themselves with securely tenured positions. Journalists and authors sold texts and photographic images about the distant "possessions"; the British Colonial Office instituted a Visual Instruction Committee after 1902. Scholars in geography, history, languages, and surveying methods formed learned societies to supply practical knowledge. To elevate their contribution and make themselves indispensable, many of these intellectual gatekeepers participated in the construction of "scientific" racism and, in an "imaginary ethnography," viewed other cultures through their own preconceptions. They "Orientalized" non-European societies, to use Edward Saïd's term.[54] The Other was seen and (mis)understood through the grids of meaning of the power-wielding intruders or, neutrally, outsiders. This skewed data collection or image production emerging from colonizer migrations has deeply influenced scholarly interpretation and analysis. For lack of other data, scholars of the present often have to rely on such collections and even on colonizer categorizations.

The quantitative data would have been available: With the change from permanently bound to temporarily bound or free-under-constraints migration, the Africa-to-the-Americas slave migration was abolished but still involved almost two million men and women in the nineteenth century. As partial replacement, the new British-imposed Asian indenture system became part of the other partially bound or free-under-constraints migration and, like the North Atlantic Europe-to-the-Americas system, involved some fifty million men and women. The equally large out-migration from north China began only in the 1880s and, with the exception of a very limited transoceanic migration under indenture, remained transcontinental. Also transcontinental was the Russo-Siberian and trans-Caspian system, with perhaps ten million involved, a system that would expand massively under Stalinism and last to the mid-1950s. In China, India, Europe, North America, and European Russia, vastly more men and women migrated internally from regions with a surplus of labor to developing urban, mining, or industrial regions. Such internal migration also occurred in Latin America, given uneven regional development, and in Africa, southern and northern, for the same reason but under colonizer impositions. All of these mass migrations involved men and women who formed families, and with few exceptions the gender ratio became balanced at the latest in the second generation. Demographic data about births—that is, "natural" population growth (as if growth by migration were unnatural)—were available all along. The view that migration is a "male thing" stemmed from gender-biased minds—research of the last two decades based on vital records and port statistics has provided the aggregate statistics.[55]

CHAPTER FOUR

# Migrations during War and Depression

From around 1900 to the 1930s the nationalization of Europe's many-cultured dynastic states—the Habsburg, Hohenzollern, Romanov, and Ottoman empires in particular—resulted in both refugee migrations and deportations of whole population segments. At first, imposition of the dominance of one ethnocultural group labeled "the nation" occurred within empires under such notions as "Germanization" or "the Turkish nation." This new domineering approach was to the detriment of numerically smaller ethnocultural groups who were labeled "minorities." At the empires' collapse in 1918, nation-states were carved out of imperial territories from regions with historically mixed settlements of peoples of many cultures. Talking heads of the times propounded the strength of their respective state in competition with neighboring ones and the importance of racial superiority. Only the League of Nations and a very few scholars addressed the refugee-generating consequences of the transition from empires to nations.[1] From Russification to Americanization, new conformity-demanding nationalism emerged across the Atlantic world—and, under Western hegemony, would become the organizing principle of former colonies after independence from the late 1940s on.

The internal changes in the Ottoman Empire, hastened by the British and French Empires' intrusion into the region, involved a new nationalism of the Turkish people. This replaced traditional interreligious and multiethnic coexistence. In the same vein, the growing intransigence of the dominant German-speakers of the Habsburg empire undercut the polity's multiple cultural-regional structures. The demands of these empires' many peoples for self-rule were quashed. Old empires and new nation-states came to advocate an "un-mixing of peoples" by involuntary mass migrations. On the two ends of the Eurasian landmass, the brinksmanship of Hohenzollern Germany (world war from 1914) and the imperialist strategies of Meiji Japan (from the war against China in 1895) were instrumental in disrupting the mass labor migrations and in generating mass refugee migrations. Contemporaries discussed the defeat of (white) tsarist Russia by (nonwhite) Meiji Japan in 1905—with arms bought from the West—in terms of race domination. Japan's aggressive expansion changed the parameters of migration in Asia and, in intention but more so in propaganda, involved a reassertion of Asia's self-determination against European and US imperialism. In this constellation, the British Empire and the re-emergent French Empire (from 1830, but especially since the 1870s), in their turn, refused to grant self-administration or independence to any but "white" colonies, the new Dominions. This imperial intransigence generated massive waves of refugees, first in the Northern Hemisphere to the late 1940s, and then in the Southern Hemisphere during and after the wars for independence from 1947 on.

In the course of their colonization, European settler and investor migrants had displaced resident or regionally mobile peoples. European peasant families from densely populated sedentary societies moved to what seemed to them thinly settled regions. Such view is never shared by those "thinly" settled: Native Americans in North America, Aborigines in Australia and New Zealand, native peoples in South Africa and, from the 1870s, East Africa. White newcomers displaced not only nomadic hunter-gatherers, as their rhetoric liked to suggest, but resident agricultural peoples. Likewise, the northward migrations of Chinese overwhelmed local Manchurians. In the 1920s, the Atlantic world's transition to industrial and urban patterns of life notwithstanding, some ideologues of white peoples' settlement in other peoples' "underused" regions suggested reducing what they considered urban congestion by further rural settlement projects in a global belt from Canada's northern Alberta via Manchuria's lowlands to southern Siberia; in a Latin American south-to-north belt along the eastern foothills of the Andes; in an African belt of cool subtropical highlands from Transvaal to Kenya; as well as in sections of Australia, Tasmania, and New Zealand. Even though all of these regions were distant from transport facilities, provisions, and markets, the population planners rhapsodized about a global "pioneer fringe" with virgin soils to be put under the plow. Influenced by racist and sexist eugenics, they divided the "white" race by extolling the virility of strong and healthy men and denigrating "slack" workers and "sickly people (especially women)." This migration planning involved a gendered "culling" of populations.[2]

One of the many migration-connected transitions of the interwar years involved a little-studied change of images: the United States, settled and urbanized as well as imperialist, became less attractive to migrants who wanted to build new societies (and the United States also sharply restricted immigration from dark Eastern Europe and olive Southern Europe). In contrast, the new Soviet Union seemed to provide vast urban-industrial frontiers as well as Siberian mining and rural frontiers full of opportunities for enterprising migrants. The project of building a new proletarian-democratic society—in the years before the Stalinist purges—offered hope and options to militants. The Soviet Union with Siberia appeared as "the other America." From the mid-1920s, with postwar economic recovery, its industrial growth did attract migrants who expected to arrive in a promising workers' republic. This image replaced the nineteenth-century hopes for an ideal American republic. To escape racism, some African-Americans from the South fled to pioneer cotton growing in Kazakhstan. Frontier opportunities, pioneer achievements, and powerful machines reflected the promises of a "youthful" culture—just as did a "young Europe" a century earlier and as "Young Turks" struggled for at the same time. The vision ended with the Soviet forced-labor camps of the 1930s and the Axis Powers' invasion in 1941.³

The late nineteenth-century realignment of imperial hegemony in the region of the contracting Ottoman Empire and the emergence of Japan as a new powerful empire initiated both refugee generation and forced-labor migrations of people designated as inferior. The declining European empires' transcontinental warfare, in 1914–1918, with the involvement of the newly—and differently—imperial United States from 1917, produced tens of millions of refugees and the deportation of peoples designated as "non-national" from their historic spaces of settlement. "Statesmen," by treaties, moved borders over them and changed their citizen status overnight from members to aliens. New forced-labor regimes were buttressed by internal militarization of societies in Africa's recently colonized segments, Europe's fascist states, the Soviet Union as a whole, Japan's internal and external economies, and South Africa. However, at the same time a combination of educational-intellectual and labor migrants moving from colonies to cores developed the foundations for anticolonial concepts and projects. Hardly noticed by white colonizers, these were to turn into movements for independence after World War II. Most involved armed struggles because the colonizer powers, though weakened, refused to withdraw, and thus from the 1950s mass refugee generation shifted from Europe to the Southern Hemisphere.

## Disintegrating and Emerging Empires

The political implementation of race-based nation-building projects in the old empires involved expulsion of whole peoples—Otherized from being accepted subjects of a dynasty to being non-nationals.⁴ Historic interethnic patterns of migration and settlement were characteristic to all borderlands: the Romance-German borderlands from Belgium to Alsace; East Central Europe from the Baltic via the Polish-Lithuanian-

Russian-German to the Polish-Ukrainian-Russian spaces; and the region from the Balkans via Anatolia to the Caucasus. Millennia of migrations had left mosaics of interspersed and cohabitating groups.[5] From the 1860s, emerging nationalist governments claimed territories of neighboring states under the pretense of incorporating co-nationals into their home. The wars of expansion and national unification of Prussia in the 1860s to 1871 and subsequent national chauvinism sent Czechs fleeing, made French Alsatians Germans, brought the expulsion of 80,000 Germans from France, and caused the departure of 130,000 Alsatians for France after annexation. Subsequently, in the east Prussia expelled 85,000 Poles. The Romanov empire's Russification sent Jewish, Mennonite, Lutheran, and Catholic German-speakers to seek shelter by westbound moves to North America. Definition of groups as minorities with lesser rights and less access to a society's resources and labor markets forced individuals and families to depart under duress. In Britain, the Alien Act of 1905 discriminated against proletarian migrants, in particular those of Russian-Jewish background.[6] Governments withdrew ordinary rights from culturally unwanted residents and denationalized them. Thus deprived of their documents of travel, they had to be relieved by the League of Nations High Commissioner on Refugees, Fridtjof Nansen, who invented the "Nansen Passport" in 1922 as a non-national travel document.

In the Ottoman Empire ethnoculturally and religiously defined peoples had lived in separate social slots (*millet* and *mahalle*) in structured and legally secure cohabitation. Since the eighteenth century, tsarist Russia's annexation of Ottoman lands had sent multiethnic Muslims fleeing, between one and two million by the 1890s. The Ottomans resettled Circassians and Chechens to Palestine to serve as border guards against Bedouin incursions. In the Balkans, the Greek people's self-rule, British, French, and Austro-Hungarian interventions, a new Turkish nationalism, and liberation struggles of resident peoples caused flight or emigration. The multiethnic and multireligious population of Istanbul doubled from the influx of Bosnian-Muslim refugees.

After 1900 the Young Turks movement called for a secular, homogenized nation-state without protected status for ethnoreligious groups. At the time of the establishment of the Turkish state, Armenians and Kurds were denied independent statehood and peoples of intercultural regions were "un-mixed." When the Christian autocephalous Armenians sought social progress, the Turkish government feared demands for autonomy. The presence of proselytizing US Protestant missionaries was seen as further imperial meddling. During World War I, Ottoman hard-liners had hundreds of thousands of Armenians deported to the Syrian and Mesopotamian deserts. In the new Soviet Union an Armenian republic was created in 1918; it had to accommodate about half a million refugees, and within a year an estimated 10 percent of its population died of starvation and epidemics. A European and North American refugee diaspora of Armenians emerged.[7]

Between Greece and Turkey, a government-imposed population exchange was legitimized by the "great powers" and left the 1.25 million Greek and 400,000 Turkish "repatriates" impoverished. The population planners neither consulted those selected for repatriation nor prepared accommodations for the "imported" co-nationals. A Turko-Bulgarian Agreement of 1925 decreed the "voluntary" exchange of Turks from Bulgaria and Bulgarians from Turkey. Such nation-state mandated migrations involved more than a million men, women, and children in the region in the 1920s and 1930s. In the western Balkans, the post-1918 new South Slav or Yugoslav state combined Serbs and Croats, Bosnian Muslims and Montenegrins, Slovenes and Dalmatians. The policies of un-mixing of peoples sprang from nationalist ideologies in which ethnocultural and ethnoreligious lifestyles were perceived as badges of political loyalty or disloyalty.[8]

Under a League of Nations mandate, formerly Ottoman Syria and Palestine were administered by the French and British governments, respectively. Palestine, according to the Balfour Declaration of November 1917, was to become "a national home" for the Jewish people without infringements on the civil and religious rights of resident Muslim and Christian peoples. Competition for land and other resources made this multicultured and interfaith region conflict-prone. In North Africa the realignment into Arab states did not involve population exchanges, but the British in Egypt had requisitioned forced laborers during wartime. When Egypt's nationalist elites responded with a project for independence, the British government deported the elite to Malta. In the Ottoman and Romanov realms, on the other hand, the British had fanned the nationalist sentiments of non-Turkish and non-Russian peoples to consolidate their hold on oil production from the Caspian Sea to Persia and to implement anti-Bolshevik policies. In the frame of Turkish nationalism and British imperialism the Ottoman Empire's dissolution turned some 8.5 million people into refugees. The region's political-territorial structures and cultural interactions have remained conflict-prone into the early twenty-first century.

Imperial Japan expanded its reach by warfare against Russia, China, and Korea starting in 1895, just as the United States had done half a century earlier against Mexico and, also in the 1890s, against Spain. With the help of hired Western advisers, the Meiji government modernized the army and pursued three expansionist strategies: modernization to win the allegiance of the population of annexed Taiwan; territorial and migratory competition in Russia's Far East; and domination, of Korea first, then Manchuria, and finally China. Taiwan, as a food-producing appendage, became a laboratory for agricultural, social, and fiscal improvements. Japanese administrators established security of landholdings and, in distinction to Western colonizers, did not introduce a plantation mode of production. Taiwanese small and middle producers benefited. Sakhalin, a contested territory with economic potential, attracted Russian newcomers who had to compete with Chinese, Korean, and Japanese migrants. The Russians, though nationals, were far from their home base, so in-migrating Chinese merchants and Japanese fishermen held a competitive advantage. According to the 1926 Russian census, one-fifth of its Far East population was of East Asian origin. South Sakhalin, valued because of its natural resources and strategic location, was annexed by Japan and renamed Karafuto. Its Japanese population of twelve thousand in 1906, working in manufacturing, commerce, and transportation, had grown to over four hundred thousand four decades later.

In Korea, in contrast to Taiwan, imperial Japan's takeover of the peasant farming economy came as a shock. Under the slogan of modernization, Japan's Society for Eastern Colonization confiscated family land for forced mass cultivation of export crops. Koreans, forced to live on inferior grains, migrated or fled to Manchuria or Russian Siberia. Japanese citizenship was imposed on them, as was modernized health care. The latter resulted in population growth at the very time when ten million "surplus" Japanese were sent to Korea, whose population density had been underestimated by Japan's population planners. The same happened in other occupied territories: two million were sent to Formosa. No sturdy agricultural pioneers, the staple of imperialist rhetoric, migrated; instead the migrants were small traders, artisans, shopkeepers, and adventurous merchants. Migration was a male middle-class and lower-middle-class project. A few women came as wives, midwives, and prostitutes. Most migrants gravitated to the cities, some became landlords. The Japanese government's rural settlement project was undercut by migrants' choice of Brazil, Peru, Hawaii, and the Philippines as destinations.

In contrast to the historic Ottoman concept of cohabitation of self-administering ethnoreligious groups within one economic-political frame, Meiji expansion employed Japanization to weld the colonized to the colonizers. Administrative personnel were sent from Japan, and Japanese education was given to sons of the Taiwanese and Korean middle classes. A Japanese-inspired youth movement was created in Korea to capitalize on intrasocietal generational differences. In all occupied regions—including, after 1937, China—the Japanese military and colonizer personnel considered "locals" as inferiors to be used to fulfill military-industrial-imperial purposes or, if women, to provide sexual services to the occupation forces.[9]

## Trans-European Warfare, 1914–1918

The Habsburg and Hohenzollern imperial bureaucracies as well as general German-culture nationalism—in Austrian and German variants—refused cultural and political autonomy to "minorities." From the 1860s, Hohenzollern Germany's unifying and expansionist warfare rearranged borders over people. Southeastern Europe was unsettled by conflict between the Habsburg and Ottoman empires as well as the expansionist aspirations of semi-independent Serbia. Many of the region's peoples demanded self-rule, but it was not evident which groups, culturally akin, formed a people. Were Macedonians a distinct people or were they Greeks? Were people in Kosovo Serb, Albanian, or a distinct group? Conflicts intensified in the 1870s. From the late nineteenth century the tsarist empire's Russification policy, which affected East Central European Baltic and Slavic peoples, as well as German-Germanization and Austrian-Germanization, attempted to deculturate the many other peoples of the imperial territories. In addition to the intracontinental conflicts, France and the United Kingdom rejected German expansion into "their" Africa and Asia, feared its new navy on the high seas, and opposed the Habsburg-Austrian ambitions in and beyond the Danube region. A minor incident in 1914 was used to declare all-out war.

The first twentieth-century European internecine war, which in its ramifications in Africa became a world war, did not "break out" but was a calculated strategy. Some sixty million men were mobilized and marched about. Women took their jobs in the aggressor or "home" states. In August 1914, about five million Europeans did not live in their state of birth. Overnight their status changed from guest, labor migrant, or immigrant to "hostile alien" or "citizen of an enemy nation": they could be interned, expelled, or repatriated. The majority, migrating workers, experienced a renationalization of the internationalized labor markets. Prevented from returning, they became captive labor forces in the Axis power states. On the side of the Allies, France relied on the labor of some 230,000 Spanish, 135,000 North Africans, Vietnamese, and Chinese, as well as neighboring Belgians or distant Malagasies. Great Britain mobilized 1.2 million non-European soldiers, mainly in India but also in northern China, and France 0.6 million mainly in North and West Africa. Thus the colonized segments of the empires supplied men and materials to the Allies, or colonial overlords, and in consequence could accelerate their process of self-liberation. The German Reich, an importer of predominantly male labor from Eastern Europe since 1885, declared as one of its war aims the achievement of permanent empire-style control over this reservoir of labor.[10]

The warfare cast the civilian populations first of Belgium, then of Poland, the Baltic provinces, and western Russia, as well as those in southeastern Europe, into nightmares of dislocation, starvation, and death. Armies and displaced civilians foraged on people who were struggling to survive. Within three months, one-fifth of the Belgian population of about seven million were refugees in the Netherlands, France, and Great Britain. Of Serbia's population of three million, one-third were refugees, one-tenth were in the army, another tenth were in camps in Hungary and Bulgaria, often as forced laborers. Typhus killed 150,000. All over Europe, families fled advancing armies,

Primary ethnolinguistic groups in the Austro-Hungarian Empire, ca. 1900.

the actual lines of fire, or the reach of distant artillery. In conquered regions, military administrators and civilian authorities expelled groups whose loyalty they questioned, whether Poles from Germany or Jews with their Yiddish-German dialect and descendants of German immigrants from Russia.

Russia's populations were particularly exposed to uprooting. To slow down the advance of German armies, retreating Russian forces pursued a scorched-earth policy. In late 1915 Russia counted 2.7 million refugees, half a year later 5 million. The 1917 armistice between Germany and Russia sent hundreds of thousands of demobilized, wounded, and sick soldiers in search of families or shelter. By the early 1920s, some 1.5 million children who had lost their parents by separation or death were said to wander about. Male and female workers who had been drafted into the war industries were let go or escaped; those who had been deported from German-occupied territories to forced labor had to find their way back. After October 1917 the Russian Revolution sent a comparatively small number of political exiles, refugee aristocrats, and bourgeois entrepreneurs into westward flight. The subsequent internal wars of 1918–1921 pitted royalists, liberals, and revolutionaries against each other and involved Ukrainian and other national liberation movements. Defeated troops, politicians, and anti-revolutionary families fled northward to Finland and the Baltic states, southward to Istanbul, Syria, and Palestine, and westward to France in particular. In the East in China, Harbin and later Shanghai became centers of perhaps sixty thousand exiles. A decade and a half later, both cities were to shelter Jewish refugees from Nazi Germany. Émigré colonies also emerged in Turkestan, Manchuria, and Mongolia.[11]

After the war, prisoners of war had to be repatriated: two million Germans from the Allies, forced laborers from the Reich, Russian prisoners from Austria and Germany, and many others. The peace treaty established new states out of the self-destructed empires. Spokespeople of millions of transatlantic migrants from the empires' disadvantaged peripheries supported independence movements and lobbied in Washington for support. Because large parts of Europe had historically mixed populations, the new borders mandated by the peace treaty forced some five million to change residence between states. The new Baltic and Polish states became the destination of returning prewar emigrants, wartime displaced, and co-nationals from outside the new borderlines. According to official data, Poland, which had been divided for a century and a half among Russia, Prussia, and Austria, and devastated by the armies of all of the belligerents, received 1.25 million returning refugees by 1920, received another 700,000 returnees by 1923, and expected a further 300,000. Hungary in its new borders received Magyar ethnics from Romania (140,000), from Czechoslovakia (57,000), and from Yugoslavia (37,000), while it expelled Hungarian-Germans. Across the war-ravaged lands, displaced civilians and demobilized soldiers returned to villages that no longer existed, to towns of which only ruins remained.[12]

The peace treaty advocated self-determination of peoples in contrast to prewar imperial domination. However, how were borders to be drawn? Centuries of migration and interaction had made almost all of East Central Europe and parts of Western Europe patchworks of interspersed settlements. None of the new states was monocultural; borders were drawn without regard to mosaics of historic settlement; people who stayed put found themselves in ethnically different states. Only national gatekeepers professed certainty about a nation's historic ethnic territories—the areas they claimed often happened to be rich in natural resources. Postwar establishment of such "nation-states" left more than twenty million people outside of the state of their ethnocultural cousins: (1) "Minorities," who in their compact, if small, territories formed the majority, could attempt to stay; (2) small groups could opt for the recently created "home" nation and leave; (3) those who did not fit the newly constructed nations could be expelled or exchanged for others considered fitting; (4) those deemed unacceptable by any state became stateless, trapped wherever they happened to lose citizen status. Multiple identities were considered a threat to the monocultures of nation-states. For the culturally reconfigured men and women, nationhood complicated lives. Borderlines between groups were fuzzy, people often rudimentarily multilingual. Nationalism was the fundamentalism of the period. There were few discourses of respect for other cultures or multicultural interaction—in fact, their existence in the past had been exorcised from memory.

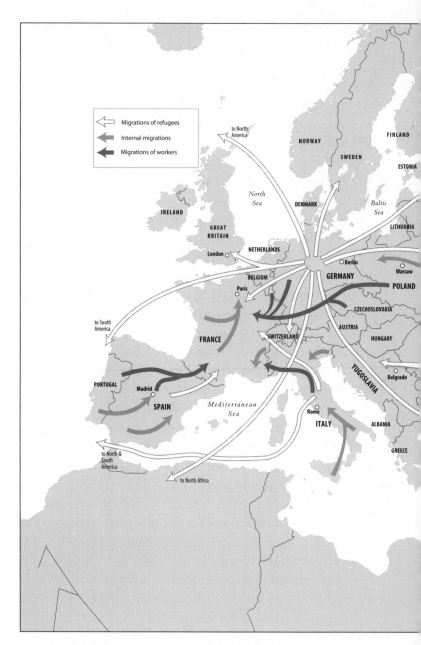

Patterns of migration and flight in Europe, 1914–1939.

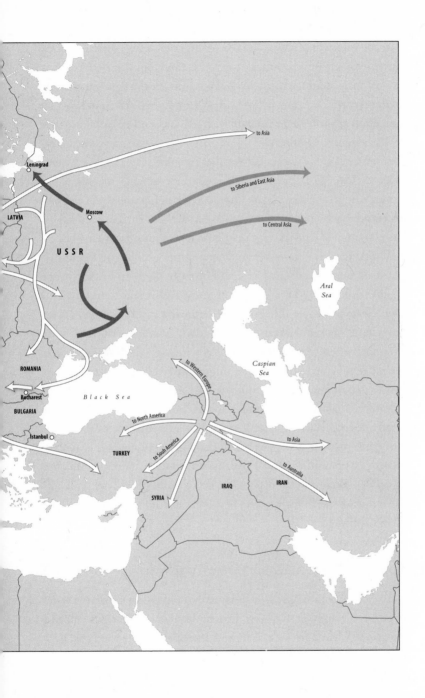

to Asia

to Siberia and East Asia

to Central Asia

Leningrad

Moscow

LATVIA

USSR

Aral
Sea

ROMANIA

Caspian
Sea

Bucharest

Black Sea

BULGARIA

to Western Europe

to North America

Istanbul

to Asia

TURKEY

to South America

to Australia

SYRIA

IRAQ

IRAN

In the interwar years thousands of migrants from North America returned to help build political institutions and to invest in the economies of "their" states, while tens of thousands left the devastated lands for the Americas. From Britain, in a last empire-migration scheme, population planners sent unemployed civilians and demobilized soldiers to "white" Dominions—men to marginal farms, women into domestic service. Working-class families emigrated after the lost general strike of 1926. To reduce ethnic antagonisms, some states improved minority rights, others pursued homogenization policies. Of the former empires, Austria became a small state without further pretensions while Germany's elites retrenched but schemed for new expansions.

In Germany, the post–World War I narrative construction of displacement and resettlement of East European German-origin groups was instrumentalized for aggression in 1939. Official terminology divided German people into those living in the Reich, *Reichsdeutsche,* those living adjacent but outside its borders, *Grenzdeutsche,* and those living farther east or southeast, *Auslandsdeutsche* or *Volksdeutsche*—descendants of three centuries of migrations. The new post-1918 German Republic included 1.5 million non-Germans, mostly Poles, and 1.3 million German-origin expellees and "voluntary" departees from Alsace, Poland, and Gdánsk (Danzig) in a population of 62.4 million. After 1933 the Nazi government augmented estimates of *Grenzdeutsche* to 10 million and began its annexation with the Sudeten region of Czechoslovakia (population 3.5 million) in 1938. Poland's and Hungary's ruling elites also began annexations. Trans-European warfare followed.[13]

## Population Displacement in the Interwar Years

In the Soviet Union, wartime devastation resulted in a disastrous decline of food supplies, millions died, and hunger migrations emptied the cities. When agricultural output increased under the New Economic Policy, 1921–1927, migratory directions reversed and industrial production resumed. After 1923 substantial population growth induced large-scale rural-to-urban migrations. The Jewish population, freed from restrictions, dispersed. Between 1926 and 1939 approximately five million migrants crossed the Urals eastbound or moved southeastward into the Central Asian peoples' republics—especially Kazakhstan, Turkestan, and Kyrgyzstan. Fewer than one-sixth still came as peasant settlers; all others were labor migrants on their way to industrial and mining frontiers. However, after 1928, when collectivization of agriculture expropriated peasants, a second mass flight from starvation, particularly in Ukraine as well as from undersupplied cities, involved millions and caused high death rates. To permit self-administration of ethnocultural groups, the Soviet government established autonomous regions or states for several of the many peoples—the Armenian republic, Birobidzhan as a Jewish enclave, and rearrangement of settlement patterns among Uzbeks, Kirgiz, and Kazakhs, to name only a few. However, in Kazakh agricultural regions self-styled "superior" Russian settler migrants appropriated lands, and in 1928 the government opened Kazakhstan to Russian settlers. The constitution of 1936 reduced self-determination of non-Russian peoples, and non-Russian peoples deemed disloyal to the Bolshevik state were deported from ancient settlement regions to Central Asia. To take the case of the Crimean Tatars, many of whom had emigrated after the Crimean Peninsula passed from Ottoman to tsarist rule, starvation in the period of the civil wars after 1917 and in particular during the state-enforced export of grain in 1921 led to death and flight, collectivization implied deportation, and the Stalinist purges led to deportation and, often, execution of non-Russian peoples' intellectual leaders.[14]

In Spain, Italy, and Germany, fascist governments caused renewed flight even before people who had been displaced by World War I were integrated. Especially during the 1930s, democratic elites fled into exile. The fascist regimes aimed at intellectual decapitation of their societies and of subjected peoples. Those fleeing had few options, both because of immigration barriers in the rest of the Western world and because of the collapse of economies during the Great Depression. Italian fascists derisively called the émigrés from liberal elites, militant unions, socialist or anarchist parties, artists and intellectuals *fuorus-citi,* "foreign fellows," just as German socialists had once been labeled "fellows without a fatherland." From 1918 to 1926, 1.5 million Italian workers continued prewar migratory patterns, then the Fascist government criminalized emigration without permission. Some nine hundred thousand Italians lived in France, the main destination, until their vibrant culture was destroyed under German occupation in 1939.

In Spain, a rebellion of army officers pitted the modernizing coastal and northern populations against the elites of the stagnant, reactionary agricultural areas. When the Fascist generals sent Moroccan, "Moorish" soldiers to fight the Republic, a racist imagery of atrocity-committing North Africans emerged. Some forty-five thousand radicals and democrats from across Europe, North America, and the Soviet Union fought for the Republic; the German and Italian Fascist governments sent "volunteers" in support of the insurgents. By August 1938, two million refugees from Fascist-controlled areas had reached Republican Spain, and after the Republic's collapse some 450,000 soldiers and civilians fled to France, where almost 390,000 refugees from Nazi Germany had already arrived.

Nazi Germany in 1933 implemented a boycott of German-Jewish businesses and professionals and expelled ten to twenty thousand Eastern European Jews. Within a year some sixty-five thousand Jewish and Christian notables and cultural leaders had fled. Because only about 1 percent of the population was "non-Aryan," German racism has been called "anti-Semitism without Jews." By 1938 some two hundred thousand impoverished Jewish and non-Jewish refugees had arrived in receiving societies, which could ill afford, or were unwilling, to offer support. The refugee-generating fascist states were surrounded by refugee-refusing democratic states in which anti-Semitism was pronounced. In 1930, 3.3 million Jews lived in Poland, 3 million in Russia, about 1.2 million in Romania and Hungary, as well as 525,000 in Germany and 180,000 in Austria. By 1939 the United States had admitted a mere 8,600 refugees, and Canadian bureaucrats had closed the doors. At the July 1938 refugee conference in Evian, France, US diplomats avoided any swift help by insisting on procedural nego-tiation through a new Intergovernmental Committee on Refugees, and Western anti-Semitic ideologues suggested deportation of Jews to French Madagascar, North Borneo, the Dominican Republic, Brit-ish Guiana, Cyprus, the Philippines, the Belgian Congo, and other destinations. Only the Soviet Union, Turkey, some Eastern European states, and China admitted refugees. The some eighteen thousand Jewish refugees who reached Harbin and cosmopolitan Shanghai could stay after Japan's takeover. In Palestine arriving refugees dis-placed local Arabs. When the German armies began to advance in 1939, a second flight carried those who had taken refuge in neighbor-ing countries farther afield.

After the German occupation of Poland in September 1939, Ger-man Jews were first transported there to be utilized as an inferior la-boring population. In a second phase, this resettlement region was to be "cleaned" of human beings of Mosaic religion. The deportees were deported again, this time to the ghettos of Polish cities where over-crowding and planned starvation caused high mortality. An estimated 200,000 to 350,000 reached the nonoccupied Soviet Union and, among neutral countries, Turkey became the most important transit route. The third deportation, labeled the "final solution," brought about six million men, women, and children to camps were they were to be worked to death in the German industry's war production or exterminated immediately. In the end, one branch of the German-language family, the Yiddish-speakers, had nearly been exterminated.[15]

## Forced Migrations

Parallel to the ethnocultural relocations, governments restricted working-class migrations through the 1920s and the Great Depression of the 1930s: entry restrictions were enacted to reduce international mobility; in many countries unemployed men, and sometimes women, were relocated to relief camps; labor activists and many of the unemployed were deported. State bureaucracies could use forced laborers on sites to which no free workers would migrate, and could shift them to wherever need arose. Relocation was cheap. Workers could be forced to construct their own camps, they received minimal wages, if any, and in economies with scarce consumer goods their confinement decreased consumption. If knowledge about forced labor was public, the system could be used to intimidate free workers. In the Americas, the US government deported labor organizers and radicals to the Soviet Union after 1917 and Mexican workers to Mexico in the 1930s. Peonage, forced labor because of alleged debt, though outlawed, continued to be imposed on African-American and Mexican-American laborers. In 1920s Canada, male harvest laborers and female domestics were sent to their destinations under police guard to work off assisted-passage contracts. In the interior of South America, the peonage system resembled slavery and landowners held the right to the part-time labor of natives. In several North African Arab states, slavery continued to be practiced, though on paper most Muslim states from Morocco to Afghanistan abolished slavery in the interwar years. Experts estimated that there were about three million slaves, worldwide, in 1930.[16]

European states, during World War I, militarized labor regimes. France relied on colonial labor and forcibly drafted African soldiers.

Britain imposed compulsory labor on colonial populations, as in Uganda. Indentured workers from China and Vietnam were sent to Britain and France. After the postwar depression and a temporary closing of the borders, France became Europe's most important destination of labor migrants, with almost two million arriving. They replaced the 1.35 million French soldiers—10 percent of the adult male population—killed in the war. When Italian peasants came to settle villages emptied of men by the wartime carnage, nationalists prohibited their arrival to reserve national soil for an "undiluted" French nation—the soil in fact was bought up by an emerging agribusiness. Polish workers, recruited by employers, had no right to change jobs or demand better conditions. Soaring unemployment after 1929, when three million Poles, Belgians, Italians, and Polish-Germans resided in the country, caused the Right to mount a campaign of xenophobia. Fascist Spain outlawed unions and workers' parties—control over workers lasted to the system's demise in 1975.

Russia, fifth among the world's industrial powers before 1914, had to reconstruct its destroyed economy, relocate industrial centers, and deal with famines. It reached prewar production levels only in 1928. The policies of the Soviet state economy were contradictory. Collectivization was to reduce the need for rural labor, but bureaucratic mismanagement and poor urban living conditions reduced out-migration and some ideologues feared infiltration of rurals as a "class-alien element" into what they constructed as the proletariat. Labor migrations were voluntary, and in the first of five phases of migration, rural-to-urban mobility assumed unprecedented proportions: 1 million annually before 1926, 2.6 million annually from 1927 to 1930, 4.3 million in 1931; by 1939 the Soviet urban population had more than doubled and had been "ruralized," because two-fifths had arrived from the countryside in twelve years. After Stalin's "Great Turning Point" in 1928, in a second phase of migration, forced collectivization sent peasants fleeing, often to industrial work; many, especially from non-Russian peoples, were shipped to deadly labor camps. During the third, consolidating, phase before 1938, some 250,000 skilled factory workers and communist educational cadres were sent to rural areas to introduce mechanization, teach reading and writing to illiterate villagers, and inculcate a new consciousness. Within five years, 12.5 million new wage workers were drawn into the urban labor forces. But free migration still failed to fill demand, and in a fourth phase, starting in February 1930, the state terminated unemployment benefits and assigned jobs by a passport system that was compulsory for urban laboring men and women. From the mid-1930s, the fifth and last migration phase involved forced recruitment, captive labor for lumbering and road and railroad construction, and the transfer of whole factories before the German armies' advance. The labor camps, gulags, were controlled by the police (NKVD). Recent research indicates that there were 2.9 to 3.5 million forced laborers in 1941, about one-tenth of them women, and at least 750,000 Polish and other deportees. Other estimates reach as high as 20 million during the peak of the system. The system was exposed in 1956 and abolished in 1960.[17]

The German Reich's labor regime had relied on harsh internal control over foreign workers since the 1880s. By 1900 the Reich ranked second among labor-importing countries. It required Eastern European workers to carry passes and expelled those who changed jobs without permission. Russian and Austrian Poles were forced to depart during a "closure period" each winter, both to prevent permanent settlement and to free agricultural employers from paying them wages. This twenty-five-year-long first phase, for reasons of German nationalist ideology and cultural purity, established the policy of a rotary labor force. The second phase, in 1914–1918, involved forced labor: with the declaration of war the 1.3 million foreign workers were prohibited from leaving, and the food rations for these "working classes of non-German nationality" were kept at starvation levels. The third phase, the 1920s, involved a "governmentalization" of labor markets, but only a few foreign workers were present. In a fourth phase, the new Nazi government restricted freedom of movement of German laborers and channeled "racially different" laborers to sectors with poor working conditions. From 1936 the state assumed complete control over mobility. Even though ideological constructions of racial purity had precluded recruitment abroad, preparation for war led the Nazi government to import agricultural laborers from Poland, where unemployment stood at 40 percent. The occupation of Poland initiated the fifth phase with a compulsory levy of 1 million Polish workers, half of them to be women, in early 1940. Eastern Europe's allegedly "subhuman" peoples became essential for the Aryan war economy. Western European civilians and prisoners of war were conscripted for labor, some 1.2 million within a year. Civilian foreign workers included Italians, Belgians, and Yugoslavs. After the attack on the Soviet Union in June 1941, employment of Russians, Byelorussians, Ukrainians, and men and women from many other ethnicities was forbidden, but by 1942 the policy was reversed. *Ostarbeiter* were captured and transported to industrial sites in the occupied and "home" territories. At the end of the war, some 1.9 million POWs and 5.7 million civilian foreign workers, about one-third of them women, slaved in Germany, as did six hundred thousand men and women in concentration camps. Together, they accounted for 20 percent of the labor force.[18]

In Japan, militarization of the economy and society increased from the mid-1920s. State bureaucrats and employer organizations determined labor relations, the National Essence Society and the Harmonization Society advocated corporatist cooperation of capital and labor, the near-fascist New Order for Labor regime was mitigated by wartime welfare legislation. Workers in the recently occupied colonies had to produce industrial and military supplies under the control of a "directive minority" of Japanese managerial personnel. Korean peasants were uprooted to form an urban industrial, low-skill, mobile proletariat. From the populous southern provinces many had to move to

Japan, where in 1917 through 1929, 1.2 million arrived and 850,000 returned. By 1945, more than 10 percent of the Korean population worked outside of Korea, and another 20 percent had been drafted for urban work or were otherwise uprooted. A type of identity-destroying labor forced Korean women to work in "comfort stations" as prostitutes for Japanese soldiers. In Manchukuo the Japanese military constructed heavy industry close to the mines in the middle of an agricultural subsistence economy of recent immigrants from China. High wages and, under Great Depression conditions, an abundant labor supply resulted in free labor markets except for ethnicized immigration policies that preferred Korean and Japanese workers over Chinese. By 1940, 1.4 million workers had been imported from Korea's north. Within Japan, policy makers allocated labor according to priorities of the military. Since 1941, labor reserves were managed centrally. In 1942 skilled workers and technicians were prohibited from changing jobs and employers were prohibited from offering wage incentives to "steal" technicians from other factories. In the occupied territories civilian and POW labor was conscripted. At the end of the war Japan's regime of forced-labor migration came to an end, but South Africa initiated a similar system a few years later to conscript Africans under its version of superior and inferior peoples in the regime of apartheid.[19]

In many of the colonized regions across the world, labor recruitment through force and taxation had been replaced by cash-related voluntary migrations. Commercial relations and mining operations—as expressions of global capitalist relationships—had penetrated deeply from ports as places of contact into hinterlands, or, from the point of those who lived there, into people's primary living spaces. Ever more transactions involved money rather than exchange, and money came from wage labor or sale of crops. With the Great Depression the demand for raw materials, and thus for labor, collapsed. At the beginning of the 1930s the population of the new towns in the copper-mining region of Northern Rhodesia and in older towns in the Belgian Congo as well as elsewhere shrank dramatically. Laboring men—and their families, if these had joined them—migrated (or drifted) back to the land to eke out their subsistence. In the northern Nigerian tin mines, wages fell rapidly, but due to the collapse of grain prices living standards did not decline as much. Surplus workers left or subsisted on income from a few days of work per week—given the by-then established cash nexus, they could not simply withdraw from wage labor. Given the power relations, the colonizers' tax rate did not fall as much as wages. As a result, in some regions whole economies collapsed, creating migrant populations in search of food or jobs. In Malayan tin mines the situation was similar. The labor recruiters, *kangani,* were no longer sent back to their home villages to recruit from a reservoir that, again under the cash nexus, was waiting to be recruited. From the rubber areas Indian workers were deported home. Thus the social costs of the Great Depression were shifted to the home communities. Across the colonies that produced raw materials, workers who had been forced to migrate in the interest of capitalist production were sent back when the capitalist system temporarily collapsed. Stable prospects for gaining income through migration demand stable economic conditions. While much of contemporary debates centered on the dramatic conditions in the First World's banking centers, dramatic food shortages imperiled most migrant families' lifeways and chances for survival.[20]

### Flight, Expulsion, and Population Transfers during World War II

In 1937 the next worldwide war began with Japan's aggression against China, called the "Second Sino-Japanese War," and in 1939 with the German aggressions in Europe. When the United States became a belligerent in 1941, the two wars, from a perspective of military efforts and political alliances, became a world war, but population movements remained largely separate. By 1945 hundreds of millions had been forced into flight or relocation camps. Population planners, who had shifted around human beings as laboring or surplus populations, reduced them to "human material." The peculiar construction of allegiance and duty to a nation in wartime made dissenters and pacifists persecuted citizens to be deported to camps, even in democratic states.

Japan's preparation for war had involved small-scale elite in-migrations and large-scale rhetoric. While military advisers were invited from Europe and the United States, military preparedness was justified as being of pan-Asian interest—Japan's expansion would counter European imperialism. In fact, Japan coveted China's raw materials and other resources, including human labor, and its (postwar) markets. Starting in 1937 it seized Shanghai and occupied large parts of China. After the fall of Nanjing, the Nationalists' capital, Japan's army massacred, raped, and looted, killing some three hundred thousand. In the countryside, both retreating Chinese and aggressing Japanese armies drove off peasants in scorched-earth campaigns or through the flooding of plains. In less than a year, a hundred million Chinese had become refugees and an estimated twelve million had fled as far as the western provinces of Yunnan, Guizhou, and Sichuan. The International Refugee Organization evacuated the small numbers of Europeans from China while Jewish refugees from Fascist persecution in Europe continued to arrive via Siberia.

In December 1941 Japan expanded the war to Southeast Asia and the Pacific by bombing the US fleet in Hawaii and occupying the Philippines, Hong Kong, Malaya, French Indochina, British Burma, Dutch Indonesia, and most of the Pacific islands. From Burma, as one example, about half a million Indians fled, perhaps fifty thousand dying en route. Bombing raids resulted in urban flight from Calcutta, and in Japan, in turn, urban populations were ordered to move to the countryside to escape Allied bombing and to produce food. After mid-1942, the Western Allies and China forced Japanese armies into slow

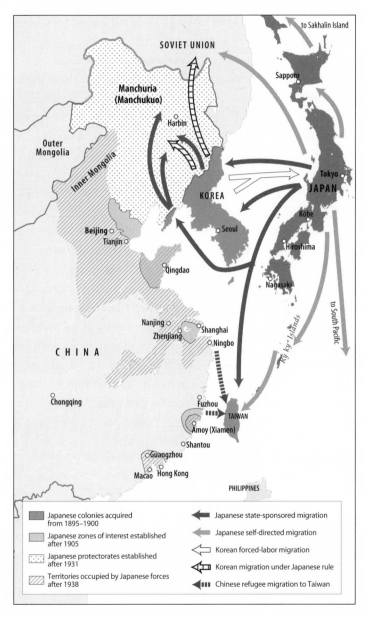

Migrations within the Japanese Empire, 1890–1940.

retreat and surviving refugees followed the armies to return to former homes, many of which no longer existed.[21]

In Europe, the German and Soviet attack on Poland caused a first mass flight toward Warsaw, across the Baltic Sea, and through Hungary or Romania for evacuation via the Middle Eastern British zone of influence. Information about German troops' atrocities sent Jews fleeing across the lines of the Soviet army. After the USSR occupied Finland's Karelia Province, it deported 420,000 to 450,000 Karelian Finns to the rest of Finland, where 11 percent of the population were refugees. More than half of them returned when Finnish troops retook Karelia in 1941, only to flee again before a renewed Soviet advance in 1944. In and from France Jews fled; in the Scandinavian countries citizens transported some of them to neutral Sweden to ensure their survival. Shortly after the westward aggression, 2 million French, 2 million Belgian, 70,000 Luxembourger, and 50,000 Dutch refugees were near destitution according to Red Cross estimates.

The Nazi bureaucracy had planned major population transfers of allegedly inferior West Slavic peoples eastward and of allegedly superior Aryan Germans into the vacated lands. Other, "lesser" peoples were to cooperate with the Reich or be used as reservoirs of cheap labor. The "General Plan East" ordered "resettlement" of 80 to 85 percent of all Poles, 75 percent of the Byelorussians, 65 percent of the Ukrainians, and 50 percent of the Czechs in interior Russia or Siberia. However, the German military, overextended from the beginning, needed "colonial auxiliaries" and resorted to local regimentation of labor. The Nazi administrative machine, intending to expand the contiguous German-settled territories five hundred kilometers eastward, divided occupied Poland into a resettlement area for Germans and a vast Polish-settled labor camp. A total of 1.2 million "Slavic" Poles were deported, at a rate of 10,000 a day. ("Potential German" Poles— designated as such by the occupation forces—could support the Nazi regime as soldiers.) In the vacated lands, diasporic German-background people from eastern and southeastern Europe were to be resettled: some 500,000 were uprooted in a region extending from the Baltic states to Bessarabia. Another 750,000 trekked westward in the next years. By the time Soviet armies advanced, most were still in camps, only a fraction had been resettled. They commenced another trek westward or, when overtaken, were deported eastward.

Soviet bureaucrats, equally unconcerned about life courses, considered many non-Russian peoples "unreliable," either because of avowed Nazi sympathies of elite segments or because they had been oppressed as minorities in the Stalinist empire. Deportations toward the interior or further east ensued: peoples from the recently occupied Baltic and Polish states, refugees from the advance of the German armies, the 1.4 million German-origin people of Russian citizenship, as well as peoples of the Caucasus, the Crimea (Tatars especially, as well as Greeks and Bulgarians), Transcaucasia, and the Caspian steppes. The USSR's massive program of transplanting industry toward and beyond the Ural Mountains as a means of self-defense for relocated workers and families meant abominable working conditions, worse living conditions, and high death tolls. Few alternatives existed: from Odessa, Moscow, and Leningrad alone, more than a million people fled or were evacuated when the German armies advanced. Still certain of victory, the German occupiers debated whether to starve whole populations, transport survivors to the Russian interior, or permit a "humanitarian" rescue by the Red Cross for resettlement somewhere else.

In southeastern Europe, where the Reich, Italy, Hungary, and Bulgaria had divided Yugoslavia among themselves, Slovenians were exchanged for German-background people, Serbs were expelled from dispersed settlements, Macedonians were expelled or Bulgarianized, and Romanians were sent into flight. The subsequent advance of Soviet armies meant new relocations; the retreat of German armies meant the flight of collaborators from among Ukrainians and other nationalities as well as anti-Soviet Cossacks. When the Soviet army reached the prewar German borders, an estimated fourteen million refugees lived behind their lines, not counting those moving before the advancing army.

Mobilization of men for nation-state armies and their interment as prisoners of war in other nation-states are not usually considered in terms of population transfer. However, they involved involuntary mobility and interaction. POWs, forced to work in the war industries and agriculture of the capturing power, interacted with local populations. During the war, when no Allied shipping was made available to transport refugee Jews out of Europe, four hundred thousand German POWs could be shipped to the United States—most returned, some emigrated subsequently. Prisoners of war from many nationalities labored throughout Germany in agriculture, mining, or factories, and German POWs labored in France and Russia. German civilians and Allied prisoners of war faced the same air raids. Germans, who worked alongside forced laborers until 1945, a mere decade later would work alongside guest workers. Would attitudes be transferred?[22]

## Intellectual Migrations

Just as colonizer migrations, small in number, have frequently been left on the sidelines of research, the limited migrations of the colonized through exile or for education have been neglected by scholars. They were of major impact. As temporary migrants, many of the intellectual leaders, statesmen, and militant fighters for independence could compare life in the colonies with life in the metropoles. Most had studied there, some received education by missionaries, a few had worked there. As prospective elites they were given privileged access to colonizer-framed education in missionary schools and in universities of Great Britain and France. There, pronouncements about the equality of all the monarch's subjects or about the integrative role of French culture notwithstanding, they experienced second-class status or even racist deprecation. Two generations, of the late nineteenth and early twentieth centuries and of the 1920s and 1930s, experienced the humanist and democratic intellectual debates as well as racializing practices. Most of the intercultural migrants formed worldviews and militancy by a fusion of their own colonized culture with Western colonizer cultures. They became reformers or radicals, nationalists, socialists or communists. Educational migration familiarized them with two cultures and provided the strategic capital to comprehend and critique colonizer rhetoric and policies in ways understandable in their societies as well as by the colonizers. They became spokespersons for independence early in the twentieth century, in the interwar years, and during decolonization.

Intellectual exchanges had been part of early contact and later colonizing, especially in the cases of complex societies that, at least initially, could influence the character of intercultural contact. In Asia, Japan and China pursued different, yet similar, courses. Japan, said to be closed before the 1850s, had always kept abreast of the latest developments in Europe through a regulated Dutch enclave in Deshima, Nagasaki. The Meiji reformers invited Western experts for colonizing agricultural development of the northern islands and for training a new army. In contrast, the Chinese court's intellectual-cultural self-sufficiency (and, perhaps, arrogance) had abrogated the scholarly contacts epitomized in the seventeenth-century presence of Jesuits and their partial Sinicization. To deal with the increasing dominance of treaty powers, the government invited US and European advisors late in the nineteenth century. Many of China's reformers and future leaders migrated for educational purposes or had to go into exile. Sun Yat-sen (1866–1935), one of the founders of the Guomindang and first president of the Republic, had lived in Hawai'i, studied in Hong Kong, and been in exile in Japan, Europe, the United States, and Canada. General Chiang Kai-shek (1887–1975) trained and served in Japan's army in 1907–1911. He staffed Nationalist China's military academies with

German and Russian instructors, and his cabinet included Harvard-trained ministers.

Women were part of these elite migrations, and the well-studied three Soong sisters may serve as examples. Their father, a Hakka Chinese, had been educated as a Methodist minister in the United States and had become wealthy in part through Bible sales. He sent his daughters to the United States for their education at Wesleyan College in Georgia. All three became politically powerful and were internationally connected. Soong Ch'ing-ling in 1949 founded the well-known international magazine *China Today* with Israel Epstein, who came from a Polish-Jewish family of labor radicals; his mother had been exiled and his father had worked in Japan. Soong May-ling—"Madam Chiang" after her marriage to Chiang Kai-Shek—became China's foremost spokesperson in the United States and in 1943 was instrumental in ending the exclusion of Chinese immigrants from the United States, which had been first instituted in the 1880s. Such contacts ended after the Communist takeover in China in 1949 and during the mind-numbing Cold War period of the 1950s in the West.

A Vietnamese young man named Nguyen Sinh Cung strove for education and as a kitchen helper departed on a vessel in 1911 for a work-study trajectory in the United States, Great Britain, and France, combining menial jobs with self-education in public libraries. He petitioned for Vietnam's independence during the Peace Conference of 1918–1919, and under the assumed name Ho Chi Minh became the leader of Indochina's struggle for independence from French rule and drafted North Vietnam's constitutions using the US Declaration of Independence as a reference. Like many colonial political intellectuals and leaders, he espoused a cultural-economic nationalism but was radicalized by the West's continuing unabashed colonial exploitation combined with grand human rights rhetoric.

In South Asia, "British India" in the colonizers' naming, the colonizers introduced Western science and English history into higher education from 1835. Sons, and to some degree daughters, of the colonized elites were to appreciate the rational and impartial government in general and England as a place of law, culture, rationality, and model literary texts in particular. By the 1880s almost half a million had graduated, and increasing numbers migrated to England (as well as to the United States, France, Germany, and the Soviet Union) for university education. Fifty years later, the British census listed seven thousand Indians in England and Wales, of which the seafaring labor migrants of the London port's lascar community were only a tiny minority. The best-known educational migrants included Dadabhai Naoroji (1825–1917), called the architect of Indian nationalism; Mahatma Gandhi (1869–1947) and Jawaharlal Nehru (1889–1964), who studied Law at the Inns of Court; Rabindranath Tagore (1861–1941), who studied at University College; Aurobindo Ghose (1872–1950), temporarily an extremist who experienced a "denationalization" and a return to Hindu culture; Bhimrao Ambedkar (1891–1956), a social revolutionary leader of the caste of untouchables and coauthor of independent India's constitution; Vinayak Damodar Savarkar (1883–1966), one of the earliest proponents of revolutionary terrorism to achieve independence; and Subhas Chandra Bose (1897–1945), an activist in the 1920s noncooperation movement. This elite congregated in India House in London and, when persecuted, moved their center to Paris. Others, influenced by the revolutionary writings of the American colonies in the 1770s, attempted to foster Indians' independence from their places of exile in the United States only to be prosecuted by US attorneys. In the context of international power rivalries, again others sought support in Germany or the Soviet Union. Several attended the seminal 1907 Stuttgart conference of the Second Socialist International. Arriving in the West, some realized that they could recite the British counties but not India's states—colonizer schooling had not considered India's history noteworthy. By living in "the West" they understood Orientalism before Edward Saïd created the term, and they established contact with European and American advocates of equality of cultures, agrarian reform, and socialist sharing. In contrast to most colonizers, they, as colonized, learned to compare the two (or more) sociocultural systems in which they lived and to analyze the gap between the rhetoric of Euro-civilization and its practices.

From African and Caribbean Francophone colonies, black students migrated to France, and in the 1920s and 1930s—after Africans had had to fight and work for France in World War I—a sailor and worker community emerged in Marseille. In the mid-1920s the sisters Paulette, Andrée, and Jeanne Nardal from Martinique established a salon in Paris as a center of debate and literary development where Antillean, US, and West African intellectuals met. Paulette Nardal, a feminist as much as an African-Caribbean "culturalist," and Leo Sajou from Haiti founded the short-lived *Revue du Monde Noir* in 1931 and published African-Americans like Claude MacKay and Langston Hughes. The migrants included Léopold Sédar Senghor (1906–2001) from Senegal, Aimé Césaire (1913–2008) from Martinique, and Léon-Gontran Damas (1912–1978) from French Guiana. Senghor served in the French army and was a prisoner of war of fascist Germany and thus experienced French culture as well as militarism, German fascism, and European warfare. The Association des Étudiants Martiniquais en France in 1934 began to publish *L'Étudiant martiniquais* but renamed it *L'Étudiant noir* in 1935 to indicate the Atlantic-wide reach of the African communities. In addition, numerous African-Americans migrated to Paris to escape racism. Influenced by both Haiti's role in the age of revolution and the Harlem Renaissance of the 1920s and 1930s, Césaire and Senghor in a reappropriation of the derogative term *nègre* developed the concept of *négritude* as conveying African identity and culture juxtaposed to colonialism and racism but using the French language and recognizing (French-) European cultural achievements. The concept was self-assertive and integrative, and it aimed at teaching white Europeans. Alioune Diop (1910–1980) founded the influential *Présence africaine* in 1947, perhaps the most influential journal to place black culture before a white audience on a par. Cheikh Anta Diop (1923–1986) also lived in Paris and was to become one of the foremost African scholars, controversial because of his racializing views of African history that remained a counterimage to European self-racialization. Many of these students became leaders in West Africa and the Caribbean.

Starting from the colonized/colonizer dichotomy, these intellectual migrants developed a critique of racism and imperialism. Another migrating group approached the issue of class and took a decidedly leftist, socialist or communist, approach to working-class and racial equality. George Padmore (1902–1959) may almost serve as prototype. Born in Trinidad, he migrated to study at Fisk and Howard Universities in the United States, then moved to Moscow where, under the auspices of the Communist International of Labour Union, he joined the leaderships of its Negro Bureau and the International Trade Union Committee of Negro Workers. Continuing to London, he cooperated with Guyanese historian C. L. R. James (1901–1989) in Pan-African and working-class activities and helped organize the 1945 Pan-African Conference in Manchester, which discussed an agenda for decolonization: independence for the "British West Indies" and for African colonies. Trinidadian Eric Eustace Williams (1911–1981) became first a historian of slavery and of the connection between capitalism and colonial underdevelopment, then prime minister of Trinidad.

In these networks these students who would become intellectual leaders received their socialization and education. They could contextualize colonized societies worldwide. At universities and law schools they developed a spectrum of approaches to change and fight unequal colonizer–colonized, white–black, or British–Indian relationships. They struggled to free the workers of capitalist and colonized societies from oppression and, occasionally, to demand equal rights for women. Observing industrial change and urbanization, they developed concepts for a transition to independence that incorporated economic development and universal human rights—the ideas of the Age of

Enlightenment freed from Eurocentrism and whites-only provincialism. They were the initiators of the many decolonization movements that would gain global dimensions from the late 1940s.

At the same time intellectuals and literati, socialized in the recently democratic Germany, had to flee Fascism and continue their work as expatriates, briefly in other European countries, then mainly in the United States and, for a smaller number, in Brazil and in Mexico. They were designated as un-German by the Fascist rulers and their student youth organizations. Some moved to Los Angeles and continued to write or to influence the film industry: Fritz Lang (Hollywood), Thomas Mann (Princeton and Pacific Palisades), and Bertolt Brecht, who, called before the House Un-American Activities Committee in 1947, fled to Switzerland. In theater, Erwin Piscator stayed in New York. The social scientists, psychologists, and literary scholars of the interdisciplinary Institute of Social Research in Frankfurt am Main (founded in 1923), after a brief relocation to Geneva, Switzerland, moved to New York, where scholars at Columbia University provided an affiliation, as did the New School for Social Research, founded in 1919 after Columbia University, like many other US institutions, demanded nationalist loyalty oaths from its faculty. The New School's graduate program began in 1933 as a university of exiles, a shelter for scholars rescued—partially with funds from the Rockefeller Foundation—from all over occupied Europe. Theodor W. Adorno, Hannah Arendt, Erich Fromm, Aron Gurwitsch, Max Horkheimer, Hans Jonas, Herbert Marcuse, Leo Strauss, Max Wertheimer, and others were associated with it. Their lasting contribution was "critical theory," an approach to scholarship that rejects positivism and national narratives for a critical understanding of societies, their material basis and cultural superstructure, and an awareness of the relatedness of knowledge and interests. The French-language École Libre des Hautes Études was also associated with the New School.[23]

As a postscript it might be added that many of the European theoreticians of postcolonialism also emerged from circuits of migration.

From the 1930s to the 1950s they experienced hierarchized interaction between colonized groups or subalterns, ready to rebel, and colonizers clinging to an imperial regime without vision, without moral foundation, and—after 1945—without the military power to support their superior position. Of the French-language theorists, Roland Barthes had lived in Romania and Egypt, Frantz Fanon in Martinique and Algeria, Jacques Derrida and Pierre Bourdieu in Algeria. Other theorists experienced two (or more) social regimes in one society: Antonio Gramsci and Mikhail Bakhtin lived through (and suffered from) the transformation of their societies' governments to Fascism and Stalinism, respectively. Michel Foucault observed the multiple discourses of schizophrenic men and women and of those who did not live according to assigned sex roles. In Britain, Stuart Hall and Catherine Hall, the former being of a color of skin other than white and of Jamaican origin, questioned imperial and national discourses. By their physical displacement or replacement, they came to live dual or multiple perspectives and thus enabled themselves to replace monocultural foundational stories and nation-state ideologies with the multiple perspectives of discourse theory. The political-societal transition of decolonization became an academic transition from nationalist historiographies to transcultural societal studies. Migrating common people throughout the ages had to negotiate two or more systems of reference and of everyday life.[24]

CHAPTER FIVE

# The Aftermath of War and Decolonization

The immediate aftermath of the Second World War gave rise to two major migrations. First was the migration of refugees, prisoners of war, forced laborers, prewar imperial colonizer migrants, and soldiers who needed to be repatriated or needed to be resettled, if "home" had been destroyed or new postwar governments made return undesirable and, perhaps, life-threatening. Second was the migration of laborers who were needed to rebuild destroyed economies. Two other important migrations were the consequence of persecutions: the migration of people of Jewish faith to Israel and the flight of Palestinians. Finally, postwar migrations also included multiple moves resulting from decolonization and forced migration of labor to meet the needs of the new regime in South Africa.

## Repatriations, Expulsions, Resettlement

After the atomic bombs were dropped on Hiroshima and Nagasaki and Japan surrendered, the internment and repatriation of the 6.5 million Japanese abroad began. The population of Karafuto (South Sakhalin Island) had become 93 percent Japanese; Nan'yō's population of 132,000 included 81,000 Japanese; in continental China, Japanese migrants had remained few; in Taiwan they accounted for 6 percent of the population; some 800,000 Japanese lived in Korea. In Europe, many displaced persons (DPs), whom the Allies estimated to total eighteen million in May 1945, walked home over hundreds of kilometers—as Chinese refugees did. Repatriation, often to homes in ruins, was completed by the end of 1946 in both macroregions. Some, however, remained in camps: Jews with no home, Baltic and Ukrainian people who had collaborated with the German occupation, East Europeans who refused to return to Stalinist Russia or other newly communist states. Nonreturning DPs did not received citizenship; in Europe they became "stateless," in Japan they were "third-country nationals."

From Japan more than a million Koreans repatriated to South Korea, another hundred thousand accepted a repatriation offer by North Korea; those remaining in Japan faced continued discrimination. At the war's beginning, Japanese migrants in the United States and Canada and their locally born children and grandchildren suffered from the warfare though living a continent off. After Japan's attack on Pearl Harbor, the migrants who purposely had left Japan became "enemy aliens." Constructed as a military threat, harassed under continuing racism, and owning modest property that could be confiscated by their Euro-American neighbors, most were relocated. Canada's security bureaucrats had all Japanese and Japanese-Canadians living within one hundred miles of the coast removed to the interior; their confiscated properties were sold. Of the 275,000 men and women of Japanese birth or ancestry in the United States and Hawai'i, more than a 100,000 were relocated to desert concentration camps. Four decades later, the US government acknowledged that the measure "was not justified by military necessity" but due to "race prejudice, war hysteria, and a failure of political leadership."

In China, warfare continued. The Nationalists (Guomindang) and the Communists received support from the Western and Soviet blocs, respectively. Thus, refugee generation continued, resettlement was delayed. The establishment of a Communist government in 1949 resulted in Nationalists' mass flight to Hong Kong as a British enclave and to Taiwan. Another 340,000 refugees, landowners, and students in particular, headed for neighboring countries, mostly to Burma and in small numbers to Laos and Portuguese Macao. In Taiwan the some two million newcomers, in an occupation-type move, overthrew societal and economic institutions. Hong Kong's population, 1.6 million in 1941, doubled by 1961. Refugees arriving in Southeast Asian countries could receive help from the diasporic Chinese, often distant family members. By mid-1953 the "Overseas Chinese" numbered 13.4 million in sixteen countries or enclaves, with another 300,000 in the Americas, Oceania, Africa, and Europe. In the Southeast Asian segment of the subsequent Cold War world, several "nationalist" movements—a misnomer, given the multiethnic population in each and every region—labeled diasporic Chinese a bridgehead of "Communist" China and targeted them for reprisals or even ferocious massacres. Many were forced to flee to the People's Republic, Taiwan, or Hong Kong or seek admission to countries with existing Chinese communities like the United States, Canada, Britain, or the Netherlands. Subsequently, abolition of racialized admission criteria in Canada (1962–1963) and in the United States (1965) made a new phase of large-scale migrations from Asia to North America possible.[1]

At the end of the war in Europe, where the number of refugees amounted to thirty million and number of dead fifty-five to sixty million, the Allies committed themselves to create conditions that would enable all refugees and displaced persons to return. In the West this was a guise for not accepting the dislocated and, from the side of Soviet Russia, a guise for depriving refugees of a choice in where to begin new lives. In the Soviet zone of liberation and occupation, given the destruction of infrastructure, refugees at first had to move by themselves. So did men and women in the post-armistice havoc of the Western zones. In the latter areas, civilian refugees, forced laborers, and Jewish survivors from the death camps, named "displaced persons" to distinguish them from POWs and demobilized soldiers, received some support from aid organizations, and several hundreds of thousands were resettled in the United States, Canada, and Australia. Polish soldiers elected to stay in Great Britain. Some two hundred thousand DPs, so-called hardcore cases, remained in West Germany as "stateless." The perhaps one million surviving men and women of Jewish faith received no recognition of their special needs after witnessing and surviving the Holocaust. Palestine remained closed because Britain had to balance Arab and Jewish interests. By the end of 1946 in Poland, where anti-Semitism remained rampant, 170,000 survivors had fled to territories administered by the Western Allies. Their hopes for admission to North America foundered on quota limitations, and "repatriation" to Palestine, the home of Muslim Arabs, emerged but slowly. The callous British request that the USSR settle Jews in Birobidzhan, the Soviet Jewish autonomous region in Central Asia, elicited but an equally callous query by the USSR government about empty spaces in the British Empire.

In the aftermath of the war, people continued to be expelled and shifted around by governments because of their allegiances during the war, ethnocultural prejudices, or redesigned "national" territories. Some 12.5 million refugees and expellees from the many eastern German and diasporic German cultures reached the four zones of Germany between 1945 and 1949. Their insertion, initially de facto segregation, was achieved only over time and under government pressure. East of the new German border, 4.5 million Poles settled, dislocated five years before by German occupation forces or fleeing from those eastern territories annexed by the USSR after the war. From 1939 to 1949 the Polish people were subjected to some twenty-five million resettlement and deportation moves, with many being shunted about repeatedly.[2]

· In the Soviet Union's southern regions, where segments of some indigenous peoples had attempted to achieve independence during the war, some six hundred thousand to one million men and women of many cultures were deported, and the prewar autonomous republics of the Crimean Tatars, the Kalmyk, the Chechen, and the Ingush were not reestablished. In-migrating Russian ethnics profited economically; Russian and Ukrainian peasants were brought in to cultivate the vacated farmlands. The territories newly acquired from Finnish Karelia, along the Polish-Byelorussian-Ukrainian borderlands to Romanian Bessarabia—like southern Sakhalin Island retaken from Japan—were vacated by flight and population transfer and resettled with Russian migrants. Many acquired deportees' possessions without having to pay recompense. In addition, a lively and mobile postwar youth movement contributed to the reallocation of individuals from the many peoples.

In East Central and southeastern Europe, Hungarians fled from Transylvania, which became part of redesigned Romania. Greece, wracked by civil war, in the fall of 1949 counted some seven hundred thousand refugees in a population of seven million. Men and women of the Yugoslav peoples fled from each other or fled from the area of mixed settlement of Venetia-Giulia and Trieste, contested between Italy and Yugoslavia. When Italian-occupied Dalmatia was reincorporated into Yugoslavia, some three hundred thousand ethnic Italians, one-third of the total population, left. From Africa, Italians who had settled in Tunisia and Ethiopia returned. Aid to refugees, at first provided by the UN Relief and Rehabilitation Administration, was coordinated by the International Refugee Organization (IRO) after December 1946. Refugee movements involved family migrations, often female-headed because men were soldiers, prisoners of war, or dead.[3]

Women's postwar migrations included departures as "war brides." The United States, to take the major recipient state as an example, had sent sixteen million men for combat or war-related activities into fifty-seven countries. Nonfraternization policies toward enemy populations were quickly undercut by human relations. From 1942 to 1952 an estimated one million soldiers married local women, and hundreds of thousands of war brides reached the United States—only occasionally did a groom remain in his wife's country. Forty-one thousand Canadian soldiers married overseas, mostly to British women. Japanese brides of US men had little hope for a lasting union because the US exclusion laws prevented them from immigrating—and African-American soldiers could not marry European women because of miscegenation laws. On the whole, however, politically mandated ethnonational hierarchies were undercut in everyday contact, through principles of humanity, and by emotional-sexual relations. In the United States, the war brides were to become the ethnocultural nuclei for postwar migrations.[4]

From destroyed Europe, emigration resumed. The Dutch government supported emigration for fear of overpopulation; the establishment of communist governments in East Central Europe caused people to flee. Because no economic recovery seemed in sight, many people headed for societies not ravaged by war. Net out-migration from Europe in 1946–1955 amounted to 4.5 million and was directed primarily to Canada, the United States, South America (from southern Europe), and Australia, as well as Israel.

## Postwar Reconstruction and the Need for Workers

From Western Europe to East Asia, devastated countries needed to be rebuilt, demobilized soldiers had to be reintegrated, industrial workers whose factories lay in ruins needed to be employed, and the gendered division of work had to be renegotiated as a result of women having migrated to industrial jobs when men were off as soldiers. In most societies, women were displaced from their wartime jobs, but their new economic clout allowed them to protest and organize. Types of migration became fluid: After the war some 30,000 German POWs were assigned to work in Belgian coal mines and 1.75 million to work in France. When return became possible, 20 percent of those in France turned the forced assignment into a migration decision and opted to stay. Elsewhere demobilized non-national soldiers or POWs decided to remain in the society of demobilization rather than return to home societies that were in ruins and that, often against their interests, had sent them into war.

The North American societies had to reintegrate millions of soldiers, migrants arriving from economies in ruin, and war brides. In Europe policy makers encouraged or retarded labor migrations. The West German labor allocation bureaucracies refused exit permits to able-bodied male prospective migrants in order to retain a labor force for reconstruction. The conservative Italian government encouraged departures to rid itself of radical and unemployed working-class voters. By the early 1950s, fast economic growth in northwestern Europe and slow development in southern Europe made imbalances of manpower evident. Governments negotiated treaties to permit controlled inter-state mobility of laborers with an implied obligation to return. The "guest worker" system came into being. In 1950s North America, Canada continued to rely on immigrants, especially from southern Europe; the United States recruited Mexican workers under the Bracero Program, expecting them to return. For ideological reasons, the communist states in East Central Europe, the Soviet Union, and the People's Republic of China permitted neither emigration nor immigration. Japan, for racist reasons, also pursued a non-immigration policy. Thus, systems of labor were redesigned. The transatlantic system came to a standstill by the mid-1950s, except for the migrations from southern Europe to Canada. A decade later there evolved a transpacific system of labor, investor, and student migration that often involved sequential family migrations. In the socialist world, bordered by the Iron Curtain in the West and Japan's exclusionism in the East, migrations remained internal to states, although later there were small-scale movements between neighboring states, such as Poland and Hungary.[5]

## Jewish and Arab Migrations

For Jewish refugees from anti-Semitism and survivors of the Holocaust, *aliyah* to Arab-settled Palestine meant ascending to the place of religious roots. It had been a spiritual and, from about 1900, a religio-nationalist state-building project. Before 1914, only 60,000 of 2.75 million Jewish migrants worldwide selected Palestine as destination, and in the interwar years, 1919–1939, only some 345,000 chose the agricultural settlement projects. In the next five years, 45,000 refugees from fascism arrived. The United Nations' November 1947 partition of Palestine envisaged a Jewish state with an Arab "minority" of almost 400,000, or 42.5 percent of the population. Statehood of Israel (1948), Israel's discrimination against the Arab-Muslim populations, the several Arab-Israel military campaigns, and state-organized Jewish immigration generated new Muslim refugee populations, some 330,000 by late 1948, some 0.9 million to 1.2 million in 1950 according to the UN Relief and Works Agency. Israel became a major region of both immigration and refugee generation. At first Holocaust survivors arrived, some 150,000 Europeans of Jewish faith. Next came an estimated 200,000 North African, Arabian Peninsula, and Iraqi men and women of Jewish faith and, according to the high rabbinate's labeling, of Jewish genetic descent through the mother's line. Third, a new exodus from Eastern Europe's rampant anti-Semitism, in 1950–1951, brought 425,000. Israel's admission and citizenship policies became as exclusionist as postwar Germany's—admission followed bloodline descent.[6]

## Racialized Labor Mobility in South Africa

After the forced-labor regimes of Germany, the Soviet Union, and Japan, the white South African government began similar policies. Before 1940 the state's increasingly interventionist Euro-origin segment expelled Chinese contract workers, restricted Indian workers, and imposed a system of labor controls and pass laws on Africans. Its restriction, since 1913, of Africans to reserves, "Homelands" or "Bantustans," brought involuntary relocation of two to three million people from territories designated for whites. In 1948, partly in reaction to labor militancy, apartheid was institutionalized under a "white supremacy" doctrine. All aspects of life were racialized: mixed marriages were prohibited (1949), interracial sexual contacts outlawed (1950), identity checks established (1952). The labor regime forced Africans to work for European-origin employers, to migrate seasonally or for extended periods of time, to leave families behind and live in camps. The powerful mining core and many utility companies drew their labor forces from a marginalized countryside. The state, which was interventionist regarding workers, guaranteed industry's labor system and, with adaptations for women and children's labor, that of white farmers. Concomitantly labor recruitment expanded to a subcontinental scale.[7]

## Decolonization and Reverse Migrations

During the interwar period, movements for self-rule or full independence had gained momentum in many colonized societies. From the beginning of war in Asia in 1937, the Euro-American colonizer powers in need of support and soldiers came up with promises for various forms of postwar partnership or independence to India (1940), Burma (1945), the Philippines (1946), and other colonies. In Africa, recruitment of soldiers, in particular by the French government in exile, was not accompanied by any negotiations for postwar rights. After the war, the political-structural frame was one of outdated and crumbling empires unwilling to negotiate transition to a new order. In consequence, wars for independence began in the 1950s—Kenya, Algeria, West Africa, to name only a few. Refugee generation and population displacement by construction of independent nation-states and imposition of arbitrary borderlines followed the European model.

Japan's and Nazi Germany's attempts at empire building, Europe's internal warfare, and US intervention left the imperial systems in shambles. French, Dutch, and US attempts to reestablish colonial rule or zones of influence in Asia only prolonged processes of dislocation. In postwar Korea, for example, a moderate prewar collaborationist elite stood opposed to an anticolonial, left-oriented elite, trained in underground activities or exile. The former was aging and established, the latter young and dynamic. Prosecution of collaborators initiated partial elite displacement, and warfare between the Communist north (population 9 million) and the West-influenced south (population 21 million) resulted in southward flight of 1.8 million.

In British India, the colonizer–colonized dualism turned into tripartite British-Hindu-Muslim negotiations, which in 1947 divided the subcontinent into (Hindu) India and (Muslim) West and East Pakistan. The 389 million people spoke fifteen official, twenty-four regional, and twenty-three indigenous languages as well as some seven hundred dialects, and thus the term *Indian* as an ethnic or cultural descriptor remained a creation of outside observer-rulers. The bulk of the Muslims, 22 percent of the population, were agriculturalists; the Hindus were predominantly shopkeepers, moneylenders, or workers in cloth and other factories. All negotiators accepted that partition would involve a projected exchange of four million men, women, and children. From Karachi, long free of intercommunal violence, almost one-third of the population departed, mainly Hindus in commerce. In the Punjab's interspersed settlements of Muslims, Sikhs, and Hindus, atrocities and massacres occurred. In the exchange between West and East Bengal (India and East Pakistan), 1.2 million of a population of 20 million Hindus and 8 million Muslims left eastbound and 4.8 million of 32 million Muslims and 10 million Hindus moved westward. Governments and armies began to speed up the movement to reduce the danger of epidemics and to resettle people in time for sowing and harvesting, to reduce the danger of famines. By the end of 1947, the two religion-based states had exchanged 7.3 million men, women, and children. An estimated one million died during the treks. Women were particularly liable to attack and robbery because they carried their traditional marriage gifts of gold and jewelry. By 1951, refugees had increased to 14.5 million. Regional populations had thus to some degree been homogenized by religion, but cultural and linguistic heterogeneity remained. State formation was a costly process for refugees.

In independent Burma (1948), in-migrating Chinese technicians who had filled the vacancies left by the flight of British Indians in 1942 faced riots after allegations that the People's Republic of China supported the state's "minority" peoples. The Karen had unsuccessfully attempted to create their own state in the late 1940s, and the Mon opposed the central government in the 1950s. In Malaya/Malaysia, which achieved independence from 1946 to 1963, a small nationalist-communist uprising was quelled by British troops in 1950 but some five hundred thousand Chinese agriculturalists were forced to resettle in order to deprive the insurgents of their produce. In Indochina (later Cambodia, Laos, and Vietnam) France reestablished colonial rule only to be defeated in a war of independence. At the time of the 1954 cease-fire, which divided the country into a nationalist-communist north and a Buddhist, Catholic-ruled, US-dependent south, 140,000 civilians opted to move to North Vietnam (population 16 million) while 860,000 moved to South Vietnam (population 11.5 million). Two more decades of warfare created further millions of refugees. French-ruled Siam/Thailand, which had survived the war years as an ally of Japan, became a refugee-receiving country.

The Netherlands East Indies declared independence immediately after Japan's surrender. British and Dutch troops, instead of interning the Japanese, fought the Indonesian People's Army. Of 240,000 residents designated as "European," more than four-fifths were of Dutch origin (1930 figures). The label veiled the other, Asian, side: 70 percent were Indos of mixed parentage. Before independence, achieved in 1949, the highest social strata left; subsequently some 15 percent of the Indos opted for Indonesian citizenship, while about one hundred thousand colonial auxiliaries, middle-level officials, and military men and their families were evacuated to the Netherlands. Most had never been there before, some did not speak Dutch and were, like the Ambonese, nonwhite. In 1957 Indonesia expelled the remaining Dutch nationals and expropriated Dutch agricultural properties.

Other wars for independence resulted in further multiple refugee streams. First, colonizers, on the defensive, deported populations; in the 1950s, the British resettled half a million Chinese in Malaya, tens of thousands of Kikuyu from Nairobi, and the Kabaka from Buganda, and the French uprooted Algerian peasants. Second, wars for independence dislocated people of whole regions. Third, in many post-independence societies factional wars between different political groups, as in Angola and Mozambique, or between divided societies, as in Vietnam and Korea, displaced millions. Conflicts exacerbated by intervention of the US and USSR superpowers or former colonial overlords took the highest death tolls and created the largest refugee movements.

Independence ended both the temporary assignments of administrators and soldiers in colonies of exploitation and the privileged position of farming families in colonies of settlement. Many would emigrate, some in immediate flight, others over time. They saw their political power crumble, their economic calculations collapse, their lifestyles vanish, and "their" subaltern native labor rise to citizenship. Most were locally born (creoles) and had never known the society of origin. Furthermore, colonial auxiliaries had to leave, whether recruited locally as in French Algeria, distributed across an empire as the Sikhs, or pitting minority against majority populations as in the case of Indochina's Hmong, whose pro-colonizer policing role made them liable to retribution from the newly sovereign people. Finally, men, women, and children of genetically mixed ancestry as well as elites with cultural affinity to a core found themselves in precarious positions. Withdrawal of elites, whether owners of capital, of skills, or of knowledge, could create havoc in the new economies. After independence, many of the new nationalist elites, in the face of multiethnic populations, pursued European-inspired models of state formation that placed one cultural group as "nation" in hegemonic position. In the metropoles the arrival of some 5.5 to 8.5 million Italian, French, British, Belgian, Dutch, and other white colonials and of nonwhite auxiliaries (before 1975) created new tensions and initiated the transition to multicolored and multicultured peoples.

The frame for further developments was set by the mid-1950s. In 1955 the Bandung, Indonesia, Conference of Non-Aligned Countries coincided with the publication of Aimé Césaire's "Discours sur le colonialisme" in the famous journal *Présence africaine* (Paris). African and Asian migrants' presence in the white world, with its many antecedents, would increase in the next decades. Former colonizer–colonized relations became migratory connections. These served life-course projects rather than nations' power interests. The migrations of the second half of the twentieth century and of the turn of the twenty-first century had their origins in the imperialist period. Although there are no figures on total short-distance, intra-state, cross-border, and transcontinental or transoceanic migrations, the extremely high levels of mobility worldwide, from the 1870s to 1945, indicate that state mobilizations and constraints, global economic inequalities, and power hierarchies mobilized and immobilized hundreds of millions.[8]

# Notes

## INTRODUCTION

1  This book is based on Dirk Hoerder, *Cultures in Contact: World Migrations in the Second Millennium* (Durham, NC: Duke University Press, 2002), chaps. 12–18. More extensive annotation can be found there.

2  Adam M. McKeown, "Global Migration, 1846–1940," *Journal of World History* 15, no. 2 (2005): 155–189.

3  Eric J. Hobsbawn and Terence Ranger, eds., *The Invention of Tradition* (Cambridge: Cambridge University Press, 1983); Benedict Anderson, *Imagined Communities: Reflections on the Origin and Spread of Nationalism* (London: Verso, 1983).

4  Adam McKeown, "Chinese Emigration in Global Context, 1850–1940," *Journal of Global History* 5 (2010): 1–30; José Moya and Adam McKeown, "World Migration in the Long Twentieth Century," in *Essays on Twentieth-Century History*, ed. Michael Adas (Philadelphia: Temple University Press, 2010), 9–52.

5  Marcus Rediker, *The Slave Ship: A Human History* (New York: Viking, 2007), 3, updating the statistics provided in Philip D. Curtin, *The Atlantic Slave Trade: A Census* (Madison: University of Wisconsin Press, 1969), and Paul E. Lovejoy, "The Volume of the Atlantic Slave Trade: A Synthesis," *Journal of African History* 23 (1982): 473–502.

6  David Northrup, *Indentured Labor in the Age of Imperialism, 1834–1922* (Cambridge: Cambridge University Press, 1995); Crispin Bates, ed., *Community, Empire and Migration: South Asian Diaspora* (Basingstoke: Palgrave, 2001).

7  Adam M. McKeown, "Conceptualizing Chinese Diasporas, 1842–1949," *Journal of Asian Studies* 58, no. 2 (1999): 306–337; Michael Mann, "Migration–Remigration–Circulation: South Asian Kulis in the Indian Ocean and Beyond, 1840–1940," in *Connecting Seas and Connected Ocean Rims: Indian, Atlantic, and Pacific Oceans and China Seas Migrations from the 1830s to the 1930s*, ed. Donna Gabaccia and Dirk Hoerder (Leiden: Brill, 2011), 108–133.

8  Dirk Hoerder, ed., *Labor Migration in the Atlantic Economies: The European and North American Working Classes during the Period of Industrialization* (Westport, CT: Greenwood, 1985).

9  Hoerder, *Cultures in Contact,* chaps. 13–15.

10  John Torpey, *The Invention of the Passport: Surveillance, Citizenship and the State* (Cambridge: Cambridge University Press, 2000); Christiane Harzig and Dirk Hoerder, with Donna Gabaccia, *What Is Migration History?* (Cambridge: Polity, 2009), 72–85.

11  Harzig et al., *What Is Migration History?*, 1–7, 69–72.

### 1. A *LONGUE-DURÉE* PERSPECTIVE

1  José C. Curto and Renée Souldore-La France, eds., *Africa and the Americas: Interconnections during the Slave Trade* (Trenton, NJ: Africa World Press, 2005).

2  Gerhard Jaritz and Albert Müller, eds., *Migration in der Feudalgesellschaft* (Frankfurt am Main: Campus, 1988); Rainer C. Schwinges, ed., *Neubürger im späten Mittelalter: Migration und Austausch in der Städtelandschaft des alten Reiches (1250–1550)* (Berlin: Duncker und Humblot, 2002).

3  David J. Robinson, ed., *Migration in Colonial Spanish America* (Cambridge: Cambridge University Press, 1990).

4  A particularly detailed study for one plantation regime is Ronald Takaki, *Pau Hana: Plantation Life and Labor in Hawaii, 1835–1920* (Honolulu: University of Hawai'i Press, 1983).

5  Paul Gilroy, *The Black Atlantic: Modernity and Double Consciousness* (Cambridge, MA: Harvard University Press, 1993), a book that is England-centered and somewhat male-biased. Two comprehensive studies are Vincent Bakpetu Thompson, *The Making of the African Diaspora in the Americas, 1441–1900* (Harlow, Essex: Longman, 1987); and John Thornton, *Africa and Africans in the Making of the Atlantic World, 1400–1800*, 2nd ed. (Cambridge: Cambridge University Press, 1998). David Patrick Geggus, *Haitian Revolutionary Studies* (Bloomington: Indiana University Press, 2002); Madison S. Bell, *Toussaint Louverture: A Biography* (New York: Pantheon Books, 2007); Emma Christopher, Cassandra Pybus, and Marcus Rediker, eds., *Many Middle Passages: Forced Migration and the Making of the Modern World* (Berkeley: University of California Press, 2007).

6  David Eltis and James Walvin, eds., *The Abolition of the Atlantic Slave Trade: Origins and Effects in Europe, Africa, and the Americas* (Madison: University of Wisconsin Press, 1981); Piet C. Emmer and Magnus Mörner, eds., *European Expansion and Migration: Essays on the Intercontinental Migration from Africa, Asia, and Europe* (New York: Berg, 1992); Seymour Drescher, *Abolition: A History of Slavery and Antislavery* (New York: Cambridge University Press, 2009);

Katia M. de Queiros Mattoso, *To Be Slave in Brazil, 1550–1880,* 4th ed. (New Brunswick, NJ: Rutgers University Press, 1994).

7  Magnus Mörner, *Race Mixture in the History of Latin America* (Boston: Little, Brown, 1967); Bonham C. Richardson, "Caribbean Migrations, 1838–1985," in *The Modern Caribbean,* ed. Franklin W. Knight and Colin A. Palmer (Chapel Hill: University of North Carolina Press, 1989), 203–228.

8  Eugene D. Genovese, *Roll, Jordan, Roll: The World the Slaves Made* (New York: Pantheon Books, 1974); Lawrence W. Levine, *Black Culture and Black Consciousness: Afro-American Folk Thought from Slavery to Freedom* (New York: Oxford University Press, 1977); Robin D. G. Kelley and Earl Lewis, eds., *To Make Our World Anew: A History of African Americans* (New York: Oxford University Press, 2000); Stephan Palmié, ed., *Slave Culture and the Cultures of Slavery* (Knoxville: University of Tennessee Press, 1995); James N. Gregory, *The Southern Diaspora: How the Great Migrations of Black and White Southerners Transformed America* (Chapel Hill: University of North Carolina Press, 2005); Chad Berry, *Southern Migrants, Northern Exiles* (Urbana: University of Illinois Press, 2000).

9  Donna Gabaccia and Dirk Hoerder, eds., *Connecting Seas and Connected Ocean Rims: Indian, Atlantic, and Pacific Oceans and China Seas Migrations from the 1830s to the 1930s* (Leiden: Brill, 2011).

10  John R. Willis, ed., *Slaves and Slavery in Muslim Africa,* 2 vols. (London: Cass, 1985); Patrick Manning, *Slavery and African Life: Occidental, Oriental, and African Slave Trades* (Cambridge: Cambridge University Press, 1990); Murray Gordon, *Slavery in the Arab World,* trans. from the French (orig. 1987; New York: New Amsterdam, 1989); W. Gervase Clarence-Smith, ed., *The Economics of the Indian Ocean Slave Trade in the Nineteenth Century* (London: Cass, 1989); Richard B. Allen, "Satisfying the Want for Labouring People: European Slave Trading in the Indian Ocean, 1500–1850," *Journal of World History* 21, no. 1 (2010): 45–73; Janet J. Ewald, "Slavery in Africa and the Slave Trades from Africa," *American Historical Review* 97 (1992): 465–485.

11  Kingsley Davis, *The Population of India and Pakistan* (Princeton, NJ: Princeton University Press, 1951); Jan C. Breman and E. Valentine Daniel, "The Making of a Coolie," *Journal of Peasant Studies* 19, nos. 3–4 (1992): 268–295; Jan Breman, *Labour Bondage in West India: From Past to Present* (New Delhi: Oxford University Press, 2007); Prasannan Parthasarathi, *The Transition to a Colonial Economy: Weavers, Merchants and Kings in South India, 1720–1800* (Cambridge: Cambridge University Press, 2001); Morris D. Morris, *The Emergence of an Industrial*

*Labour Force in India: A Study of the Bombay Cotton Mills, 1854–1947* (Bombay: Oxford University Press, 1965); Ranajit Das Gupta, "Factory Labour in Eastern India: Sources of Supply, 1855–1946," *Indian Economic and Social History Review* 13 (1976): 277–330; Dietmar Rothermund and D. C. Wadhwa, eds., *Zamindars, Mines, and Peasants: Studies in the History of an Indian Coalfield and Its Rural Hinterland* (New Delhi: Manohar, 1978).

12  Philip A. Kuhn, *Chinese among Others: Emigration in Modern Times* (Lanham: Rowman and Littlefield, 2008); Alfonso Felix Jr., ed., *The Chinese in the Philippines,* 2 vols. (Manila: Solidaridad, 1966–1969); Victor Purcell, *The Chinese in Southeast Asia,* 2nd rev. ed. (London: Oxford University Press, 1965); Wong Kwok-Chu, *The Chinese in the Philippine Economy, 1898–1941* (Quezon City: Ateneo de Manila University Press, 1999).

13  Harry G. Gelber, *Opium, Soldiers and Evangelicals: Britain's 1840–42 War with China and Its Aftermath* (New York: Palgrave Macmillan, 2004); Timothy Brook and Bob Tadashi Wakabayashi, eds., *Opium Regimes: China, Britain, and Japan, 1839–1952* (Berkeley: University of California Press, 2000).

14  Ping-ti Ho, *Studies on the Population of China, 1368–1953* (Cambridge, MA: Harvard University Press, 1959), 153–158; Jonathan D. Spence, *The Search for Modern China* (New York: Norton, 1990), 167–242.

15  Lynn Pan, gen. ed., *The Encyclopedia of the Chinese Overseas* (Richmond, UK: Curzon, 1999); Lynn Pan, *Sons of the Yellow Emperor: The Story of the Overseas Chinese* (London: Secker and Warburg, 1990), esp. 3–22; Wang Gungwu, *The Chinese Overseas: From Earthbound China to the Quest for Autonomy* (Cambridge, MA: Harvard University Press, 2000); Amarjit Kaur, *Wage Labour in Southeast Asia since 1840: Globalisation, the International Division of Labour and Labour Transformations* (Basingstoke: Palgrave Macmillan, 2004).

16  Irene B. Taeuber, *The Population of Japan* (Princeton, NJ: Princeton University Press, 1958), 173–190; Neville Bennett, "Japanese Emigration Policy, 1880–1941," in *Asians in Australia: The Dynamics of Migration and Settlement,* ed. Christine Inglis et al. (Singapore: Institute of Southeast Asian Studies, 1992), 23–43; Marius B. Jansen, "Japanese Imperialism: Late Meiji Perspectives," in *The Japanese Colonial Empire, 1895–1945,* ed. Ramon H. Myers and Mark R. Peattie (Princeton, NJ: Princeton University Press, 1984), 61–79; Douglas R. Howland, *Translating the West: Language and Political Reason in Nineteenth-Century Japan* (Honolulu: University of Hawai'i Press, 2002).

17  France had lost its first empire to Britain, resumed colonization in nearby Algeria in the 1830s, and began a new imperial expansion after its defeat by Prussia in 1871.

18  Hugh Tinker, *A New System of Slavery: The Export of Indian Labour Overseas, 1830–1920* (London: Oxford University Press, 1974); David Northrup, *Indentured Labor in the Age of Imperialism, 1834–1922* (Cambridge: Cambridge University Press, 1995); Kay Saunders, ed., *Indentured Labour in the British Empire, 1834–1920* (London: Croom Helm, 1984).

19  Kenneth McPherson, Frank Broeze, Joan Wardrop, and Peter Reeves, "The Social Expansion of the Maritime World of the Indian Ocean: Passenger Traffic and Community Building, 1815–1939," in *Maritime Aspects of Migration*, ed. Klaus Friedland (Cologne: Böhlau, 1989), 427–440. The numerous studies on specific regions of destination include: Surendra Bhana, ed., *Essays on Indentured Indians in Natal* (Leeds: Peepal Tree Press, 1990); Uttama Bissoondoyal and S. B. C. Servansing, eds., *Indian Labour Immigration* (Moka, Mauritius: Mahatma Gandhi Institute, 1986); Marina Carter, *Voices from Indenture: Experiences of Indian Migrants in the British Empire* (Leicester: Leicester University Press, 1997); Adam McKeown, *Chinese Migrant Networks and Cultural Change: Peru, Chicago, Hawaii, 1900–1936* (Chicago: University of Chicago Press, 2001).

20  Dirk Hoerder, *Cultures in Contact: World Migrations in the Second Millennium* (Durham, NC: Duke University Press, 2002), 199–200, 211–215.

21  For a summary of the literature, see ibid., 191–199, 200–210, 216–227. For the postcolonial period, the best summary appears in José C. Moya, "A Continent of Immigrants: Postcolonial Shifts in the Western Hemisphere," *Hispanic American Historical Review* 86, no. 1 (2006): 1–28.

22  Mark Wyman, *Round-Trip to America: The Immigrants Return to Europe, 1880–1930* (Ithaca, NY: Cornell University Press, 1993).

23  Dirk Hoerder and Nora Faires, eds., *Migrants and Migration in Modern North America: Cross-Border Lives, Labor Markets, and Politics in Canada, the Caribbean, Mexico, and the United States* (Durham, NC: Duke University Press, 2011), esp. chaps. 2, 4, 6, 8, 10.

24  Case studies of migration internal to the United States include: Thomas Dublin, *Women at Work: The Transformation of Work and Community in Lowell, Mass., 1826–1860* (New York: Columbia University Press, 1979); Joe W. Trotter Jr., ed., *The Great Migration in Historical Perspective: New Dimensions of Race, Class, and Gender* (Bloomington: Indiana University Press, 1991). The flight of white sharecroppers from Depression and dustbowl conditions has been documented by the photographers of the US Farm Security Administration and is the theme of John Steinbeck's *Grapes of Wrath* (1939).

25  Hoerder, *Cultures in Contact*, 357–361.

26  Donald W. Treadgold, *The Great Siberian Migration: Government and Peasant in Resettlement from Emancipation to the First World War* (Princeton, NJ: Princeton University Press, 1957); Michael Khodarkovsky, *Russia's Steppe Frontier: The Making of a Colonial Empire, 1500–1800* (Bloomington: Indiana University Press, 2002); Andrew A. Gentes, *Exile to Siberia, 1590–1822* (New York: Palgrave Macmillan, 2008).

27  James H. Bater, *St. Petersburg: Industrialization and Change* (London: Arnold, 1976); Barbara A. Anderson, *Internal Migration during Modernization in Late Nineteenth-Century Russia* (Princeton, NJ: Princeton University Press, 1980); Inge Blank, "A Vast Migratory Experience: Eastern Europe in the Pre- and Post-Emancipation Era (1780–1914)," in *Roots of the Transplanted,* ed. Dirk Hoerder et al., 2 vols. (New York: Columbia University Press, 1994), 1:201–251.

28  Ben Eklof and Stephen P. Frank, eds., *The World of the Russian Peasant: Post-Emancipation Culture and Society* (Boston: Unwin Hyman, 1990).

## 2. THE GLOBAL AND THE LOCAL

1  The theoretical and methodological approaches to migration are summarized in Christiane Harzig and Dirk Hoerder, with Donna Gabaccia, *What Is Migration History?* (Cambridge: Polity, 2009). See also Caroline B. Brettell and James F. Hollifield, eds., *Migration Theory: Talking across Disciplines* (London: Routledge, 1999); Jan Lucassen and Leo Lucassen, eds., *Migration, Migration History, History: Old Paradigms and New Perspectives* (Frankfurt am Main: Lang, 1997; rev. ed. 2005). Migrant insertion and acculturation from a sociological perspective are best summarized in Wsevolod W. Isajiw, *Understanding Diversity: Ethnicity and Race in the Canadian Context* (Toronto: Thompson, 1999). The Canadian case can be transposed to other societies.

2  Arjun Appadurai, "Global Ethnoscapes: Notes and Queries for a Transnational Anthropology," in *Recapturing Anthropology: Working in the Present,* ed. Richard Fox (Santa Fe, NM: School of American Research Press, 1991), 191–210; Allen F. Roberts, "La 'Géographie Processuelle': Un nouveau paradigme pour les aires culturelles," *Lendemains* 31, nos. 122–123 (2006): 41–61. See, in general, Henri Lefebvre, *The Production of Space,* trans. Donald Nicolson-Smith (French orig., 1974; Oxford: Blackwell, 1991).

3  Adam M. McKeown, "Global Migration, 1846–1940," *Journal of World History* 15, no. 2 (2005); and José Moya and Adam McKeown, "World Migration in the Long Twentieth Century," in *Essays on Twentieth-Century History,* ed. Michael Adas (Philadelphia: Temple University Press, 2010).

4  The regional approach is developed in Sylvia Hahn, *Migration–Arbeit–Geschlecht: Arbeitsmigration in Mitteleuropa vom 17. bis zum Beginn des 20. Jahrhunderts* (Göttingen: V&R Unipress, 2008), 18, 32–33, 157–244; and by Lynn Pan, *Sons of the Yellow Emperor: The Story of the Overseas Chinese* (London: Secker and Warburg, 1990), esp. 3–22; as well as many others.

5  Dirk Hoerder, *"To Know Our Many Selves": From the Study of Canada to Canadian Studies* (Edmonton: Athabasca University Press, 2010), 260–390; and Hoerder, "Transnational–Transregional–Translocal: Transcultural," in *Handbook of Research Methods in Migration,* ed. Carlos Vargas-Silva (Cheltenham, UK: Edward Elgar, 2012), 69–91.

6  Harzig et al., *What Is Migration History?,* 66–69.

7  Dirk Hoerder, "From Migrants to Ethnics: Acculturation in a Societal Framework," in *European Migrants: Global and Local Perspectives,* ed. Dirk Hoerder and Leslie P. Moch (Boston: Northeastern University Press, 1996), 211–262.

8  Pierre Bourdieu, *Questions de sociologie* (Paris: Éditions de Minuit, 1980); Raymond Williams, *Culture and Society, 1780–1950* (London: Chatto and Windus, 1958).

9  James H. Jackson Jr. and Leslie Page Moch, "Migration and the Social History of Modern Europe," *Historical Methods* 22 (1989): 27–36, reprinted in Hoerder and Moch, *European Migrants,* 52–69; Harzig et al., *What Is Migration History?,* 87–114. See also Ewa Morawska and Michael Bommes, eds., *International Migration Research: Constructions, Omissions, and Promises of Interdisciplinarity* (Aldershot: Ashgate, 2005).

10 Raymond Breton, "Institutional Completeness of Ethnic Communities and Personal Relations of Immigrants," *American Journal of Sociology* 70 (September 1964): 193–205; John Goldlust and Anthony H. Richmond, "A Multivariate Model of Immigrant Adaptation," *International Migration Review* 8 (1974): 193–225.

11 Robin Cohen, *Global Diasporas: An Introduction* (Seattle: University of Washington Press, 1997); Khachig Tölölyan, "Rethinking *Diaspora(s):* Stateless Power in the Transnational Moment," *Diaspora* 5, no. 1 (1996): 9–36.

12 Michael R. Marrus, *The Unwanted: European Refugees in the Twentieth Century* (Oxford: Oxford University Press 1985), quotation at 51.

13 See, in general, Ernest Gellner, *Nations and Nationalism* (Oxford: Blackwell, 1983); Anthony D. Smith, *National Identity* (Reno: University of Nevada Press, 1991); and Smith, *Myths and Memories of the Nation* (Oxford: Oxford University Press, 1999).

14 Donna R. Gabaccia, "The 'Yellow Peril' and the 'Chinese of Europe': Global Perspectives on Race and Labor, 1815–1930," in Lucassen and Lucassen, *Migration, Migration History,* 177–196.

15 Ann L. Stoler, "Making Empire Respectable: The Politics of Race and Sexual Morality in 20th-Century Colonial Cultures," *American Ethnologist* 16 (1989): 634–660; Frederick Cooper and Ann L. Stoler, eds., *Tensions of Empire: Colonial Cultures in a Bourgeois World* (Berkeley: University of California Press, 1997); Anne McClintock, *Imperial Leather: Race, Gender and Sexuality in the Colonial Context* (New York: Routledge, 1995); Margaret Strobel, *Gender, Sex, and Empire* (Washington, DC: American Historical Association, 1993); Mary Louise Pratt, *Imperial Eyes: Travel Writing and Transculturation* (London: Routledge, 1992).

16 Mrinalini Sinha, *Colonial Masculinity: The "Manly Englishman" and the "Effeminate Bengali" in the Nineteenth Century* (Manchester: Manchester University Press, 1995).

17 See, for more detail, Dirk Hoerder, *Cultures in Contact: World Migrations in the Second Millennium* (Durham, NC: Duke University Press, 2002), chap. 16 and references.

18 Talal Asad, ed., *Anthropology and the Colonial Encounter* (New York: Humanities Press, 1973); Peter Pels, "The Anthropology of Colonialism: Culture, History, and the Emergence of Western Governmentality," *Annual Review of Anthropology* 26 (1997): 163–183; Sylvia Van Kirk, *"Many Tender Ties": Women in Fur Trade Society in Western Canada, 1670–1870* (Winnipeg: Watson, 1980).

## 3. MIGRATIONS, FREE AND BOUND

1 Carey McWilliams, *Factories in the Field: The Story of Migratory Farm Labor in California* (Boston: Little, Brown, 1935); Eric R. Wolf, *Europe and the People without History* (Berkeley: University of California Press, 1982).

2 Isabelle Vagnoux, *Les États-Unis et le Mexique* (Paris: L'Harmattan, 2003); Steven C. Topik, "When Mexico Had the Blues: A Transatlantic Tale of Bonds, Bankers, and Nationalists, 1862–1910," *American Historical Review* 105 (2000): 714–738.

3 José C. Moya, "A Continent of Immigrants: Postcolonial Shifts in the Western Hemisphere," *Hispanic American Historical Review* 86, no. 1 (2006); Donald Denoon, *Settler Capitalism: The Dynamics of Dependent Development in the Southern Hemisphere* (Oxford: Oxford University Press, 1983). "Dependency theory" developed as analysis of Latin American economies in relation to more

powerful economic actors in the Northern Hemisphere. André Gunder Frank, *Capitalism and Underdevelopment in Latin America* (New York: Monthly Review Press, 1969); Ian Roxborough, *Theories of Underdevelopment* (London: Macmillan, 1979); Ronald H. Chilcote, ed., *Dependency and Marxism: Toward a Resolution of the Debate* (Boulder, CO: Westview Press, 1982).

4 Thomas R. Gottschang and Diana Lary, *Swallows and Settlers: The Great Migration from North China to Manchuria* (Ann Arbor: University of Michigan Press, 2000); Isaiah Bowman, *The Pioneer Fringe* (New York: American Geographical Society, 1931); W. L. G. Joerg, ed., *Pioneer Settlement: Cooperative Studies by Twenty-Six Authors* (New York: American Geographical Society, 1932); David Wolff, *To the Harbin Station: The Liberal Alternative to Russian Manchuria, 1898–1914* (Stanford, CA: Stanford University Press, 1999); James H. Carter, *Creating a Chinese Harbin: Nationalism in an International City, 1916–1932* (Ithaca, NY: Cornell University Press, 2002).

5 Wilbur Zelinsky, "The Hypothesis of the Mobility Transition," *Geographical Review* 61 (1971): 219–249; Jan Lucassen and Leo Lucassen, "The Mobility Transition Revisited, 1500–1900: What the Case of Europe Can offer to Global History," *Journal of Global History* 4 (2009): 347–377; José Moya and Adam McKeown, "World Migration in the Long Twentieth Century," in *Essays on Twentieth-Century History*, ed. Michael Adas (Philadelphia: Temple University Press, 2010).

6 Brinley Thomas, *Migration and Economic Growth: A Study of Great Britain and the Atlantic Economy* (Cambridge: Cambridge University Press, 1954); Dirk Hoerder, ed., *Labor Migration in the Atlantic Economies: The European and North American Working Classes during the Period of Industrialization* (Westport, CT: Greenwood Press, 1985).

7 *The Cambridge Economic History of Europe from the Decline of the Roman Empire*, ed. Michael M. Postan and John Habakkuk (Cambridge: Cambridge University Press, 1941–1969), and its second edition, edited by John H. Clapham and Eileen Power (from 1966), still emphasized the continuity from agriculture to textile and thus included family labor, in particular women's sphere. With the turn to industrialization, for which Eric J. Hobsbawm's classic *Industry and Empire* (London: Weidenfeld and Nicolson, 1968) stands as a core text, the steel industry came to be viewed as a lead industry and women's labor got lost. Hobsbawm, *Labouring Men: Studies in the History of Labour* (London: Weidenfeld and Nicolson, 1964). Parallel, Walt Rostow, *The Stages of Economic Growth: A Non-Communist Manifesto* (New York: Cambridge University

Press, 1960), added another evolutionary approach. Throughout the period of industrialization and to the present, more men and women have been employed in textile and food production than in "heavy" industry. Sven Beckert, *The Empire of Cotton: A Global History* (New York: Knopf, forthcoming), chap. 9. See also "A Global History of Textile Workers, 1650–2000," International Institute of Social History, Amsterdam, November 2004, coordinators Lex Heerma van Voss, Els Hiemstra, and Elise van Nederveen Meerkerk, unpublished "Preliminary Papers."

8 Peter Kriedte, *Peasants, Landlords and Merchant Capitalists: Europe and the World Economy, 1500–1800*, trans. V. R. Berghahn (German orig. 1980; Cambridge: Cambridge University Press, 1983); Peter Kriedte, Hans Medick, and Jürgen Schlumbohm, *Industrialization before Industrialization: Rural Industry in the Genesis of Capitalism* (Cambridge: Cambridge University Press, 1981); Sheilagh C. Ogilvie and Markus Cerman, eds., *European Proto-Industrialization: An Introductory Handbook* (Cambridge: Cambridge University Press, 1996).

9 Gianfausto Rosoli, ed., *Un Secolo di Emigrazione Italiana, 1876–1976* (Rome: Centro studi emigrazione, 1980); and Rosoli, "Italian Migration to European Countries from Political Unification to World War I," in Hoerder, *Labor Migration*, 95–116; Donna R. Gabaccia and Fraser Ottanelli, eds., *Italian Workers of the World: Labor, Migration and the Making of Multi-Ethnic States* (Urbana: University of Illinois Press, 2001); Donna R. Gabaccia and Franca Iacovetta, eds., *Women, Gender, and Transnational Lives: Italian Workers of the World* (Toronto: University of Toronto Press, 2002).

10 Peter Doeringer and Michael J. Piore, *Internal Labor Markets and Manpower Analysis* (Lexington, MA: Heath, 1971); Edna Bonacich, "A Theory of Ethnic Antagonism: The Split Labor Market," *American Sociological Review* 37 (1972): 547–559; F. C. Valkenburg and A. M. C. Vissers, "Segmentation of the Labour Market: The Theory of the Dual Labour Market—The Case of the Netherlands," *Netherlands Journal of Sociology* 16 (1980): 155–170; Randy Hodson and Robert L. Kaufmann, "Economic Dualism: A Critical Review," *American Sociological Review* 47 (1982): 727–739.

11 Hoerder, *Labor Migration*, 3–31.

12 Dirk Hoerder, *Cultures in Contact: World Migrations in the Second Millennium* (Durham, NC: Duke University Press, 2002), 332–334.

13 Heinz Fassmann, "Emigration, Immigration and Internal Migration in the Austro-Hungarian Monarchy, 1910," in *Roots of the Transplanted*, ed. Dirk Hoerder et al., 2 vols. (New York: Columbia University Press, 1994), 1:253–307;

Sylvia Hahn, *Migration-Arbeit-Geschlecht: Arbeitsmigration in Mitteleuropa vom 17. bis zum Beginn des 20. Jahrhunderts* (Göttingen: V&R Unipress, 2008).

14 Heinz Fassmann and Rainer Münz, *Einwanderungsland Österreich? Historische Migrationsmuster, aktuelle Trends und politische Maβnahmen* (Wien: Wissenschaft, Jugend und Volk, 1995); Monika Glettler, *Die Wiener Tschechen um 1900: Strukturanalyse einer nationalen Minderheit in der Groβstadt* (Munich: Oldenbourg, 1972); Michael John and Albert Lichtblau, *Schmelztiegel Wien einst und jetzt: Zur Geschichte und Gegenwart von Zuwanderung und Minderheiten,* 2nd ed. (Vienna: Böhlau, 1993).

15 Matthew Frye Jacobson, *Whiteness of a Different Color: European Immigrants and the Alchemy of Race* (Cambridge, MA: Harvard University Press, 1998); Cheryl I. Harris, "Whiteness as Property," *Harvard Law Review* 106 (1993): 1707–1791; "Whiteness and the Historians' Imagination," topical issue of *International Labor and Working-Class History* 60 (Fall 2001): 1–92. The imposition of whiteness was far more violent in other parts of the world. John W. Cell, *The Highest Stage of White Supremacy: The Origins of Segregation in South Africa and the American South* (Cambridge: Cambridge University Press, 1982); Ruth Frankenberg, *White Women, Race Matters: The Social Construction of Whiteness* (Minneapolis: University of Minnesota Press, 1993); George M. Fredrickson, *The Black Image in the White Mind: The Debate on Afro-American Character and Destiny, 1817–1914* (New York: Harper and Row, 1971). And in the US South: Johnpeter Horst Grill and Robert L. Jenkins, "The Nazis and the American South in the 1930s: A Mirror Image?," *Journal of Southern History* 58 (1992): 667–694; Grace E. Hale, *Making Whiteness: The Culture of Segregation in the South* (New York: Pantheon, 1998).

16 An overview is provided in Roger Daniels, *Coming to America: A History of Immigration and Ethnicity in American Life,* rev. ed. (New York: HarperCollins, 2002); and Ronald Takaki, *A Different Mirror: A History of Multicultural America* (Boston: Little, Brown, 1993). John Bodnar, *The Transplanted: A History of Immigrants in Urban America* (Bloomington: Indiana University Press, 1985), deals with the proletarian mass migration and counters the term *uprooted* migrants posited by Oscar Handlin in the early 1950s. James R. Barrett, "Americanization from the Bottom Up: Immigration and the Remaking of the Working Class in the United States, 1880–1930," *Journal of American History* 79 (1992): 997–1020.

17 Jean R. Burnet with Howard Palmer, *"Coming Canadians": An Introduction to a History of Canada's Peoples* (Toronto: McClelland and Stewart, 1988); Franca Iacovetta with Paula Draper and Robert Ventresca, eds., *A Nation of*

*Immigrants: Women, Workers, and Communities in Canadian History, 1840s–1960s* (Toronto: University of Toronto Press, 1998); Bruno Ramirez, *On the Move: French-Canadian and Italian Migrants in the North Atlantic Economy, 1860–1914* (Toronto: McClelland and Stewart, 1991); John J. Bukowczyk, Nora Faires, David Smith, and Randy William Widdis, *Permeable Border: The Great Lakes Basin as Transnational Region, 1650–1990* (Pittsburgh: University of Pittsburgh Press; Calgary: University of Calgary Press, 2005).

18 Moisés Gonzáles Navarro, *Los extranjeros en México y los mexicanos en el extranjero, 1821–1970,* 3 vols. (Mexico City: Colegio de México, 1993–1994); Dolores Pla, Guadelupe Zárate, Mónica Palma, Jorge Gómez, Rosario Cardiel, and Delia Salazar, *Extranjeros en México (1821–1990): Bibliografía* (Mexico City: INAH, 1994); Jaime R. Aguila and Brian Gratton, "Mirando atrás: Mexican Immigration from 2008 to 1876," and Delia Gonzàles de Reufels and Dirk Hoerder, "Migration to Mexico, Migration in Mexico: A Special Case on the North American Continent," both in *Migrants and Migration in Modern North America: Cross-Border Lives, Labor Markets, and Politics in Canada, the Caribbean, Mexico, and the United States,* ed. Dirk Hoerder and Nora Faires (Durham, NC: Duke University Press, 2011), 188–209.

19 Bonham C. Richardson, "Caribbean Migrations, 1838–1985," in *The Modern Caribbean,* ed. Franklin W. Knight and Colin A. Palmer (Chapel Hill: University of North Carolina Press, 1989), 203–228; Howard Johnson, ed., *After the Crossing: Immigrants and Minorities in Caribbean Creole Society* (London: Cass, 1988); Elizabeth Maclean Petras, *Jamaican Labor Migration: White Capital and Black Labor, 1850–1930* (Boulder, CO: Westview Press, 1988); Lara Putnam, "Undone by Desire: Migration, Sex across Boundaries, and Collective Destinies in the Greater Caribbean, 1840–1940," in Hoerder and Faires, *Migrants and Migration,* 99–126.

20 A comparative perspective on South and North America is provided by Walter Nugent, *Crossings: The Great Transatlantic Migrations, 1870–1914* (Bloomington: Indiana University Press, 1992).

21 Nancy P. Naro, "The Transition from Slavery to Migrant Labour in Rural Brazil," in *Unfree Labour in the Development of the Atlantic World,* ed. Paul E. Lovejoy and Nicholas Rogers (Ilford, UK: Cass, 1994), 183–196; Magnus Mörner, "Immigration into Latin America, Especially Argentina and Chile," in *European Expansion and Migration: Essays on the Intercontinential Migration from Africa, Asia, and Europe,* ed. Piet C. Emmer and Magnus Mörner (New York: Berg, 1992), 217–231; Mörner, *Adventurers and Proletarians: The Story of*

*Migrants in Latin America* (Pittsburgh: University of Pittsburgh Press, 1985); Elizabeth Kuznesof, "A History of Domestic Service in Spanish America, 1492–1980," in *Muchachas No More: Household Workers in Latin America and the Caribbean,* ed. Elsa M. Chaney and Mary Garcia Castro (Philadelphia: Temple University Press, 1989), 17–35.

22  José C. Moya, *Cousins and Strangers: Spanish Immigrants in Buenos Aires, 1850–1930* (Berkeley: University of California Press, 1997); Samuel Baily, *Immigrants in the Land of Promise: Italians in Buenos Aires and New York City, 1870–1914* (Ithaca, NY: Cornell University Press, 1999); Fernando J. Devoto and Gianfausto Rosoli, eds., *L'Italia nella società argentina* (Rome: Centro Studi Emigrazione, 1988).

23  Pierre-Michel Fontaine, ed., *Race, Class and Power in Brazil* (Los Angeles: Center for African-American Studies, University of California, 1985); Thomas H. Holloway, *Immigrants on the Land: Coffee and Society in São Paulo, 1886–1934* (Chapel Hill: University of North Carolina Press, 1980).

24  The first conceptualization of transculturation was Fernando Ortiz, "Del fenómeno de la transculturación y su importancia en Cuba," *Revista Bimestre Cubana* 27 (1940): 273–278 (numerous reprints and translations); of the reaction to Yankee self-elevation, José Vasconcelos, *Raza cósmica* (1925), bilingual edition *The Cosmic Race: La raza cósmica* (Baltimore: Johns Hopkins University Press, 1997). For one of many late twentieth-century contributions, see Néstor Garcia Canclini, *Culturas híbridas: Estrategias para entrar y salir de la modernidad* (Mexico, D.F.: Grijalbo, 1989); English translation: *Hybrid Cultures: Strategies for Entering and Leaving Modernity,* trans. Christopher L. Chiappari and Silvia L. López (Minneapolis: University of Minnesota Press, 1995).

25  Michael Mann, "Migration–Re-migration–Circulation: South Asian Kulis in the Indian Ocean and Beyond, 1840–1940," in *Connecting Seas and Connected Ocean Rims: Indian, Atlantic, and Pacific Oceans and China Seas Migrations from the 1830s to the 1930s,* ed. Donna Gabaccia and Dirk Hoerder (Leiden: Brill, 2011), 108–133; Moya and McKeown, "World Migration."

26  Samuel Truett and Elliott Young, eds., *Continental Crossroads: Remapping U.S.-Mexican Borderlands History* (Durham, NC: Duke University Press, 2003); Carlos G. Vélez-Ibáñez, *Border Visions: Mexican Cultures of the Southwest United States* (Tucson: University of Arizona Press, 1996); Daniel D. Arreola, ed., *Hispanic Spaces, Latino Places: Community and Cultural Diversity in Contemporary America* (Austin: University of Texas Press, 2004); Evelyn

Hu-DeHart, "Racism and Anti-Chinese Persecution in Mexico," *Amerasia Journal* 9, no. 2 (1982): 1–27.

27  Rita J. Simon and Caroline B. Brettell, *International Migration: The Female Experience* (Totowa, NJ: Rowman, 1986); M. D. North-Coombes, "Indentured Labour in the Sugar Industries of Natal and Mauritius, 1834–1910," in *Essays on Indentured Indians in Nepal*, ed. Surendra Bhana (Leeds: Peepal Tree Press, 1990), 12–88; Christiane Harzig, ed., *Peasant Maids, City Women: From the European Countryside to Urban America* (Ithaca, NY: Cornell University Press, 1997).

28  Hugh Tinker, *A New System of Slavery: The Export of Indian Labour Overseas, 1830–1920* (London: Oxford University Press, 1974); David Northrup, *Indentured Labor in the Age of Imperialism, 1834–1922* (Cambridge: Cambridge University Press, 1995); Moya and McKeown, "World Migration."

29  Brij V. Lal, Peter Reeves, and Rajesh Rai, eds., *The Encyclopedia of the Indian Diaspora* (Singapore: Millet, 2006); Crispin Bates, ed., *Community, Empire and Migration: South Asian Diaspora* (Basingstoke: Palgrave, 2001).

30  K. Hazareesingh, *History of Indians in Mauritius* (London: Macmillan, 1975); Uttama Bissoondoyal and S. B. C. Servansing, eds., *Indian Labour Immigration* (Moka, Mauritius: Mahatma Gandhi Institute, 1986); Marina Carter, "Strategies of Labour Mobilisation in Colonial India: The Recruitment of Indentured Workers for Mauritius," *Journal of Peasant Studies* 19, nos. 3–4 (1992): 229–245; Marina Carter, *Voices from Indenture: Experiences of Indian Migrants in the British Empire* (Leicester: Leicester University Press, 1997); Tinker, *New System of Slavery.*

31  Hilda Kuper, *Indian People in Natal* (Pietermaritzburg: University of Natal Press, 1960; repr. Westport, 1974); Bhana, *Indentured Indians in Natal.*

32  Bridglal Pachai, *The International Aspects of the South African Indian Question, 1860–1971* (Cape Town: Struik, 1971); Surendra Bhana and Joy B. Brain, *Setting Down Roots: Indian Migrants in South Africa, 1860–1911* (Johannesburg: Witwatersrand University Press, 1990); Patrick Harries, *Work, Culture, and Identity: Migrant Laborers in Mozambique and South Africa, c. 1860–1910* (Portsmouth, NH: Heinemann, 1994); Martin Legassick and Francine de Clerq, "Capitalism and Migrant Labour in Southern Africa: The Origins and Nature of the System," and Peter Richardson, "Coolies, Peasants, and Proletarians: The Origins of Chinese Indentured Labour in South Africa, 1904–1907," both in Shula Marks and Peter Richardson, eds., *International Labour Migration: Historical Perspectives* (Hounslow, UK: Temple Smith, 1984), 140–166, 167–185;

Melanie Yap and Dianne L. Man, *Colour, Confusion and Concessions: The History of the Chinese in South Africa* (Hong Kong: Hong Kong University Press, 1996).

33  Usha Mahajani, *The Role of Indian Minorities in Burma and Malaya* (Bombay: Vora, 1960; repr. Westport, CT: Greenwood Press, 1973); Michael Adas, *The Burma Delta: Economic Development and Social Change on an Asian Rice Frontier, 1852–1941* (Madison: University of Wisconsin Press, 1974); Amarjit Kaur, *Wage Labour in Southeast Asia since 1840: Globalisation, the International Division of Labour and Labour Transformations* (Basingstoke: Palgrave Macmillan, 2004).

34  Gabaccia and Hoerder, *Connecting Seas,* esp. essays in sections 1 and 2.

35  Kirti N. Chaudhuri, *Asia before Europe: Economy and Civilization of the Indian Ocean from the Rise of Islam to 1750* (Cambridge: Cambridge University Press, 1990); Milo Kearney, *The Indian Ocean in World History* (London: Routledge, 2003); G. Balachandran, "Circulation through Seafaring: Indian Seamen, 1890–1945," in *Society and Circulation: Mobile People and Itinerant Cultures in South Asia, 1750–1950,* ed. Claude Markovits, Jacques Pouchepadass, and Sanjay Subrahmanyam (Delhi: Permanent Black, 2003), 89–130; Sugata Bose, *A Hundred Horizons: The Indian Ocean in the Age of Global Empire* (Cambridge, MA: Harvard University Press, 2006); Thomas R. Metcalf, *Imperial Connections: India in the Indian Ocean Arena, 1860–1920* (Berkeley: University of California Press, 2007).

36  Jagdish S. Gundara, "Fragments of Indian Society in Zanzibar: Conflict and Change in the 19th Century," *Africa Quarterly* 21, nos. 2–4 (1981): 23–40; Michael Twaddle, "East African Asians through a Hundred Years," in *South Asians Overseas: Migration and Ethnicity,* ed. Colin Clarke, Ceri Peach, and Steven Vertovec (Cambridge: Cambridge University Press, 1990), 149–163.

37  Ranajit Das Gupta, "Plantation Labour in Colonial India," *Journal of Peasant Studies* 19, nos. 3–4 (1992): 173–198.

38  Hoerder, *Cultures in Contact,* 380–383.

39  Kaur, *Wage Labour,* 3–58.

40  Ramon H. Myers and Mark R. Peattie, eds., *The Japanese Colonial Empire, 1895–1945* (Princeton, NJ: Princeton University Press, 1984); Edward R. Beauchamp and Akira Iriye, eds., *Foreign Employees in Nineteenth-Century Japan* (Boulder, CO: Westview Press, 1990); Irene B. Taeuber, *The Population of Japan* (Princeton, NJ: Princeton University Press, 1958), 173–190; Keizo Yamawaki, "Foreign Workers in Japan: A Historical Perspective," in *Japan and Global*

*Migration: Foreign Workers and the Advent of a Multicultural Society,* ed. Michael Douglass and Glenda S. Roberts (New York: Routledge, 2000), 38–51.

41  Clarence E. Glick, *Sojourners and Settlers: Chinese Migrants in Hawaii* (Honolulu: University of Hawai'i Press, 1980); John M. Liu, "Race, Ethnicity, and the Sugar Plantation System: Asian Labor in Hawaii, 1850 to 1900," in *Labor Migration under Capitalism: Asian Workers in the United States before World War II,* ed. Lucie Cheng and Edna Bonacich (Berkeley: University of California Press, 1984), 186–209; Ronald Takaki, *Pau Hana: Plantation Life and Labor in Hawaii, 1835–1920* (Honolulu: University of Hawai'i Press, 1983).

42  Walton L. Lai, *Indentured Labor, Caribbean Sugar: Chinese and Indian Migrants to the British West Indies* (Baltimore: Johns Hopkins University Press, 1993), 1–18; Keith O. Laurence, *Immigration into the West Indies in the 19th Century* (Barbados: Caribbean Universities Press, 1971).

43  Evelyn Hu-DeHart, "Latin America in Asia-Pacific Perspective," in *What Is in a Rim? Critical Perspectives on the Pacific Region Idea,* 2nd ed., ed. Arif Dirlik (Lanham, MD: Rowman and Littlefield, 1998), 251–282; Hu-DeHart, "Coolies, Shopkeepers, Pioneers: The Chinese of Mexico and Peru, 1849–1930," *Amerasia Journal* 15, no. 2 (1989): 91–116; Adam McKeown, *Chinese Migrant Networks and Cultural Change: Peru, Chicago, Hawaii, 1900–1936* (Chicago: University of Chicago Press, 2001).

44  Cheng and Bonacich, *Labor Migration under Capitalism;* Erika Lee, *At America's Gates: Chinese Immigration during the Exclusion Era, 1882–1943* (Chapel Hill: University of North Carolina Press, 2003); Peter S. Li, *The Chinese in Canada,* 2nd ed. (Toronto: Oxford University Press, 1998).

45  Ping-ti Ho, *Studies on the Population of China, 1368–1953* (Cambridge, MA: Harvard University Press, 1959), 153–158; Gottschang and Lary, *Swallows and Settlers.*

46  Hoerder, *Cultures in Contact,* 369–373; Jonathan D. Spence, *The Search for Modern China* (New York: Norton, 1990), 117–268; Michael R. Godley, "China's Policy towards Migrants, 1842–1949," in *Asians in Australia: The Dynamics of Migration and Settlement,* ed. Christine Inglis et al. (Singapore: Institute of Southeast Asian Studies, 1992), 1–21; Ching-huang Yen, *Coolies and Mandarins: China's Protection of Overseas Chinese during the Late Ch'ing Period (1851–1911)* (Singapore: Singapore University Press, 1985), 32–36; Yen, "Ch'ing Changing Images of Overseas Chinese," *Modern Asian Studies* 15 (1981): 261–285.

47  Andreas Kappeler, *The Russian Empire: A Multiethnic History* (London: Longman Pearson, 2001); Donald W. Treadgold, *The Great Siberian Migration: Government and Peasant in Resettlement from Emancipation to the First World War*

(Princeton, NJ: Princeton University Press, 1957); Daniel R. Brower and Edward J. Lazzerini, eds., *Russia's Orient: Imperial Borderlands and Peoples, 1700– 1917* (Bloomington: Indiana University Press, 1997); Inge Blank, "A Vast Migratory Experience: Eastern Europe in the Pre- and Post-Emancipation Era (1780–1914)," in Hoerder, *Roots of the Transplanted.*

48  Barbara A. Anderson, *Internal Migration during Modernization in Late Nineteenth-Century Russia* (Princeton, NJ: Princeton University Press, 1980); Ben Eklof and Stephen P. Frank, eds., *The World of the Russian Peasant: Post-Emancipation Culture and Society* (Boston: Unwin Hyman, 1990); Robert E. Johnson, *Peasant and Proletarian: The Working Class of Moscow in the Late Nineteenth Century* (New Brunswick, NJ: Rutgers University Press, 1979); Jeffrey Burds, *Peasant Dreams and Market Politics: Labor Migration and the Russian Village* (Pittsburgh: University of Pittsburgh Press, 1998); Lewis H. Siegelbaum, "The Odessa Grain Trade: A Case Study in Urban Growth and Development in Tsarist Russia," *Journal of European Economic History* 9, no. 1 (Spring 1980): 113–151.

49  Nancy L. Green, ed., *Jewish Workers in the Modern Diaspora* (Berkeley: University of California Press, 1998); Jack Wertheimer, *Unwelcome Strangers: European Jews in Imperial Germany* (Oxford: Oxford University Press, 1987); Irving Howe, *The World of Our Fathers* (New York: Simon and Schuster, 1976); Susan A. Glenn, *Daughters of the Shtetl: Life and Labor in the Immigrant Generation* (Ithaca, NY: Cornell University Press, 1990); Hasia R. Diner, *The Jews of the United States, 1654–2000* (Berkeley: University of California Press, 2004); Elena Shulman, *Stalinism on the Frontier of the Empire: Women and State Formation in the Soviet Far East* (Cambridge: Cambridge University Press, 2008).

50  Ahmet İçduygu and Kemal Kirişçi, eds., *Land of Diverse Migrations: Challenges of Emigration and Immigrations in Turkey* (Istanbul: MiReKoc, 2008); Reşat Kasaba, *A Moveable Empire: Ottoman Nomads, Migrants, and Refugees* (Seattle: University of Washington Press, 2009).

51  John D. Ruedy, *Modern Algeria: The Origins and Development of a Nation* (Bloomington: Indiana University Press, 1992), 22–29; Neil MacMaster, "Labour Migration in French North Africa," in *The Cambridge Survey of World Migration,* ed. Robin Cohen (Cambridge: Cambridge University Press, 1995), 190–195; Michael J. Heffernan, "The Parisian Poor and the Colonization of Algeria during the Second Empire," *French History* 3 (1989): 377–403; Michael J. Heffernan and Keith Sutton, "The Landscape of Colonialism: The Impact of French Colonial Rule in the Algerian Rural Settlement Pattern, 1830–1987," in *Colonialism and Development in the Contemporary World,* ed. Chris Dixon and Michael J. Heffernan (London: Mansell, 1991), 121–152.

52 Alan Jeeves, *Migrant Labour in South Africa's Mining Economy: The Struggle for the Gold Mines' Labor Supply, 1890–1920* (Montreal: McGill-Queen's University Press, 1985); Jonathan Crush, Alan Jeeves, and David Yudelman, *South Africa's Labor Empire: A History of Black Migrancy to the Gold Mines* (Boulder, CO: Westview Press, 1991); Patrick Harries, *Work, Culture, and Identity: Migrant Laborers in Mozambique and South Africa, c. 1860–1910* (Portsmouth, NH: Heinemann, 1994).

53 Babacar Fall, *Le travail forcé en Afrique Occidentale française (1900–1945)* (Paris: Karthala, 1993); Sheldon Gellar, *Structural Changes and Colonial Dependence: Senegal, 1885–1945* (Beverly Hills: Sage, 1976), 36–48; Martin A. Klein, *Slavery and Colonial Rule in French West Africa* (Cambridge: Cambridge University Press, 1998); Sharon B. Stichter, *Migrant Labour in Kenya: Capitalism and African Response, 1895–1975* (Harlow, UK: Longman, 1982); François Manchuelle, *Willing Migrants: Soninke Labor Diasporas, 1848–1960* (Athens: Ohio University Press, 1997).

54 Edward W. Saïd, *Orientalism* (London: Henley, Routledge, and Kegan Paul, 1978).

55 Hoerder, *Cultures in Contact*, 419–442; Mrinalini Sinha, *Colonial Masculinity: The "Manly Englishman" and the "Effeminate Bengali" in the Nineteenth Century* (Manchester: Manchester University Press, 1995); Waltraud Ernst, *Mad Tales from the Raj: The European Insane in British India, 1800–1858* (London: Routledge, 1991); Catherine Hall, *White, Male, and Middle Class: Explorations in Feminism and History* (London: Routledge, 1991); Dirk Hoerder, *Creating Societies: Immigrant Lives in Canada* (Montreal: McGill-Queen's University Press, 1999), chap. 16; Antoinette Burton, *At the Heart of the Empire: Indians and the Colonial Encounter in Late Victorian Britain* (Berkeley: University of California Press, 1998); Frederick Cooper and Ann Laura Stoler, eds., *Tensions of Empire: Colonial Cultures in a Bourgeois World* (Berkeley: University of California Press, 1997); Ann L. Stoler, "Making Empire Respectable: The Politics of Race and Sexual Morality in 20th-Century Colonial Cultures," *American Ethnologist* 16 (1989): 634–660; Strobel, *Gender, Sex, and Empire* (Washington, DC: American Historical Association, 1993); Nupur Chaudhuri and Margaret Strobel, eds., *Western Women and Imperialism: Complicity and Resistance* (Bloomington: Indiana University Press, 1992); Linda Bryder, "Sex, Race, and Colonialism: An Historiographic Review," *International History Review* 20 (1998): 806–822.

## 4. MIGRATIONS DURING WAR AND DEPRESSION

1 The League of Nations, under Fridtjof Nansen, established the International Office for Refugees.

2 Isaiah Bowman, *The Pioneer Fringe* (New York: American Geographical Society, 1931), v–vii, quotation at 200; W. L. G. Joerg, ed., *Pioneer Settlement: Cooperative Studies by Twenty-Six Authors* (New York: American Geographical Society, 1932), quotation at 362–363. These studies had a French equivalent in the proceedings of the *Congrès de la Colonisation Rurale, Alger, 26–29 mai 1930*, 4 vols. (Algiers: V. Heintz, 1931). Vol. 4, *La colonisation rurale dans les principaux pays de peuplement,* provided a comparative perspective.

3 Sean Callahan, ed., *The Photographs of Margaret Bourke-White* (New York: Bonanza, 1972), 69–89; Christine Hoffmeister, *Heinrich Vogeler: Die Komplexbilder* (Worpswede: Worpsweder Verlag, 1980); Otto Heller, *Sibirien: Ein anderes Amerika* (Berlin: Neuer Deutscher Verlag, 1930); Fridtjof Nansen, *Sibirien, ein Zukunftsland* (Leipzig: Brockhaus, 1914).

4 A concise discussion of the nation-to-refugee-generation continuum is provided by Michael R. Marrus, *The Unwanted: European Refugees in the Twentieth Century* (Oxford: Oxford University Press, 1985), 9–60; Robin Cohen, "Shaping the Nation, Excluding the Other: The Deportation of Migrants from Britain," in *Migration, Migration History, History: Old Paradigms and New Perspectives,* ed. Jan Lucassen and Leo Lucassen (Frankfurt am Main: Lang, 1997; rev. ed., 2005), 351–373; Andrew Bell-Fialkoff, *Ethnic Cleansing* (New York: St. Martin's Press, 1996), 7–49.

5 Klaus J. Bade, Pieter C. Emmer, Leo Lucassen, and Jochen Oltmer, eds., *Encyclopedia of Migration and Minorities in Europe: From the Seventeenth Century to the Present* (Cambridge: Cambridge University Press, 2011), xxv–xxxix.

6 William Cunningham, *Alien Immigrants to England* (London: Swann Sonnenschein, 1897), provided a solitary call to appreciate the economic contributions of migrants. A thoughtful discussion of alienation is Georg Simmel, "The Stranger," in *The Sociology of Georg Simmel,* trans. Kurt Wolff (New York: Macmillan, 1950), 402–408. Other renowned scholars joined the anti-immigrant campaigns: Max Weber considered Poles inferior, demographer Friedrich Burgdörfer advocated deportation of non-German peoples, George Mauco in *Les étrangers en France* (1932) equated Frenchness with natural superiority and was a population planner both under the Fascist Vichy regime and in the French Republic of the 1950s. Bernard Gainer, *The Alien Invasion: The Origins of the Alien Act of 1905* (London: Heinemann, 1972).

7  Gérard Chaliand and Yves Ternon, *Le Génocide des Arméniens* (Brussels: Éditions Complexe, 1980).

8  Fikret Adanir and Hilmar Kaiser, "Migration, Deportation, and Nation-Building: The Case of the Ottoman Empire," in *Migrations and Migrants in Historical Perspective: Permanencies and Innovations,* ed. René Leboutte (Brussels: Centre for Migration Law of the University of Nijmegen, 2000), 373–393; Daniela Bobeva, "Emigration from and Immigration to Bulgaria," in *European Migration in the Late Twentieth Century: Historical Patterns, Actual Trends, and Social Implications,* ed. Heinz Fassmann and Rainer Münz (Aldershot, UK: Elgar, 1994), 221–237; Joseph B. Schechtman, *The Refugee in the World: Displacement and Integration* (New York: Barnes, 1963), 54–67; André Wurfbain, *L'Échange greco-bulgare des minorités ethniques* (Lausanne: Payot, 1930); Stephen P. Ladas, *The Exchange of Minorities: Bulgaria, Greece and Turkey* (New York: Macmillan, 1932); Charles B. Eddy, *Greece and the Greek Refugees* (London: Allen and Unwin, 1931); Ludger Kühnhardt, *Die Flüchtlingsfrage als Weltordnungsproblem: Massenzwangswanderungen in Geschichte und Politik* (Vienna: Braumüller, 1984).

9  Ramon H. Myers and Mark R. Peattie, eds., *The Japanese Colonial Empire, 1895–1945* (Princeton, NJ: Princeton University Press, 1984); Chih-ming Ka, *Japanese Colonialism in Taiwan: Land Tenure, Development, and Dependency, 1895–1945* (Boulder, CO: Westview Press, 1995); Andrew C. Nahm, ed., *Korea under Japanese Colonial Rule: Studies of the Policy and Techniques of Japanese Colonialism* (Kalamazoo, MI: Center for Korean Studies, Western Michigan University, 1973), 261–269; Irene B. Taeuber, *The Population of Japan* (Princeton, NJ: Princeton University Press, 1958), 123–170, 198–203; International Labour Office, *Industrial Labour in Japan* (Geneva: ILO, 1933).

10  Fritz Fischer, *Griff nach der Weltmacht: Die Kriegszielpolitik des kaiserlichen Deutschland 1914/18* (Düsseldorf: Droste, 1961), 128–133, 310–321, 601; David Stevenson, *1914–1918: The History of the First World War* (London: Allen Lane, 2004), 3–43; Babacar Fall, *Le travail forcé en Afrique Occidentale française (1900–1945)* (Paris: Karthala, 1993), 126–145.

11  Peter Gatrell, *A Whole Empire Walking: Refugees in Russia during World War I* (Bloomington: Indiana University Press, 1999).

12  See Dirk Hoerder, *Cultures in Contact: World Migrations in the Second Millennium* (Durham, NC: Duke University Press, 2002), chap. 17, sec. 1; Eugene M. Kulischer, *Europe on the Move: War and Population Changes, 1917–1947* (New York: Columbia University Press, 1948), 64–128.

13  *Statistik des Deutschen Reichs,* vol. 401 (Berlin, 1930), 412–423, 491–492, 623–640; Marrus, *The Unwanted,* 52–61.

14  Kulischer, *Europe on the Move,* 64–88, 99–128.

15  Frank Caestaecker and Bob Moore, eds., *Refugees from Nazi Germany and the Liberal European States* (New York: Berghahn, 2010); Dariusz Stola, "Forced Migrations in Central European History," *International Migration Review* 26 (1992): 324–341.

16  Kulischer, *Europe on the Move,* 206–225 (Italy), 227–239 (Spain); Walter Wilson, *Forced Labor in the United States* (New York: International, 1933), 28–83, passim; Pete Daniel, *The Shadow of Slavery: Peonage in the South, 1901–1969* (Urbana: University of Illinois Press, 1972), 21, passim; Donald H. Avery, *Reluctant Host: Canada's Response to Immigrant Workers, 1896–1994* (Toronto: McClelland and Stewart, 1995), chaps. 4–5.

17  Marcel van der Linden, "Forced Labour and Non-Capitalist Industrialization: The Case of Stalinism (ca. 1929–ca.1956)," in *Free and Unfree Labour,* ed. Tom Brass et al. (Amsterdam: IISG, 1993), 19–30; Brass and van der Linden, eds., *Free and Unfree Labour: The Debate Continues* (Bern: Lang, 1997); Lewis H. Siegelbaum and Ronald G. Suny, eds., *Making Workers Soviet: Power, Class, and Identity* (Ithaca, NY: Cornell University Press, 1994), 1–26; Kulischer, *Europe on the Move,* 88–93; Robert A. Lewis and Richard H. Rowland, *Population Redistribution in the USSR: Its Impact on Society, 1897–1977* (New York: Praeger, 1979), 158–198; Andrea Graziosi, "Foreign Workers in Soviet Russia, 1920–1940: Their Experience and Their Legacy," *International Labor and Working-Class History* 33 (1988): 38–59; Edwin Bacon, " 'Glasnost' and the Gulag: New Information on Soviet Forced Labour around World War II," *Soviet Studies* 44 (1992): 1069–1086. Numerous memoirs of internees and forced laborers have been published.

18  Ulrich Herbert, *A History of Foreign Labor in Germany, 1880–1980* (German orig., 1986; Ann Arbor: University of Michigan Press, 1990), 9–119; Lothar Elsner and Joachim Lehmann, *Ausländische Arbeiter unter dem deutschen Imperialismus, 1900–1985* (Berlin: Dietz, 1988).

19  Louise Young, *Japan's Total Empire: Manchuria and the Culture of Wartime Imperialism* (Berkeley: University of California Press, 1998), 307–411; Joseph B. Schechtman, *Population Transfers in Asia* (New York: Hallsby Press, 1949); Taeuber, *The Population of Japan,* 173–190; Narihiko Ito, "Eine Skizze über Kolonialherrschaft, Invasionskrieg und Arbeiterbewegung unter dem japanischen Imperialismus," in *Internationale Tagung der Historiker der Arbeiterbewegung,*

ed. Hans Hautmann (Vienna: ITH, 1989), 436–441; Ehud Harari, *The Politics of Labor Legislation in Japan: National-International Interaction* (Berkeley: University of California Press, 1973), 10–50; Andrew Gordon, *Labor and Imperial Democracy in Prewar Japan* (Berkeley: University of California Press, 1991), 302–342; Ramon H. Myers, *The Japanese Economic Development of Manchuria, 1932 to 1945* (New York: Garland, 1982), 158–200; George Hicks, *The Comfort Women: Sex Slaves of the Japanese Imperial Forces* (Sydney: Allen and Unwin, 1995); Ustinia Dolgopol and Snehal Paranjape, *Comfort Women: An Unfinished Ordeal—Report of a Mission* (Geneva: International Commission of Jurists, 1994).

20  Bill Freund, *The African Worker* (Cambridge: Cambridge University Press, 1988), 40; Freund, *Capital and Labour in the Nigerian Tin Mines* (London: Longman, 1981), 82–84; Amarjit Kaur, *Wage Labour in Southeast Asia since 1840: Globalisation, the International Division of Labour and Labour Transformations* (Basingstoke: Palgrave Macmillan, 2004), 68, 106, passim.

21  Diana Lary and Stephen R. MacKinnon, *Scars of War: The Impact of Warfare on Modern China* (Vancouver: University of British Columbia Press, 2001); MacKinnon, *Wuhan, 1938: War, Refugees, and the Making of Modern China* (Berkeley: University of California Press, 2008).

22  Joseph Schechtman, *European Population Transfers, 1939–1945* (New York: Oxford University Press, 1946); Grzegorz [Gregory] Frumkin, *Population Changes in Europe since 1939* (New York: Allen and Unwin, 1951); Malcolm J. Proudfoot, *European Refugees, 1939–52: A Study of Forced Population Movement* (London: Faber and Faber, 1956); Marrus, *The Unwanted*, 174–204; Norman Davis, *Heart of Europe: A Short History of Poland* (Oxford: Oxford University Press, 1986), 63–83.

23  Jarrell C. Jackman and Carla M. Borden, eds., *The Muses Flee Hitler: Cultural Transfer and Adaptation, 1930–1945* (Washington, DC: Smithsonian Institution Press, 1983); Claus-Dieter Krohn, *Intellectuals in Exile: Refugee Scholars and the New School for Social Research* (Amherst: University of Massachusetts Press, 1993); Aristide R. Zolberg, "The École Libre at the New School, 1941–1946," *Social Research* 65, no. 4 (Winter 1998): 921–951.

24  Bernd-Peter Lange and Mala Pandurang, "Dialectics of Empire and Complexities of Culture: British Men in India, Indian Experiences of Britain," in *The Historical Practice of Diversity: Transcultural Interactions from the Early Modern Mediterranean to the Postcolonial World,* ed. Dirk Hoerder with Christiane Harzig and Adrian Shubert (New York: Berghahn, 2003), 177–200; Karen J. Leong, *The China Mystique: Pearl S. Buck, Anna May Wong, Mayling Soong,*

*and the Transformation of American Orientalism* (Berkeley: University of California Press, 2005).

## 5. THE AFTERMATH OF WAR AND DECOLONIZATION

1 Bruno Lasker, *Asia on the Move: Population Pressure, Migration and Resettlement in Eastern Asia under the Influence of Want and War* (New York: Holt, 1945).

2 Wolfgang Jacobmeyer, *Vom Zwangsarbeiter zum Heimatlosen Ausländer: Die Displaced Persons in Westdeutschland, 1945–1951* (Göttingen: Vandenhoeck und Ruprecht, 1985); Göran Rystad, ed., *The Uprooted: Forced Migration as an International Problem in the Post-War Era* (Lund: Lund University Press, 1990); Mark Wyman, *DP: Europe's Displaced Persons, 1945–1951* (Philadelphia: Balch, 1988).

3 Keith Sword, "The Repatriation of Soviet Citizens at the End of the Second World War," in *The Cambridge Survey of World Migration*, ed. Robin Cohen (Cambridge: Cambridge University Press, 1995), 323–325.

4 Elfrieda B. Shukert and Barbara S. Scibetta, *War Brides of World War Two* (New York: Presidio, 1988).

5 Dirk Hoerder, *Cultures in Contact: World Migrations in the Second Millennium* (Durham, NC: Duke University Press, 2002), chaps. 17.3, 19.2, 19.3.

6 Raul Hilberg, *The Destruction of the European Jews* (Chicago: Quadrangle, 1961); Eliezer Ben-Rafael, *The Emergence of Ethnicity: Cultural Groups and Social Conflict in Israel* (New York: Greenwood, 1982); Benny Morris, *Righteous Victims: A History of the Zionist-Arab Conflict, 1881–1999* (New York: Knopf, 1999).

7 Hoerder, *Cultures in Contact,* chap. 18.4.

8 Ibid., chap. 18.3.

# Selected Bibliography

Appadurai, Arjun. "Global Ethnoscapes: Notes and Queries for a Transnational Anthropology." In *Recapturing Anthropology: Working in the Present,* edited by Richard G. Fox. Santa Fe, NM: School of American Research Press, 1991.

Bade, Klaus J. *Europa in Bewegung: Migration vom späten 18. Jahrhundert bis zur Gegenwart.* Munich: C. H. Beck, 2000.

Bade, Klaus J., Pieter C. Emmer, Leo Lucassen, and Jochen Oltmer, eds. *The Encyclopedia of European Migration and Minorities: From the Seventeenth Century to the Present.* Cambridge: Cambridge University Press, 2011.

Balachandran, G. "Circulation through Seafaring: Indian Seamen, 1890–1945." In *Society and Circulation: Mobile People and Itinerant Cultures in South Asia, 1750–1950,* edited by Claude Markovits, Jacques Pouchepadass, and Sanjay Subrahmanyam. Delhi: Permanent Black, 2003.

Belich, James. *Replenishing the Earth: The Settler Revolution and the Rise of the Anglo-World, 1783–1939.* Oxford: Oxford University Press, 2009.

Bell-Fialkoff, Andrew. *Ethnic Cleansing.* New York: St. Martin's Press, 1996.

Bose, Sugata. *A Hundred Horizons: The Indian Ocean in the Age of Global Empire.* Cambridge, MA: Harvard University Press, 2006.

Breman, Jan. *Labour Bondage in West India: From Past to Present.* New Delhi: Oxford University Press, 2007.

———. *Taming the Coolie Beast: Plantation Society and the Colonial Order in Southeast Asia.* Delhi: Oxford University Press, 1989.

Breman, Jan, and E. Valentine Daniel. "Conclusion: The Making of a Coolie." *Journal of Peasant Studies* 19, nos. 3–4 (1992): 268–295.

Brettell, Caroline B., and James F. Hollifield, eds. *Migration Theory: Talking Across Disciplines.* Rev. ed. London: Routledge, 2008.

Chaudhuri, Nupur, and Margaret Strobel, eds. *Western Women and Imperialism: Complicity and Resistance.* Bloomington: Indiana University Press, 1992.

Cheng, Lucie, and Edna Bonacich, eds. *Labor Immigration under Capitalism: Asian Workers in the United States before World War II.* Berkeley: University of California Press, 1984.

Christopher, Emma, Cassandra Pybus, and Marcus Rediker, eds. *Many Middle Passages: Forced Migration and the Making of the Modern World.* Berkeley: University of California Press, 2007.

Cohen, Robin, ed. *The Cambridge Survey of World Migration*. Cambridge: Cambridge University Press, 1995.

Coniff, Michael L., and Thomas J. Davis. *Africans in the Americas: A History of the Black Diaspora*. New York: St. Martin's Press, 1994.

Cooper, Frederick, and Ann Laura Stoler, eds. *Tensions of Empire: Colonial Cultures in a Bourgeois World*. Berkeley: University of California Press, 1997.

Curto, José C., and Renée Soulodre-LaFrance. "Introduction: Interconnections between Africa and the Americas during the Era of the Slave Trade." In *Africa and the Americas: Interconnections during the Slave Trade,* edited by José C. Curto and Renée Soulodre-LaFrance. Trenton, NJ: Africa World Press, 2005.

Daniels, Roger. "No Lamps Were Lit for Them: Angel Island and the Historiography of Asian American Immigration." *Journal of American Ethnic History* 17 (1997): 3–18.

Drescher, Seymour. *Abolition: A History of Slavery and Antislavery*. New York: Cambridge University Press, 2009.

Dupeux, Georges, ed. *Les Migrations internationale de la fin du XVIIIe siècle à nos jours*. Paris: Centre National de la Recherche Scientifique, 1980.

Eltis, David, ed. *Coerced and Free Migration: Global Perspectives*. Stanford, CA: Stanford University Press, 2002.

Fahrmeir, Andreas, Olivier Faron, and Patrick Weil, eds. *Migration Control in the North Atlantic World: The Evolution of State Practices in Europe and the United States from the French Revolution to the Inter-War Period*. New York: Berghahn, 2003.

Feys, Torsten, Lewis R. Fischer, Stéphane Hoste, and S. en Vanfraechem, eds. *Maritime Transport and Migration: The Connections between Maritime and Migration Networks*. St. John's, NL: International Maritime Economic History Association, 2007.

Gabaccia, Donna R. *Italy's Many Diasporas*. Seattle: University of Washington Press, 2000.

Gabaccia, Donna R., and Dirk Hoerder, eds. *Connecting Seas and Connected Ocean Rims: Indian, Atlantic, and Pacific Oceans and China Seas Migrations from the 1830s to the 1920s*. Leiden: Brill, 2011.

Gatrell, Peter. *A Whole Empire Walking: Refugees in Russia during World War I*. Bloomington: Indiana University Press, 1999.

Gilroy, Paul. *The Black Atlantic: Modernity and Double Consciousness*. Cambridge, MA: Harvard University Press, 1993.

Gottschang, Thomas R., and Diana Lary. *Swallows and Settlers: The Great Migration from North China to Manchuria*. Ann Arbor: Center for Chinese Studies, University of Michigan, 2000.

Green, Nancy L., and François Weil, eds. *Citizenship and Those Who Leave: The Politics of Emigration and Expatriation*. Urbana: University of Illinois Press, 2007.

Harzig, Christiane, and Dirk Hoerder, with Donna Gabaccia. *What Is Migration History?* Cambridge: Polity, 2009.

Harzig, Christiane, and Danielle Juteau, with Irina Schmitt, eds. *The Social Construction of Diversity: Recasting the Master Narrative of Industrial Nations.* New York: Berghahn, 2003.

Ho, Engseng. *The Graves of Tarim: Genealogy and Mobility across the Indian Ocean.* Berkeley: University of California Press, 2006.

Hoerder, Dirk. *Cultures in Contact: World Migrations in the Second Millennium.* Durham, NC: Duke University Press, 2002.

———, ed. *Labor Migration in the Atlantic Economies: The European and North American Working Classes during the Period of Industrialization.* Westport, CT: Greenwood Press, 1985.

Hoerder, Dirk, with Christiane Harzig and Adrian Shubert, eds. *The Historical Practice of Diversity: Transcultural Interactions from the Early Modern Mediterranean to the Postcolonial World.* New York: Berghahn, 2003.

Jackson, James H., Jr. and Leslie Page Moch. "Migration and the Social History of Modern Europe." *Historical Methods* 22 (1989): 27–36.

Karras, Alan L., and J. R. McNeill, eds. *Atlantic American Societies: From Columbus through Abolition, 1492 to 1888.* London: Routledge, 1992.

Lal, Brij V., Peter Reeves, and Rajesh Rai, eds. *The Encyclopedia of the Indian Diaspora.* Singapore: Didier Millet/National University of Singapore, 2006.

Lary, Diana, and Stephen MacKinnon, eds. *The Scars of War: The Impact of Warfare on Modern China.* Vancouver: UBC Press, 2001.

Lucassen, Jan, and Leo Lucassen, eds. *Migration, Migration History, History: Old Paradigms and New Perspectives.* Bern: Peter Lang, 1997.

Markovits, Claude. *The Global World of Indian Merchants, 1750–1947: Traders of Sind from Bukhara to Panama.* Cambridge: Cambridge University Press, 2000.

Marrus, Michael R. *The Unwanted: European Refugees in the Twentieth Century.* Oxford: Oxford University Press, 1985.

McClintock, Anne. *Imperial Leather: Race, Gender, and Sexuality in the Colonial Contest.* New York: Routledge, 1995.

McKeown, Adam. "Chinese Emigration in Global Context." *Journal of Global History* 5 (2010): 95–124.

———. *Chinese Migrant Networks and Cultural Change: Peru, Chicago, Hawaii, 1900–1936.* Chicago: University of Chicago Press, 2001.

———. "Global Migration, 1846–1940." *Journal of World History* 15, no. 2 (2004): 155–189.

———. *Melancholy Order: Asian Migration and the Globalization of Borders.* New York: Columbia University Press, 2008.

McPherson, Kenneth. "Processes of Cultural Interaction in the Indian Ocean: An Historical Perspective." *Great Circle* 6, no. 2 (1984): 78–92.

Metcalf, Thomas R. *Imperial Connections: India in the Indian Ocean Arena, 1860–1920*. Berkeley: University of California Press, 2007.

Midgley, Clare, ed. *Gender and Imperialism*. Manchester: Manchester University Press, 1998.

Moch, Leslie Page. *Moving Europeans: Migration in Western Europe since 1650*. 2nd ed. Bloomington: Indiana University Press, 2003.

Moya, José C. "A Continent of Immigrants: Postcolonial Shifts in the Western Hemisphere." *Hispanic American Historical Review* 86, no. 1 (2006): 1–28.

Moya, José C., and Adam McKeown. "World Migration in the Long Twentieth Century." In *Essays on Twentieth-Century History*, edited by Michael Adas. Philadelphia: Temple University Press, 2010.

Ness, Immanuel, ed. *The Encyclopedia of Global Human Migration*. Oxford: Wiley-Blackwell, 2013.

Northrup, David. *Indentured Labor in the Age of Imperialism, 1834–1922*. Cambridge: Cambridge University Press, 1995.

Nugent, Walter. *Crossings: The Great Transatlantic Migrations, 1870–1914*. Bloomington: Indiana University Press, 1992.

Pan, Lynn, ed. *The Encyclopedia of the Chinese Overseas*. Cambridge, MA: Harvard University Press, 1999.

Pearson, Michael. *The Indian Ocean*. London: Routledge, 2003.

Pierson, Ruth Roach, and Nupur Chaudhuri, with Beth McAuley, eds. *Nation, Empire, Colony: Historicizing Gender and Race*. Bloomington: Indiana University Press, 1998.

Rediker, Marcus. *The Slave Ship: A Human History*. New York: Viking, 2007.

Roberts, Allen F. "La 'Géographie Processuelle': Un nouveau paradigme pour les aires culturelles." *Lendemains* 31, nos. 122–123 (2006): 41–61.

Said, Edward W. *Orientalism*. New York: Vintage, 1994.

Sharpe, Pamela, ed. *Women, Gender, and Labour Migration: Historical and Global Perspectives*. London: Routledge, 2001.

Sinha, Mrinalini. *Colonial Masculinity: The 'Manly Englishman' and the 'Effeminate Bengali' in the Late Nineteenth Century*. Manchester: Manchester University Press, 1995.

Skeldon, Ronald. "International Migration within and from the East and Southeast Asian Region: A Review Essay." *Asian and Pacific Migration Journal* 1 (1992): 19–63.

Smith, Alan K. *Creating a World Economy: Merchant Capital, Colonialism, and World Trade, 1400–1825*. Boulder, CO: Westview Press, 1991.

Stola, Dariusz. "Forced Migrations in Central European History." *International Migration Review* 26 (1992): 324–341.

Stoler, Ann Laura. *Capitalism and Confrontation in Sumatra's Plantation Belt, 1870–1979.* New Haven, CT: Yale University Press, 1985.

———. "Making Empire Respectable: The Politics of Race and Sexual Morality in 20th-Century Colonial Cultures." *American Ethnologist* 16 (1989): 634–660.

———. *Race and the Education of Desire: Foucault's History of Sexuality and the Colonial Order of Things.* Durham, NC: Duke University Press, 1995.

Strobel, Margaret. *Gender, Sex, and Empire.* Washington, DC: American Historical Association, 1993.

Thornton, John. *Africa and Africans in the Making of the Atlantic World, 1400–1800.* Rev ed. New York: Cambridge University Press, 1998.

Tinker, Hugh. *A New System of Slavery: The Export of Indian Labour Overseas, 1830–1920.* London: Institute of Race Relations/Oxford University Press, 1974.

Torpey, John. *The Invention of the Passport: Surveillance, Citizenship, and the State.* Cambridge: Cambridge University Press, 2000.

Van Kirk, Sylvia. *"Many Tender Ties": Women in Fur-Trade Society in Western Canada, 1670–1870.* Winnipeg: Watson and Dwyer, 1980.

Vargas-Silva, Carlos, ed. *Handbook of Research Methods in Migration.* Cheltenham, UK: Edward Elgar, 2012.

Vecoli, Rudolph J., and Suzanne M. Sinke, eds. *A Century of European Migrations, 1830–1930.* Urbana: University of Illinois Press, 1991.

Vidal, Cécile. "La Nouvelle histoire atlantique: Nouvelle perspectives sur les relations entre l'Europe, l'Afrique et les Amériques du XVe au XIXe siècle." *Revue internationale des livres et des idées* 4 (2008): 23–28.

Wang Gungwu, ed. *Global History and Migrations.* Boulder, CO: Westview Press, 1997.

Willcox, Walter F., ed. *International Migrations.* 2 vols. New York: National Bureau of Economic Research, 1929–1931.

Williams, Raymond. *Culture and Society, 1780–1950.* New York: Columbia University Press, 1958.

Wolf, Eric R. *Europe and the People without History.* Berkeley: University of California Press, 1982.

Yu, Henry. *Thinking Orientals: Migration, Contact, and Exoticism in Modern America.* Oxford: Oxford University Press, 2001.

Zolberg, Aristide R. *A Nation by Design: Immigration Policy in the Fashioning of America.* New York: Russell Sage Foundation/Harvard University Press, 2006.

# Index